OUR AMERICAN DREAM

By: David and Linda Goodsell

Published
by
Brown Bear Publications (Sussex)

OUR AMERICAN DREAM

Authors: David and Linda Goodsell

First published in 2006
by
Brown Bear Publications (Sussex)

ISBN Numbers: 0-9552722-0-3
: 978-0-9552722-0-2

CONTENTS

HINTS AND TIPS

Appendix

INTRODUCTION

Reading this book could significantly change **YOUR LIFE** if you have any desire to purchase or alternatively hire an American Recreational Vehicle in the United Sates of America and then travel while there to experience first hand the lifestyle as well as the freedom that it presents.

This book is therefore a factual account of our own personal American Dream that we would very much like to share with you as we recount how we became hooked and eventually flew many thousands of miles all the way to Oregon in the USA to purchase our own 'A' Class Safari Trek and while there use it to travel to numerous interesting and fascinating locations.

You are therefore invited to join us as we tour in the Trek through Oregon, Nevada, Arizona, California and Utah visiting such exotic and famous areas including Las Vegas, The Valley of Fire, The Grand Canyon, Lake Mead, Crater Lake, Virginia City, Carson City, Monument Valley as well as the National Parks of Zion, Bryce Canyon and Yosemite and many more fantastic venues.

The book is also literally packed with invaluable information together with a host of 'hints and tips' on locating and purchasing an American RV in the USA together with a whole range of important parameters that really should be very carefully considered and thoroughly evaluated prior to making that all important buying decision.

We provide hints on how to double check vehicle ownership, vehicle prices and provide an insight into US driving rules and regulations as well as an introduction into the basics of exporting and importing a vehicle.

There is an appendix containing a whole range of extremely useful web site addresses that should prove invaluable for anyone that may wish to conduct further research of their own.

However please be fully aware that you could become consumed by the potential thrill of the open road and you may become infatuated by the experience, so once that happens there may be no turning back. The real danger is that you could be hooked for the rest of your life!!!!!

We sincerely trust that the contents of our book will prove interesting and invaluable so may hopefully encourage you to live out your very own American Dream.

Linda

PS

Another book entitled **'On the Road Again'** is scheduled to follow shortly covering the journey of some 3,250 miles all the way across the United States of America from Oregon on the West Coast to Baltimore on the East Coast. It includes yet more valuable and in-depth information regarding the export and import process as well as vehicle licensing and registration procedures in the UK. Probably a 'must read' book for anyone that would like to do the same and avoid some of the pitfalls.

Acknowledgements

It is appropriate to take this opportunity to acknowledge the extremely valuable role played by Jim and Carol our American hosts, friends and previous owners of our Safari Trek without whose help and assistance our American Dream may not have been possible.

In addition we are also extremely grateful for the warm welcome given to us along the way by the many new American friends we encountered, including David and his wife Janet who presented us with a very detailed US map and along with Don and his wife Chiyo who kindly provided a host of very useful web site information on the Safari Trek and of course Swiss Pete and his wife Debbie who befriended us while we were in Las Vegas. Nor can we forget Frank and his wife Judy who we met at the Grand Canyon and again while at Monument Valley.

Furthermore we owe a duty of thanks to Christopher as well as his wife Helen plus their two children Jasmine and Saffron for taking good care of our two small whippets Tigger and Willow, as well as Martin and June for looking after one or two automobile chores at home and to everyone else that helped make Our American Dream become a reality.

Along the way we encountered many very friendly Americans all of whom were real nice characters who welcomed us to their country and with whom we still remain in contact and hopefully they will never be forgotten.

It is also necessary to acknowledge the help and valuable support provided by Kevin Norman, a talented and friendly 'IT Guru' for his advise on numerous word processing queries and a special 'thanks' must also be extended to Ryan O'Hara for using his extensive graphic design skills and expertise to dramatically improve the visual layout and appeal of this publication.

Finally it is of course necessary to fully acknowledge the help, encouragement and assistance provided by my lovely wife Linda, who proved to be a very capable chief photographer and whose navigational skills ensured that we did not get lost on too many occasions!!!!

Graphic Design by: Ryan O'Hara (www.rhinobytes.co.uk)

Printed by: Lancaster Print Services Ltd

OUR AMERICAN DREAM

Most of us have dreams, so we are not unusual in that respect and like many our dream started a number of years ago, but at that time we did not fully appreciate the long-term implications or impact that our dream was really going to have. As readers will already appreciate there are defining moments in time where one is say at the crossroads in ones life, when important decisions need to be made but at that time it is not fully appreciated how significant and important those decisions may prove to be in the future.

Well it was not so much at the crossroads where my wife Linda and I started to formulate and make such a decision it was at the ferry port in Calais as we were returning to Sussex from a super and very elaborate wedding in Paris, followed by a short break with friends in the Toulouse area of France. Sitting in our car at the docks in the early evening waiting to catch the ferry back to Dover we settled down for what turned out to be a long session as our ship was not due to sail until the following day, for some reason we could not get on an earlier one so decided to spend the night in the car. On reflection probably not the best of ideas as it was cold and uncomfortable in the car so we needed to leave the vehicle frequently to go for short walks. As expected the car park was fairly full and continued to fill with a variety of cars, motorcycles, vans, lorries and also some attractive looking motorhomes parked on the quayside.

Judging by the mouth-watering aroma coming from some of the 'homes on wheels' it appeared that their owners were no-doubt cooking delicious meals, while others were probably relaxing, perhaps even watching television or reading a good book?

Unfortunately our car seemed even less welcoming as the cold night progressed so felt very envious as we imagined the motorhome dwellers snuggling down in warm comfortable beds, so this experience soon had us considering the merits of owning such a vehicle, so much so that when we returned home we purchased one or two magazines and before long began to appreciate that we were getting fairly serious.

We even attended some of the major shows at Shepton Mallet as well as Peterborough and also went to look round some gorgeous vehicles at selected dealers and although we did see quite an attractive array of 'homes on wheels', their price was beyond our fairly modest budget; nevertheless we kept searching in the hope that one day we would find something to meet our high and possibly unrealistic expectations.

Then one day we just happened to visit our local Land Rover dealer to obtain an oil filter for our trusty old Land Rover County and there parked at the back of the garage was a magnificent twenty two foot long coach-built Swift Kon-Tiki, similar in style to an American 'C' Class RV.

It transpired that the vehicle was owned by the elderly chairman of the company who wanted to sell it, initially we could not believe our good fortune as it was just a few years old and was in immaculate condition having covered only around 6,500 miles.

Our hopes were soon dashed when the sales manager confirmed how much the sales price was, in fairness we should not have been so optimistic as the motorhome was in good condition and so was fairly priced so we had no alternative but to leave the garage without concluding a deal as the price was much higher than our meager budget allowed.

Several weeks later we happened to be passing the same garage so could not resist calling in just to see if the Kon-Tiki was still there or if it had been sold to some lucky new owner and surprise, surprise it was still sitting there waiting for a buyer and guess what?

Surprisingly the price shown on the windscreen had been reduced by quite a few thousand pounds, but it was sadly still beyond our budget, nevertheless we again spoke with the sales manager, who unexpectedly said that he would make enquiries to find out whether an even lower sales price might just be acceptable, as the owner was keen to sell. To our utter amazement he returned with a proposed deal that would see the vehicles price reduced by yet another very substantial amount of money and to our delight, that actually brought the price within our budget, so a deal was agreed there and then. Was that luck or just fate? We will probably never know.

Over the next eight or so years we travelled extensively in the UK in our Kon-Tiki 640/6, enjoying the thrill of the open road, the freedom that the lifestyle afforded and explored much of the West Country, Scotland and Wales.

The motorhome proved to be ideal and was much loved by our three whippets Fred, Annie and Sammy who became avid campers over the years and whenever possible we attended the various RV trade shows at Peterborough, Shepton Mallet, Malvern and several in Kent. While there we started to look more and more closely at the numerous American RV's that were on display and spoke to dealers, owners and anyone that was willing to provide us with valuable information.

We even attended one excellent and very useful seminar held during one of the Malvern Shows specifically related to purchasing an RV in the USA and then using it tour while over there.

This exposure had a tremendous impact on us both as we began to dream of crossing the Atlantic and living the dream ourselves, but at the time we were not at all sure when or even if we would be able fulfill that dream. However we did appreciate that if we could make our dream come true, we would be following in the footsteps of the many RV enthusiasts that had gone before so would not be real pioneers, nevertheless the prospect did seem to be somewhat daunting but non the less very appealing.

Eventually the time came when we had to part company with our much loved Kon-Tiki and spent probably too many years without the benefit of having a motorhome, although we never gave up the hope or desire to acquire another vehicle as soon as we had sufficient funds. We still dreamed of being able to own an American RV but really did not think that would be possible, unless our Premium Bonds were to come up or we could have a substantial Lottery win; to be honest our luck was never going to be that good anyway! Nevertheless in the back of our minds we still kept on dreaming of flying to the USA to buy our very own RV and see some of that vast and varied country.

We still purchased the occasional motorhome magazine and our thoughts always returned to the possibility of actually fulfilling what could be by now described as a fantasy, which seemed so far away and possibly no longer achievable.

Nevertheless after far too many years our fortunes improved a little and no the Premium Bonds did not come up nor did we win the Lottery, but we were able to at least consider purchasing a second hand American 'A' Class RV in the UK, so eagerly commenced our quest to find an appropriate vehicle. Although we located some very nice motorhomes advertised by various RV dealers and even saw one or two at the various RV shows, finding our preferred RV, a Safari Trek proved extremely difficult.

The 'A' class Trek was our first choice because it is a fairly small RV compared with many RV's of American origin, measuring just about 25/26 feet long by 98 inches wide, so in theory if used with caution should be reasonably at home on most roads in the UK and also viable in Europe.

Treks are fitted with a space saving electrically operated 'ElectroMajic' bed that stores very neatly in the ceiling when not in use and therefore offers an extremely good living/lounging area that would normally only be found in much larger vehicles. Furthermore the RV is also comprehensively and very well equipped to ensure the total comfort of the occupants in almost any situation so it has automatic transmission with cruise control, full air conditioning and heating system, double glazed windows, solar charging system, inverter, generator, reversing camera, hydraulic levelling system, and much, much more. The generous sized kitchen is equipped with Corian worktops, solid wood cabinetry and a generous sized refrigerator with combined deep freeze plus micro-convection oven. In keeping with the vehicle's design concept the bathroom is naturally also very generous in size and is extremely well equipped so should not disappoint even the most demanding owner. The main exterior panels of the RV are produced from aircraft grade aluminum that are fully painted in attractive eye catching colours, under a clear coat of lacquer to give that deep down shine. Some Treks even have beautiful and professionally produced air brushed murals on the rear exterior, frequently featuring animals or animal scenes that tend to create a great deal of interest and attention. Interior storage is really excellent with a multitude of well-designed quality cabinets, while the under floor exterior storage is adequate for most normal needs.

At one stage we even thought that we had found the ideal vehicle that was advertised for sale privately in the UK, but fate again reared its head as the vehicle turned out to be a major disappointment. It was not in what we would have described as in good condition as it had more badly applied mastic on the roof than we considered appropriate for a vehicle that had a mere 6,000 miles on the clock, so it was back to square one again.

We were of course very disappointed, but all was not lost, as we had done a little previous homework on the Internet so had found a few excellent American web sites that showed vast ranges of American RV's for sale, so the decision was therefore taken to do a little more browsing and before long came across a whole range of Treks of varying ages, mileages, specifications and prices.

Then as if by magic found what appeared to be a very nice looking Safari Trek with a 6.5ltr Turbo Diesel engine, apparently quite rare in the USA as most of the smaller vehicles have gas (petrol) engines, that was being offered for sale by the owner.

The advertisement showed pictures of the Trek emerging from its garage; yes a real garage and more than large enough to house a sizeable RV, built beside the owner's home.

As far as could be ascertained the vehicle looked in really good condition and the owner described the Trek's condition 'as new', with just 9,000 miles on the clock, so wondered if this could be 'the one' and if it would be worthy of further investigation?

When Linda returned home that evening the Trek became the topic of conversation and we then took the decision to e-mail the owner that night, as they say nothing ventured nothing lost, so we drafted our e-mail and asked for more data on the vehicle and even had the audacity to request more photographs then pressed the send button and for some reason held our breath but felt quite excited. We were uncertain whether the message would even get through or whether the owner would bother to respond, but thought it was worth a try at least.

The next day we eagerly turned on the computer to check our e-mail system and there right in front of our eyes saw that we did have a reply from the Trek's owners and yes there were even some photographs as well so we enthusiastically read the message and our excitement grew even more as the information unfolded and eventually we both looked at each other and said in unison 'could it be the vehicle for us'?

The e-mail from the owners, Jim and Carol, who lived in Oregon, stated that they had purchased the vehicle new in the year 2000 and had used it during the summer months for short vacations only and that the vehicle had always been garaged so was of course very well looked after.

The age of the vehicle also meant that it would have a gross vehicle weight of under 7,500kg so that it could be driven in the UK on a normal car C1 licence compared to the more recent Safari Treks that appear to exceed this weight limit and therefore fall into a different driving licence category.

Over the next few weeks' e-mails were exchanged between the UK and the USA, on almost a daily basis, both sellers and potential buyers exchanging details of our respective families, homes and interests etc.

By now we were fairly convinced that this was probably going to be 'the vehicle', but as it was in Oregon it was not going to be quite such an easy process to purchase the vehicle as if it had been in the UK, but for some reason both Linda and I were convinced this was 'the one for us' and that for once fate was possibly working in our favour.

Jim and Carol were extremely helpful answering all our questions as well as also providing much needed advice regarding driving licence requirements and also helped guide us through the maze of vehicle insurance.

At the same time we started to investigate the rules and regulations about importing the

RV from the US into the UK and spoke to two well-respected American RV dealers in the UK and concluded that it should be feasible, but possibly reasonably costly to get the vehicle into the country.

However we found out that not only would we have to pay all the required import duties but we would also need to have the vehicle modified to meet UK Specifications and this would involve modifications to the vehicles front and rear lights etc.

Furthermore if we wanted to run a 240 volt electrical system we would need to have a suitable transformer and the necessary wiring and socket outlets added, the TV would need to be changed, as the US version would not work in the UK, but it could still be used if we wanted with the vehicle's reversing camera and possibly the reversing camera itself may have to be changed.

In addition as the vehicle was over three years old it would have to pass an MOT test as well and it would also need to be registered and of course taxed for use in the UK.

Contact was also made with H M Customs and Excise via the Internet to ascertain how they would levy taxes on the RV and how much this was likely to cost and at this stage things got a little more complex, as it transpired that we would have to pay duty based on the price we paid for the vehicle plus shipping and insurance at the rate of 10% and then on top of that would have to pay VAT at 17.5%——-ouch!!!!

However it transpired that as the vehicle was over six months old and had done more than six thousand miles, the rules could be slightly different, so if the vehicle had been owned by us for up to one month the above tax rates based on the price we paid for the vehicle would apply, but if it were owned for two months or more before importing it into the UK then the basis for assessing the vehicle's value would probably be based on the RV's 'Wholesale Value', which is understood to be equivalent to the 'Trade Price' which of course should of course be lower.

We attempted without any luck to get H M Customs and Excise to provide their assessment of the likely 'Wholesale Value' of the vehicle, but were told they could only do this once the vehicle had landed in the UK, not terribly helpful as we needed to evaluate if the whole project was feasible and within our limited budget!!!!!

It also appeared that if we owned the vehicle for just over a year and could prove that we also had been out of the EC for that same amount of time then we could possibly import the vehicle into the UK without having to pay the import duty and VAT, regrettably this was not really an option for us.

Meanwhile Jim suggested that we should look on the Oregon Driver and Motor Vehicle Services (DMV) web site to double check the driving licence requirements and this revealed that an International Driving Permit would enable us to drive in the USA for up to one year without having to take a US driving test, so that was very good news but we had been prepared to take a test if that had been necessary. So far everything seemed to be going pretty well, probably too well we thought and soon encountered our first major difficulty.

On scanning the 'Oregon DMV' web site again we noticed some data related to vehicle ownership and became very concerned when we read that only people who had been residents of Oregon for six months or more could gain the title to a motor vehicle, if correct this was a serious setback and could again bring the whole project to a big halt. To double check we contacted the Oregon DMV via e-mail and were horrified to receive their reply a day or so later as it confirmed that only Oregon residents with a permanent address could gain title to a vehicle.

A hurried e-mail on this matter was sent to Jim and Carol and their reply confirmed that they were aware of this problem, but Jim confirmed that he had spoken with the local DMV in Redmond and had been assured this should not be a real problem!!!!!!!

Still very concerned, but a little more confident by Jim's positive response that "things could be sorted" when we arrived, we started to make positive moves to make it all happen.

Linda and I looked very closely at our finances and concluded that we could just afford to purchase the vehicle, but would probably have to defer it's importation into the UK for another year, to allow us to save the necessary funds, in addition we reasoned that by that time the vehicle's value, used as a basis for calculating the import duties and taxes would be lower.

We were hooked by now so negotiated a deal over the Internet, something we would never have contemplated before as we are extremely cautious people, but we felt the owners were sincere and honest and that the vehicle was just what we wanted, so it was an opportunity that was just too good to miss. At one stage Jim was even asked to take pictures of the vehicle's roof, which he did without hesitation and to our relief everything looked to be in very good condition, furthermore as part of the deal Jim agreed that the Trek could be stored safely on his land if needed and that we could stay with them until we were ready to start Our American Dream, so we quickly accepted this very kind and generous offer.

In addition it was agreed that we would send a small deposit which would be refundable if the vehicle did not meet our full expectations, so reasoned that we were minimising our risks and if the vehicle lived up to it's description and photographs this was possibly our one and only opportunity to acquire the vehicle we had desired for such a long time. We began to check the dollar/pound exchange rates on a daily basis and arranged to send the deposit in dollars, from our bank electronically directly into Jim and Carols 'Trek bank account'.

Linda and I went down to Brighton in Sussex, which is close to our home to obtain our International Driving Permits and at the same time (through the Post Office) made applications to also obtain UK Photo Card Driving Licences.

We decided that as we were going to spend quite a lot of money going all the way to the United States, then we had better make the very best of the opportunity and stay there for a reasonably long period and use the Trek to see some of the sights we had always dreamed about, such as Las Vegas and the Grand Canyon.

We spent time on the Internet looking at the cost of flights, but in the end went to our local travel agent and booked the flights through them, with a planned departure date in late March and the return trip to the UK scheduled for early June 2004. The travel agents came up with a very good deal that cost around four pounds sterling return per person flying with United Airlines from Heathrow to San Francisco and then on to Redmond in Oregon, a journey time of some 22 hours or more!!!!

We also began to look more closely at the logistics of exporting the vehicle and found that most RV's were actually shipped out of the US from the East Coast, which was somewhat disappointing as our Trek and the Safari factory were not far from the West Coast Ports. We established that it would be best to get the vehicle across to Baltimore for eventual shipping, a distance of some 3,000 miles. Again we initially thought that new vehicles leaving the Safari factory, bound for the UK would have been transported overland by rail or on the back of a 'low loader lorry', but we were incorrect in our assumption as it transpired that even a new Safari RV would actually be driven overland to Baltimore. At this stage it appeared that we had two choices, to get a company to arrange to transport the vehicle for us, at a cost of something like $2/mile probably plus expenses, or to drive the vehicle across ourselves. So we considered that the latter option was preferable as this would give us the opportunity to see much more of the US, although this would need further research before a final decision could be taken.

It was decided that we really needed to arrange suitable personal medical/accident insurance for both of us, but found that many companies were reluctant to provide cover for the length of time required, but after much research we obtained suitable cover from the Automobile Association. We also contacted Saga our household insurers to advise them of the planned trip, fortunately they were happy to provide cover at an additional premium providing someone would visit the house regularly to ensure everything was OK. Next forms were acquired from the Post Office to enable our mail to be redirected to our youngest son for the duration of our adventure and within a few days confirmation was received from the Post Office but luckily we double-checked the dates only to find that one of them was incorrect, however a quick telephone call soon corrected this error.

Jim suggested that we contact The Good Sam Club to obtain an insurance quotation for the Trek, this we did via the Internet, but several days later were horrified to receive their reply, which indicated that they wanted $1,133 for just six months. This sounded extremely high so we contacted them again by e-mail and explained that the Trek would be actually used for less than three months then it would then be securely stored on private premises, we also stressed that we both had extremely good driving records and that this could be substantiated in writing if necessary. Even today we still cannot trace any acknowledgement or any response to our e-mail!

Again a quick e-mail was sent to Jim, advising him of the insurance situation and he subsequently suggested we contact Bill Pearce Insurance in Redmond for a quotation, this we did and were quoted around $1,200 for a full twelve months, at least this seemed better, that is until we learnt that Jim paid around $400/year for the same RV.

Jim did yet more research on our behalf and confirmed that he had spoken with his current insurance provider AARP (understood to be similar to Saga in the UK) and that they had advised that they would be able to insure the vehicle at a competitive price, but as we were due to travel to the US fairly soon, it would be better to wait until we were in the USA to put this into effect.

At the same time all this was happening Linda investigated the most appropriate and cost effective ways that could be used to communicate with family and friends as well as how we could monitor our expenditure with the bank back in the UK. Following her in-depth study and acting on the advice she was given purchased a Tri-Band mobile telephone, but had to inform all concerned that text messages were really the only way for us to send and receive messages economically, as a short text to or from the UK would cost us only about 25 pence compared to a phone call which would cost us over one pound sterling per minute. Linda's research indicated that we should consider the purchase a pre-paid 'phone card' once we were in the USA as this would enable economical calls to be made within the US and would also enable calls to be made back to the UK at a cheaper rate than via the mobile.

In addition following more advice, it was decided that a lap top computer was an essential accessory as it should enable e-mails to be sent and received and could also be used to download the many digital photographs we planned to take, in addition we hoped to be able to have sufficient time to record a daily diary of Our American Dream.

We also considered the advantages and disadvantages of purchasing the laptop either in the UK or in the US, but in the end the decision was taken to purchase one in the United States, as we believed this may be more cost effective and that there should be a greater choice of Centrino models with Wi-Fi facilities, furthermore we were led to believe that if we went to a Starbucks Coffee Shop with the laptop we should be able to gain access to the Internet.

During the latter part of May, Linda handed in her notice terminating her employment and left with mixed feelings as she had built up a very good rapport with her customers and many were sad to learn of her departure.

However quite a number did ask to be kept fully informed of our great American Dream as they said they would really like to do a similar trip themselves in the future.

The decision was made to take a bankers draft to pay for the balance due for the purchase of the RV and that we would only carry a small amount of US currency to pay for incidentals and would rely on our credit card for the majority of our expenditure.

A close watch was kept on exchange rates in an attempt to get the most advantageous rate and actually completed our financial transactions almost at the very last minute.

By now as our departure date was approaching rapidly we sincerely hoped that we had completed all the necessary tasks to ensure a successful trip, all that really was left was to complete our packing and make sure the house was safe and secure just before leaving.

LIVING THE DREAM

Tuesday 23 March – Monday 30 March

After leaving our current two whippets, Tigger and Willow, at the home of our youngest son, he kindly drove us to Heathrow Airport and luckily we did not encounter too much traffic or delays on the notorious M25, nevertheless as we had to go through the tight security checks introduced following 9/11 were pleased that we had ample time to spare.

Eventually we boarded the United Airlines flight bound for that very exotic sounding destination known as San Francisco and once in the air were able to follow the aircraft's progress on the GPS monitors on the rear of the seats and noted with great interest that the route took us over Baffin Island, Greenland and then over Canada before entering US airspace. The flight passed slowly and to help time go by we watched several in-flight films, did a little reading and of course a little snoozing, this was no-doubt also helped by the friendly cabin staff, good food and naturally a few in-flight drinks.

Somewhat jet lagged and more than little tired we arrived many hours later at San Francisco and when we disembarked from the aircraft were greeted by unbelievable cloud free vivid blue skies and very welcoming warm temperatures—absolute magic. Unfortunately we had to wait around six hours before we could catch our onward flight to our destination of Redmond in Oregon, so after clearing immigration and customs and that was a slow process due to increased airport security, then spent too much time in the airport lounge. Fortunately we came across a company demonstrating some of the Centrino laptop computers, so with their help were able to send a few free of charge e-mails to family members back in the UK to let them know of our progress. After what seemed ages we eventually boarded an exceedingly small turbo-prop aircraft for the rather bumpy and crowded ride on the last leg of our journey to Redmond. We arrived in darkness some two hours later, even more tired and jet lagged, but extremely relieved that the marathon outward journey was almost over and luckily the airport proved to be smaller than we had anticipated, so managed to locate our hosts and new friends Jim and his wife Carol without any trouble. In no time at all we were in their large four by four vehicle heading for their home in the very Western sounding location of 'Crooked River Ranch', so some twenty-four hours after leaving our own home in the UK we arrived at our new temporary home in Oregon. As we drew alongside Jim and Carol's quite spectacular Eco Dome style home, they explained that they had purchased the land and had constructed the dwelling themselves to blend in with the rugged canyon area and to cope with the extremes of temperature.

For the record Crooked River Ranch is a high desert community resting between the Crooked River and the Deschutes River and is at an elevation of almost 3,000 feet above sea level and the ranch was officially registered back in the 1950's and was then operated as a cattle ranch by the ZZ Cattle Company. However it is now a Rural Residential Ranch with its own golf course and many other facilities including, tennis courts, swimming pool, basketball and baseball pitches as well as several RV camping grounds.

The ranch occupies some 12,000 acres and is visually very spectacular as it looks as if it is the backdrop to a Western movie, with a range of scattered dwellings being some hundred feet below the rim with the Crooked River just about 200 yards or so from the house but around 150 feet lower down in the canyon.

Although it was dark we could not resist taking a quick peak at 'our' Safari Trek and from what we could see it looked just as Jim had described and was in immaculate condition inside and out.

Carol and Jim had even laid the table for two people complete with two bottles of wine, but there were even more surprises in store as we were presented with a super bottle opener, a beautiful basket of edible goodies, an American map covering all the US states and there were even some cold beers in the spacious refrigerator plus new wine glasses inscribed with the words 'Crooked River Ranch' as well as tee shirts and baseball hats bearing the same logo.

We spent the night in the comfortable guest room Jim and Carol had kindly prepared for us in their delightful and very spacious home, but did not sleep particularly well as we were still 'travelling' and were really still far too excited.

When we awoke on the first morning, a large herd of deer could be seen grazing in the garden of the house next door and remembered encountering a large stag on the roadside during our journey to the ranch on the previous evening that could be clearly seen in the vehicle's headlights.

Our first day was spent in a very relaxed manner around the house and grounds so that we could recover from the flight, although we did travel with Jim and Carol to Redmond to do a little shopping.

On the second morning we awoke to see to our left, a cloud of dust rising in the distance from the canyon and with our newly acquired binoculars, costing less than $70, could just make out the very well known figure of Big John, 'G'it on your horse', Wayne as he raced across the parched land on his horse. We noticed that he was heading straight towards some soldiers and could make out one very distinguished figure, yes it really was, non other than Colonel Custer with his troops, who were preparing to mount-up and move out. But just then we heard gun shots and looked to the right where we thought they came from and riding very fast were the unmistakable figures of William Cody, yes Wild Bill himself and Kit Carson who were trying to signal to the Colonel and Big John to look at the ridge of the canyon, but they did not appear to see them. However from our vantage point we could see what Bill and Kit were so concerned about, for on the ridge of the canyon there was non other than Chief Sitting Bull and Geronimo with hundreds of warriors all dressed in full war paint.

Were we dreaming or was it real?

We just did not know as every experience was surely a dream, we had travelled many thousands of miles to buy our very own American RV and planned to travel to places that had only been a dream before, now in a few days we would be on our way to actually live our very own personal American Dream.

Unfortunately it did take us several days to recover from the flight, so we did not venture very far from the ranch and could still not believe that we were actually in the USA, nevertheless we took full advantage to become better acquainted with the gleaming Safari Trek parked outside Jim's garage. Wow, what a garage it measured some 50 feet wide by 40 feet deep that had been specifically built to house their RV, Sports Utility Vehicle, Carol's 200 HP sparkling red high-speed boat that they use for competition fishing, a trailer and would you believe it, an unbelievable pristine workshop that looked more like an operating theatre, where Jim does stained glass work.

Jim took time out to explain how to use the Trek's comprehensive range of equipment and we were pleased and relieved to find that everything had been very well maintained so consequently functioned just as it should.

The vehicle's engine oil had been changed frequently at intervals of 2,000 to 3,000 miles, as Jim reasoned that this was prudent engineering practice, particularly as a gallon of good quality oil in the USA cost only about $20. We double checked the vehicle from stem to stern, inside and out, we even borrowed a large step ladder to cast an eye over the vehicle's roof paying particular attention to the roof structure and joints, we even investigated the condition of all the components fitted on it such as the solar panel, air conditioning unit, retractable TV aerial etc.

Fortunately everything was extremely clean as it had been well cared for so passed our inspection with flying colours so this was naturally quite a relief as we did not want anything to go wrong at this stage so soon agreed that this was indeed the vehicle for us. We were pleased to observe first hand the Trek's really eye catching African animal mural on the rear of the vehicle known as 'Sunset' depicting a range of elephants, giraffes and lions etc.

The African theme was also carried through to the vehicle's interior with similar animals adorning the fabric covering on the settee cushions, dining chairs as well as the sleep sack and there were even elephants etched on the glass of the shower door.

We prepared a bill of sale for the Trek and wishing to conclude the deal went with Jim and Carol to the bank in the nearby city of Redmond to deposit the final payment then called into the Oregon DMV, where we encountered what appeared to be a major problem.

Once inside the DMV Jim took the lead, as he had recently spoken to them personally to explain that we were currently living with them and that he sold the Trek to us so therefore wanted to transfer ownership and hence the title of the vehicle to Linda and myself, so far so good. However the clerk started to ask questions, how long had we lived at Jim's address and did we have Oregon driving licences and did we have any service bills to substantiate our claim to residency?

Being honest characters, we told the truth and explained that we were in the USA for about three months and would then return to the UK for a while, but in the near future planned to return to the USA and drive the Trek to Baltimore then ship it back to the UK. The clerk did not really seem to understand, so stated again that we needed to prove that we had been residents of Oregon for at least six months and possess an Oregon driving licence if we wanted to gain title to the vehicle.

He also added a final sting in the tail by proclaiming that our International Driving Permits were not an acceptable alternative to an Oregon driving licence.

Somewhat depressed, deflated and dejected to say the least, we left the DMV and felt that the hand of fate was going to call a halt to our ownership of the Trek and scupper our scheduled American Dream. We returned to Crooked River Ranch with what appeared to us as a very big problem, Jim was naturally extremely concerned as he reconfirmed several times that he had been to the DMV only recently and had explained the situation to another clerk, only to be informed that there should be no problems.

Naturally the topic of conversation back at the ranch was how best to overcome what seemed to be an insurmountable hurdle so a lot of the time was taken up with conversations revolving around 'what if we try? Fortunately Jim then revealed his next plan, 'plan B', which he had also discussed with the DMV at an earlier meeting and this involved Carol transferring her title to the vehicle to Linda and myself, while Jim would remain on the title documents himself, although this seemed like a good idea, we still thought that the DMV may not go along with the plan and may also insist that we acquire Oregon driving licences.

The following day we visited the DMV again and all felt more than a little apprehensive about the possible result, we duly completed the necessary documentation and with hearts pounding handed over the forms to a different clerk to the one we encountered the previous day, to our surprise and utter amazement everything seemed to go through without any major problems!!!

This clerk confirmed that our International Driving Permits would be perfectly acceptable for up to twelve months so like lightening we quickly paid the transfer and vehicle licence fee of just under $300 and quickly left, to say we were relieved, would have been an understatement.

We later learnt that because Oregon is currently a zero rated sales tax haven, many potential RV buyers from other US states, where they do have sale tax, have been making significant savings, sometimes amounting to thousands of dollars, by purchasing, titling and registering their RV's in Oregon. It appears that the DMV are now being more vigilant and stringent with respect to these transactions, nevertheless it transpired that if we had just wanted to buy a car, then title and register that in Oregon then that would probably not have presented any real problem!!!

This whole situation seemed even more confusing when we subsequently purchased a copy of the US magazine called 'MotorHome' only to discover several advertisements by RV dealers based in the state of Montana actively encouraging buyers to 'pay no sales tax' and save thousands of dollars by buying in that state. We could not help wondering if those buyers would then encounter similar difficulties to those we had met in Oregon when they came to title and register their vehicles?

However subsequent research has revealed that the state on Montana may now be considering the introduction of some form of vehicle tax for out of state RV purchasers.

Nevertheless, despite this success we still needed to obtain suitable vehicle insurance but as it was now late on Friday decided that we would leave this to be resolved early the following week.

Over the weekend we took the opportunity to travel with Jim and Carol to Portland so joined Highway 97 North as far as Madras, where we turned off on to Highway 26 then went through Warm Springs Indian Reservation, unfortunately we did not see any Indians, only a few cowboys.

On our journey we climbed the sweeping pine tree lined wide road of Mount Hood, the tallest mountain in Oregon rising to a height of approximately 11,240 feet which is popular with skiers, hikers and climbers and is situated some forty five miles East Southeast of Portland. We were fascinated to learn that Mount Hood is a Stratovolcano made of lava flows, domes and volcanic deposits and in the last 15,000 years it has erupted four times, the most recent eruption being only about 200/250 years ago. Apparently this snow capped mountain, the forth highest peak in the Cascades, has a number of down hill ski runs and cross country tracks and was named after a British Admiral and is surrounded by the Mount Hood National Forest. On route we encountered sun, hail, rain and snow all in the space of a few miles but were not too disappointed as the scenery was really magnificent and we could see people skiing on the distant slopes.

At Sandy we stopped at Fred's RV World so that Jim could obtain a replacement component for his new 'C' class Lexington. While there we were introduced to Mike, one of the company's sales staff and were a little surprised to find him dressed in baseball hat, traditional chequered cowboy shirt, high heeled Western boots and a very nice rodeo style belt with the customary large silver buckle, not quite the attire an RV salesperson would probably wear in the UK, however as expected he was of course in the true American way very polite and helpful.

While in Portland we visited a number of computer stores but found a surprisingly poor selection of laptops and very few Centrino models, so had to return to the ranch empty handed.

On our homeward journey Jim stopped at a garage to add some gas to the 4x4's large tank, adding 171/2 gallons at a cost of just $1.77/gallon and that seemed pretty good value, but Jim and Carol said that the price of gas had risen recently, but they were absolutely staggered to learn how much more expensive it was in the UK.

During this eventful week Jim was kind enough to let Linda and I drive the family automatic 4x4, so that we could get used to driving on the right hand side of the road as well as become more familiar with the road signage and traffic lights etc. We could not have had a better tutor, as Jim was an ex-fire chief so was used to supervising, instructing and putting new recruits through their paces.

Soon we became quite comfortable about the actual driving process but remained a little apprehensive about the different driving rules, regulations and terminology used in the USA compared to the UK. For example in the US, the traffic light sequence is slightly different, as the red and amber lights do not appear together prior to going green, they just change from red to green. It is even acceptable practice turn right and proceed against a red traffic light, after briefly slowing or stopping to ensure that it is clear and safe to proceed, then it is OK to turn in the direction of the traffic, when entering a two way street or junction, although it is necessary to yield to pedestrians, bicycles and other traffic or unless restricted from doing so by a turn sign or police officer.

Initially the American terminology seemed a little strange as they tend to refer to the indicators on a vehicle as 'blinkers', pavement becomes 'sidewalk', drive through becomes 'pull through' and a short overtaking lane becomes a 'turnout'. OK not impossible to come to terms with, but still different and if it had been necessary to take a vehicle test that includes a theory and actual practical driving assessment it would be advantageous to also 'speak their language'. So some homework was called for with much reference being made to the Oregon Driver Manual we had collected at the DMV.

Over the next few days we went to Redmond and then on to the larger city of Bend to do some essential shopping for our forthcoming adventure and while there managed to locate a small computer store where we were able to purchase a very nice wide screen Centrino Wi-Fi laptop computer at a fairly modest price. Fortunately we had done our homework and appreciated that as we wanted to use the machine initially in the United States where 115/120 volt 60 cycles supply is normal and also when we returned home to the UK where a 230/240-volt 50cycle supply is standard, we needed a model that would be compatible with the electrical mains power supplies in both countries, so we took care to select a model that would operate successfully with a 100 to 240 voltage with a 50 to 60 Hertz supply.

Back at Crooked River Ranch we took the opportunity to explore some of the area on foot and were pleasantly surprised by the number of people, that we did not know, who wanted to stop and speak with us, cars that were passing would pull alongside and the occupants would engage in a brief chat before resuming their journey, even the larger vehicles that could not stop on the narrow roads would 'toot their horn' or give a friendly wave of the hand as they drove by and that even included the local sheriff.

During such conversations our accent soon indicated that we were not American and were often mistaken for Canadian or Australian, although a few people did quickly appreciate that we were from the UK but it was mostly those that had visited our home country at some time in their life.

Eventually we had to get down to the serious business of finding vehicle insurance and so recommenced our search for a company willing to insure the Trek for an acceptable and not an exorbitant premium.

In reality this proved more difficult than anticipated, for example when Jim telephoned AARP he was told they would not insure us, furthermore as soon as they found out that Jim now shared ownership of the Trek with us, they immediately cancelled his existing insurance!!

Next we tried Camping World, who use GMAC Insurance and were quoted $1,249 for just six-months which was similar to the premium quoted by the Good Sam Club!!!!

We then made a telephone call to Bill Pierce Insurance Inc in Redmond who re-confirmed that they could arrange insurance for us and it should not be a major problem and to our utter surprise and delight they stated that the premium, via Progressive Insurance, would still only be $1,112 for a whole twelve months, success at long last!!!

The final arrangements were eventually falling into place and after all the recent traumas could now start to look forward to hitting the road in our very own RV in the next day or so.

Later in the day we visited the insurance company and quickly obtained the necessary insurance cover that also included breakdown cover and concluded the deal there and then.

Luckily they were quite happy to accept our International Driving Permits however they explained that we would need to hold an Oregon driving licence, with a clean accident free driving record for three years or more before we would be eligible for a lower insurance premium.

While at their offices we also took the opportunity to get our bill of sale for the Trek stamped by a member of staff who also acts as a Notary Public.

Tuesday 30 March

While Linda and Carol went off to Redmond to obtain some essential food items in preparation for our forthcoming trip, Jim suggested we take the Trek out for the first short run to ensure everything was OK before setting out on Our American Dream. So after adjusting the driver's seat, the mirrors and fastening the seat belts, the ignition key was inserted and a check made to ensure that the automatic gearbox selector was in 'park'. The key was very cautiously turned and almost instantly the large 6.5 litre turbo diesel engine burst into life and began to clatter, as if excitedly talking to us about what was going to happen next. After a short period of time the engine note changed and became much quieter, as it began to get warmer, then with one foot on the brake reverse gear was selected so that we could move the vehicle on to the driveway. All went well and once this had been successfully achieved came to a halt and then with one foot on the brakes selected 'drive' and then very, very gently edged forward. When the Trek reached the tarmac road at the end of the short driveway, we accelerated and were pleasantly surprised by the way the vehicle changed gear extremely smoothly, so well in-fact that it was very difficult to initially detect that another gear had been selected. As the road was narrow, it was advisable to keep the speed down, especially as it was necessary to negotiate some acute almost blind bends as we left the ranch area but driving was not as difficult as originally anticipated although considerable care was needed to correctly position this 'monster' on the road and the tension increased as we encountered a large truck coming the other way so almost came to halt to allow it to pass as there was not a great deal of clearance on either side. As the journey progressed, Jim continued to provide useful hints and tips so that my confidence increased so much that I soon became quite at home and started to enjoy the experience. We drove slowly through the adjacent countryside and then returned to the ranch safely and without incident having covered about twenty-eight miles and parked the Trek near to Jim's garage. When Linda and Carol returned later that day the opportunity was taken to fill the vehicle's tank with fresh water and all the food was stowed safely away in the generous cupboards, refrigerator and deep freezer. The following day was spent at the ranch where time was taken to do a few last minute checks on the vehicles as well as to peruse the maps and plan the route that we would be taking the following day, that night we did not sleep very much as we were too excited.

VIVA LAS VEGAS

Las Vegas Bound

Thursday 1 April

Having finished an early breakfast we all climbed into our respective RV's, accompanied by Jim and Carol's dog Mattie and their cat Homer, as they certainly did not intend missing out on the adventure.

Soon Jim's 'C' class Lexington burst into life, as did the Trek's, but as the Lexington had a gas engine it seemed much quieter than that of the Trek.

After waiting a few moments to allow the engines to 'wake-up' we followed Jim and edged the vehicles down the short drive then made our way slowly through the winding road away from the Crooked River Ranch area to join Highway 97 South.

Shortly after joining the highway we stopped at a garage in Terrebonne to fill the RV's with fuel and were surprised to learn that in the State of Oregon that the garage attendant has to operate the pumps and deliver the fuel. This being the case we were pleased that we did not have to get our hands dirty and it was a great experience to be able to say 'fill her up' without having to worry unduly about the cost, something we would probably not be able to do in the UK. The Trek's tank eagerly gulped down 21.98 gallons at $1.8/gallon then we rejoined the highway and drove through Redmond where our speed had to reduced as the roads seemed extremely narrow especially as there were quite a few cars and some trucks parked by the roadside. At this point the Trek seemed incredibly wide and we thought possibly too wide at some stages, so much so that Linda had to provide feedback on the available clearance on her side of the vehicle. With nerves a little on edge after the narrow roads of Redmond we were relieved to find Highway 97 improved as we passed through Bend and drove on through the Deschutes National Forest, which Linda said was quite spectacular, although the driver was far too concerned about keeping the Trek safely on what became quite a fast road. Even at around 55mph fairly moderate imperfections in the road's surface could send the Trek dancing all over the place and this could be very alarming at times and this came as an unwelcome surprise as our Swift Kon-Tiki had been far better mannered with firmer suspension and superior road holding.

About one hundred miles south of Bend on Highway 97 we stopped at the Collier Memorial State Park and Logging Museum, that was started back in 1947 when the Collier brothers donated a collection of logging equipment. The very interesting outdoor collection shows the evolution of logging equipment from oxen to axes, as well as trucks to chain saws and also highlights the significant role the railroad contributed to the industry. We were all naturally very eager to see as much as possible in the short time available so took the opportunity to stretch our legs and stroll in just a small section of the vast 146 acre site and read from the display boards that years ago the Pacific Northwest used to be covered by dense forest of pine and fir with some trees measuring as much as four feet in diameter with bark up to one foot thick.

Back in the 1800's the loggers often from far away places such as Michigan, Wisconsin and Minnesota brought their specialised equipment with them and according to history led a very tough life, working 10 or more hours per day for six days a week earning only about $30 or if they were really lucky $40 per month. They lived a primitive existence housed in small timber dwellings heated by wood burning stoves and had little to occupy themselves after their shift or on their one day off per week. Logging was often a hazardous occupation and the men were expected to work tirelessly with equipment that was very similar to that used by the early settlers to the British Colonies in the 1660's. In the early days oxen were used to pull the logs directly to the mills or to the river where they could be floated to the mill, but by the 1880's horses had taken the place of the oxen but with the introduction of steam power and wire rope, less men and horses were needed and by the early 1920's the horses were replaced by gas powered engines. These machines proved to be more efficient and economical than the horse and it appears that the inventors eventually merged their operations to adopt the now well-known name of the Caterpillar Company.

It seemed as we had taken a step back in time as we gazed at just some of the machinery on display that included the Ground Hog Sawmill Engine, the Horse Powered Drag Saw, the Austin Rip Snorter Pull Grader and the McGiffert Quarter-Boom Log Loader etc, a truly very interesting collection of machinery and equipment that would be worthy of another visit if we are ever in the area again. Regrettably all too soon we had to return to our RV's to resume our journey on Highway 97 South and our journey took us close to the Klamath Falls where we joined Highway 39 South passing through Merrill, then joined Highway 139 South, then turned on to Highway 359 passing the Madoc National Forest on our right. After two hundred and fifty eight miles our small convoy pulled off the road at Canby adjacent to a small and very picturesque fast flowing narrow river and as it was now fairly late in the evening Linda prepared some really excellent buffalo burgers for us all to eat as we all settled down in the large, comfortable living/lounge area of the Trek to discuss the day's journey and consult the map to reconfirm our route for the following day.

We were all tired after what appeared to be a long journey, so soon Jim and Carol retreated to their own RV and we settled down for the night or that was the plan!! However we did not really appreciate how cold the night was going to be or how ferocious the wind was to become, the Trek was buffeted continually so much so we were both concerned that we may be blown over, the wind was really that strong and as it was extremely cold did not get much sleep!!

Friday April 2

On waking early in the morning Linda looked out of the Trek's side window and was delighted, but a little surprised to see a small herd of around ten or so mule deer swimming across the river and then graze on the lush drew covered green grass that was in the sun adjacent to the two RV's, the grass not far away was by contrast still white as it was in the shade and had not yet recovered from the hard overnight frost.

After a quick breakfast we resumed our journey but were concerned that the Lexington was able to leave the Trek standing when we approached any real gradient but thought this was probably because a gas and not a diesel engine powered it.

Nevertheless when Jim and the Lexington pulled in to refuel sometime later, we continued on and as we attempted the next long climb soon realised that all was not well with the Trek, as our speed continued to fall dramatically until we were moving at a mere 3 to 4 mph with the accelerator pressed hard to the floor and with a rapidly growing stream of traffic behind we just had no alternative but to pull off the road, to take refuge in the car park of a nearby hotel.

We used our hand held 'walkie-talkie' to alert Jim to our problem and luckily by the time the Lexington arrived had managed to restart the Trek which seemed as if by some miracle to have recovered from it's apparent problem. We spent some time discussing and analysing the apparent symptoms that had almost brought the Trek to a complete standstill, concluding that there may have been some water in the diesel fuel purchased from the garage back in Terrebonne. Fortunately at this stage the Trek appeared to be a running little better, so continued our journey and followed behind the Lexington through Susanville on to Highway 395 and a little later crossed the border into Nevada.

However the Trek still seemed to be very sluggish when any significant incline was encountered and Jim was so concerned about the RV's apparent lack of performance; that he elected to drive the vehicle for a few miles. During this test drive it was not possible to detect any obvious lack of performance, but on this section of the journey we did not encounter any really significant inclines, nevertheless, we were still not too impressed with the Trek's ability to climb hills but still managed to reach Reno where we stopped to refuel. As we were now in Nevada we had to refuel the vehicles ourselves and at this point discovered the possible cause of the Trek's lack of performance!!!! We found that the filler cap was missing and concluded that it had not been replaced when we had stopped for fuel at Terrebonne or that it had been incorrectly fitted so had possibly fallen off somewhere along the road!!!!

After refuelling we drove immediately to a nearby auto store to purchase a replacement fuel cap, but this proved to be a little more difficult than we had hoped, as they could not identify from their records which cap should be fitted to the Trek, so had to try a number of options that looked about right until we found what Jim believed to be the correct one. While in the store we also took the opportunity to purchase some fuel additive to clean the fuel injectors just incase the problem was actually still due to dirty or watery fuel.

As we continued our journey to Las Vegas, we suddenly found that Jim had guided us via one of the cities featured in many well known Western films, yes it was Virginia City, which is just about twenty five miles southeast of Reno at the base of the Sierra Nevada Mountains and is some fourteen miles east of nearby Carson City off Highway 50.

After parking the Lexington and Trek safely in a large car park, it was really magical to walk on the wooden sidewalks, to see and occasionally touch some of the frontier style saloons, restaurants and buildings that had been restored and/or recreated following a devastating fire of 1875 when around 2,000 structures were destroyed. Virginia City is a very photogenic location that will probably leave a lasting magical memory for years to come and was a very, very memorable experience and one not to be missed by anyone visiting the area.

During our all too brief stay, we learnt that much of the city's wealth along with that of Carson City and San Francisco came from the silver mines of the Comstock Lode, a solid seam of pure silver discovered beneath Mount Hamilton in 1859. During the 1870's Virginia City became the mining metropolis of the West with 30,000 residents, banks, churches, theatres and around 110 saloons and the Comstock Lode mines eventually yielded over $400 million in gold and silver so still remains the richest known US silver deposit.

Apparently Virginia City is the largest Federal designated historical district in America and that the brothers Ethan and Hosea Grosh discovered gold in six mile canyon in 1857, unfortunately they died before they could register their claim and according to legend fellow miner Henry Comstock stumbled across their incredible find but claimed it was his.

Miner James Finney is said to have christened the newly 'tent and dug out town' as 'Old Virginny Town' in honor of himself and his birthplace, however rich deposits of gold and silver ore helped to turn the name into Virginia City. William Ralston and James Crocker founders of the bank of California made their first fortunes in the city, as did Leland Stanford, George Hurst, John Mackay and William Flood, other famous residents were Mark Twain and Brete Hart who both wrote for the Territorial Enterprise—Nevada's first newspaper.

In 1898 the excavations along the fissures vein that descended more than 3,000 feet was flooded by water and this plus the halt in silver dollar coinage eventually brought operations to a somewhat sad end.

After this brief history lesson we had to leave this historic location and resume our journey leaving Virginia City behind us as we headed North East on Highway 50 as far as Silver Springs, where we joined Alternative Highway 95, leading to Las Vegas.

As we had been on the road most of the day we were all very tired and to save having to do any cooking in the RV's, stopped in Hawthorne at a well-known hamburger establishment to enjoy some burgers and chips. Later we travelled just a mile or so down the road to spend the night at the El Capitan Casino and when we pulled into their large free parking area noted that we had covered three hundred and seventeen miles during the day. We were lucky enough to find a reasonably quite space adjacent to some very large RV's that included a few very tasty Monaco and Beaver RV's, their owners also doing a little dry camping for the night. Just before dark we walked round the car park looking, with a little envy, at many of the really beautiful RV's and wondered where they had come from and where they were going.

OK we did appreciate that the vehicles' place of registration is normally displayed on their registration plates, but that may not actually be where the owners actually lived, after all our Trek had Oregon plates but it's new owners were based in the UK.

Later in the evening we ventured into the El Capitain Casino, in the naive hope of winning a fortune at the tables, but with only a few dollars to play with this seemed most unlikely. Bright lights bombarded us from all directions as we ventured through the doors and we were greeted by the metallic tinkling and clattering of coins being feverishly inserted in the vast array of slot machines and could just see through the haze of smoke all the gamblers intently looking at the screens, waiting to see and hear the joyful sound of money tumbling into the tray below.

It was not however necessary to use a computer or even a calculator to quickly work out that the gamblers were not really on the winning side and that more money was going to the casino coffers compared to that being won by the punters.

Undeterred and still full of hope, Linda and Carol played a few slot machines, but as luck did not seem to be on their side both called a halt to the proceedings when they had won a little and then lost it all and concluded that gambling all of $5 each was going to be their limit. At the same time Jim and I walked round to check out some of the other gambling activities that were going on and listened for a while to the live music and observed the many the gamblers who came from all walks of life. Some were dressed in full Western attire, complete with obligatory white Stetson and they could have just walked off the set of a Western movie, while others looked as is they had just left the farm and others the office, unfortunately the atmosphere was too smoky and as they say 'the air could be cut with a knife' so decided to call it a night and return to the RV's.

Saturday 3 April

We were all ready to go early, but were a little surprised to see that quite a number of the other RV's had already departed from the El Capitain obviously eager to beat the rush.

Pulling out of the car park it was possible to see the Excelsior Mountains in the distance as we rejoined Highway 95 South on the last leg of our journey to Las Vegas. Both Linda and I had been surprised at the ever-changing scenery that had been encountered so far, that ranged from beautiful forest areas of pine and fir to remote desert planes with little or no vegetation or any obvious signs of life with roads that were almost totally empty so it was a real joy to travel in such a stress free environment soaking up the atmosphere as we settled into our new home on wheels. As the roads were generally very good and as we were becoming more familiar with the Trek's handling characteristics it was possible to take time out to look at the scenery a little more and really enjoyed seeing some of the large RV's we encountered on route. These immaculate vehicles were frequently around 40 feet long or more and seemed to be travelling effortlessly at around 60mph while towing a car, possibly a Cadillac or something similar!!!

Nevertheless concentration was still needed to keep the Trek firmly on track, as it was all too easy for the RV to wander on the road and veer on to the verge on the passenger side, which prompted Linda to issue a sharp word of warning in the hope that things would be rectified before it was too late. Under these circumstances it was very important to not over correct the steering as this could lead to rapid movement towards any traffic coming the other way, but believe it or not, with practice we were actually getting much better.

Later we stopped for a break and Carol said that she had been trying to use her mobile phone to contact Circus Circus, our next planned overnight stop, but due to poor reception had not been successful but Linda was not able to get any signal on her mobile so luckily it was not an emergency. During our stop Carol did manage to make contact with Circus Circus only to be told that they were currently fully booked for this coming Saturday as a motor racing event was taking place at a nearby circuit, however they would accept our booking for the two RV's from Sunday for three nights, but we were told that the fee would be around $35/night for a fully serviced hard standing pitch and this was more expensive than Carol had been previously told.

We were left wondering where we could spend the night and after a short discussion decided that we would head for the Wal-Mart supermarket near Las Vegas, so continued our journey south on Highway 95 passing close to the Nellis Air Force Bombing and Gunnery Range, but could not see any activity. Later we passed Scotty's Junction and crossed Sarcobatus Flat, through Beatty and across the Amargosa Desert region and on our right could see signs to Death Valley National Park, so agreed that we would try to make a short visit there if we returned along the same route.

Our journey took us close to the Toiyabe National Forest, Indian Springs Air Force Base as well as the Mount Charleston Wilderness Area then on towards Las Vegas but needed to stop to add a little more diesel to the Trek's tank taking on board 10.25 gallons that cost $20 as it was almost on the red line.

After five hundred and five miles the small convoy pulled into Wal-Mart on Tropical Boulevard and easily found ample parking, away from the store entrance, so as not to inconvenience any of the other customers. There a thoroughly enjoyable quick snack was prepared and eaten, later we ventured into the supermarket and were extremely surprised at the immense size of the store, we really needed a map plus a Navajo guide to ensure we did not get lost. The store was just incredible, at one end of the supermarket it was possible to buy a set of automobile tyres, have them fitted, while a mechanic completed an oil change, walk further through to purchase a gun, ammunition, canoe or fishing gear, then continue on to buy a whole range of electrical equipment, then stop to acquire a range of shoes or clothes and then load up with vast amounts of food, stopping of course to select the appropriate live lobster, before emerging at the exit fully laden.

Later in the day two people stopped to speak to Jim and Carol so before long we were drawn into the conversation with our friends and introduced to Dave and his wife Janet, who had recently purchased a newer Safari Trek so were keen to speak with other owners.

During the conversation Linda happened to mention that we wanted to purchase a more detailed map that would cover the rest of our journey and this was enough to prompt David, a Good Sam's Club member, to head off in the direction of the adjacent Sam's Club (part of Wal-Mart) only to resurface a little later with a super map that also contained the addresses of all the Wal-Mart stores throughout the US and this would prove invaluable for the remainder of our trip.

We were extremely pleased and thought that this was a brilliant gesture by David, so were only too pleased to reimburse him and then later exchanged home e-mail addresses. Walking back to our RV we just could not believe how friendly and helpful some Americans could be not only had we obtained a super map at a very good price, David promised to e-mail some useful information related to Treks.

The Vegas experience

Sunday 4 April – Wednesday 7April

After making an early start to avoid as much local traffic as possible we drove from our overnight Wal-Mart stop towards Vegas and soon found ourselves on a fast, very busy freeway, which was intimidating, as the Trek was being forced along by the traffic at speeds higher than we would have wished to travel, particularly as we were not too certain of our route, even with a map. Approaching our destination we could see what must have been a mirage rising out of the desert right before our eyes, but no, as we drove closer could clearly see it was in-fact Las Vegas with its high rise 'Disney' like buildings towering before us.

After around sixteen hectic miles or so, we eventually arrived safely at Circus Circus, one of the major hotels with its own casino conveniently located right on Las Vegas Boulevard where Linda booked us into the Circusland RV Park at the rear of the complex, but nothing could really have prepared us for the sight that unfolded before our eyes. There were literally hundreds of RV's already parked there, ranging from vehicles as small as the Trek right up to the large and very luxurious American Eagles, Monaco Windsors, Dutch Stars, Bounders, Prevosts and of course quite a few Trailers and Fifth Wheelers. From our site plan we concluded there were over three hundred and fifty pitches all fully serviced with their own 50 amp power supplies, fresh water plus waste disposal points, in addition there were also laundry facilities, a store, video arcade, three swimming pools and probably much, much more.

We were told that inside Circus Circus there were actually three full size casinos, numerous restaurants as well as snack bars, too many shops to visit and the 'Adventuredome' that claims to be the world's largest indoor theme park, the venue therefore seemed suitable for children and adults alike with just so much to do and see without even leaving the complex.

With the booking in procedure completed we slowly made our way through the park along Midway Boulevard to our own pitch, number 360 on Ringling Drive and quickly made all the necessary connections to the Trek from the adjacent island services.

Although it was our first full 'hook-up' everything was fairly simple, nevertheless it was necessary to fight with the Trek's inbuilt heavy-duty landline mains power cable as it seemed to have a mind of its own and was difficult to manoeuvre due to it's very large diameter necessary to cope with a current of up to 50 amps, happily Jim and Carol were on hand as always to provide valuable help and assistance should it have been needed.

It soon became apparent that the circus theme had been carried through to all of the roadway names within the complex that included Big Top Drive, Clown Street, Dumbo Drive and Ring Master Drive.

With fantastic blue skies all around and the temperatures nearing seventy degrees Fahrenheit, we changed into suitable attire, tee shirts plus shorts and headed off to the main lobby of the Circus Circus hotel to meet some friends of Jim and Carol.

After the formal introductions, we set off via taxi to the 'Bellagio', a really luxurious hotel some two or so miles away to really enjoy our time in the unbelievable, beautiful indoor Conservatory and Botanical Gardens. We strolled through the complex and were really taken by the sight and aroma of more than 10,000 blooming flowers that included lilies, tulips, chrysanthemums plus cherry trees, ferns and weeping willows. The focal point of the exhibit was the 'Temple of Love' in the West garden, a structure designed to recreate a temple built at Versailles for Marie Antoinette by Louis XVI in 1778 to house many live giant butterflies and in keeping with this theme and suspended from the ceiling throughout the building were many artistic and eye catching model butterflies, a really fantastic sight.

Before long, we were quickly ushered outside so as not miss the fountain display and from our vantage point stood shoulder to shoulder patiently alongside hundreds of other visitors that had gathered to see the show. At four pm, the display commenced and everyone was treated to a mesmerizing ballet of water fountains rising high into the air, choreographed to the music of Celine Dion, this was truly a magnificent and unforgettable sight; a photographic opportunity not to be missed if ever in the area.

Returning to the Trek we were greeted by Don, a very nice jovial gentleman who was casting a discerning eye over our RV and it transpired that he owned a more recent model and during the subsequent conversation invited Linda and myself over to see his vehicle. It turned out that Don was a retired ex-military man and with his wife Chiyo had travelled extensively in their RV all over the US and seemed to have literally been to every US state at least once. Don and Chiyo were great Trek enthusiasts and were staying at Circus Circus prior to setting off in a few days to attend a forthcoming Safari Trek Convention. Apparently these Conventions can be attended by several hundred Trek owners and are a great place to exchange ideas and to learn more about the vehicles, it was a real shame that we did not have sufficient time to join in all the fun.

While at Circus Circus and with temperatures of around 60/70 degrees Fahrenheit, we walked the Strip each day and attempted to take in all the sights, leaving early in the morning and returning just before or after dark each evening absolutely exhausted but exhilarated by the experience.

It proved impossible in the time available to cover many of the fabulous attractions, as it was quite easy to spend a considerable amount of time at each Casino/Hotel visited just soaking up the atmosphere, looking at the sights, window shopping of course and then trying to find the way out!!! No mean task, as many of the buildings are exceptionally large extending over multiple floors, so it is all too easy to get lost in a big way.

The food in Vegas is extremely enticing so each evening we were spoilt for choice as there were just so many places to choose from and then the decision had to be made about what to order, the burgers were mouthwatering as was the pizza and of course there were the famous gigantic American steaks.

One evening the four of us ordered a steak meal in one of restaurants in Circus Circus where there was the choice of soup or salad as a starter, followed by a very large and extremely succulent Rib Eye Steak Meal all for the price of just under $9 plus tax per person.

Time just seemed to race by and all too soon we had to say goodbye to our friends Carol and Jim, as they had to return to Oregon and their home at Crooked River Ranch. Very soon we realised that from now on that we were on our own, initially quite a daunting prospect as we still had a long way to go and did not even relish the thought of finding our own way out of Vegas when the time eventually came to leave, nevertheless we remained in a good positive frame of mind.

A little research while in Vegas revealed that it was founded in 1905 as a stop over for the Union Pacific Railway as it was conveniently situated between Los Angeles and Salt Lake City so when in 1931 gambling was made legal it was frequented by many of the workers from the nearby Hoover Dam. Although it did not take long before it became the gambling centre for the entire country and is regarded by many as an endless playground of bright lights, countless hotels and casinos, topless revues and live entertainment so has attracted stars such as Frank Sinatra, Liberace and of course Elvis to perform there.

For anyone doing some serious Las Vegas sightseeing a visit to the Stratosphere really should be high on the agenda and it is certainly recommended to anyone fortunate enough to visit the Strip, this large hotel/casino can be seen from Circusland and so was only a short walk away so it did not take us long to agree that it was a 'must see' opportunity. The 'Stratosphere' is in-fact a rather special hotel/casino built below a very tall tower rising some 1,149 feet above the Las Vegas Boulevard and we wondered and asked ourselves many times, if we would be brave enough to take the lift to the top observation platform, but of course we would and thoroughly enjoyed the truly panoramic 360-degree view from both the indoor and outdoor observation decks.

The views over the Strip were just awesome and should not to be missed as they present numerous photographic opportunities and provide breathtaking views across Las Vegas so with clear skies it is possible to see as far as the mountains in the distance, we could even see our very own RV parked at Circus Circus, although it did look exceedingly small.

Linda took some remarkable photographs of the Stratosphere's very own window cleaner merrily cleaning the windows on the outside of the building at around 1,000 feet in the air and although he was in a special cage of course, he was still a very brave man nonetheless.

In addition Linda managed to get some unbelievable photographic shots of some incredibly brave or was it foolish people above us on the outside of the building on the 'High Roller-Coaster' a device that twists and turns over and above the observation deck. Then there was 'Big Shot' that literally shoots the riders some 160 feet vertically in the air before falling back to the launch pad. If these rides were not scary enough, there were super brave people, we would possibly categories them as 'completely crazy or insane', that were prepared to ride on 'X Scream'.

This terrifying device looked like a large green sled that travelled from somewhere outside and above our vantage point up the tower then transported the seated occupants way over the side of the building at around 30 mph and then just at the last minute dipped as if to tip the riders down to the ground many hundreds of feet below. Just watching scared us and even the journey back down in the lift at 21 mph was fast enough as our ears popped during the decent and so were really pleased to land safely.

In the afternoon we met another very nice couple called Peter and Debbie who were staying on the next pitch to ourselves at Circus Circus, in their 34 foot long Gulfstream along with their German Shepherd dog called Vilo. On several occasions they were kind enough to take us in their Honda CRV that they towed behind their RV, further along the Strip than we had managed to walk before to visit 'Excalibur', a themed medieval castle with knights in armour and dragons lurking in the darkness. Adjacent to this remarkable building even more photographic opportunities presented themselves and some good shots of 'New York' and the 'MGM' entertainment complex were soon captured on camera. One large poster proclaimed that the world famous band, the "Eagles", would be flying in to performing yet another farewell tour in May, but unfortunately we would be far away by then.

While in the area it proved impossible to resist the temptation to purchase a rather large and intoxicating pair of 'Margarita's for just one dollar each and felt that was pretty good value for money!!!!!!

During one of our marathon walking trips we noticed quite a number of RV's parked in the very large car park at the rear of the New Frontier Hotel/Casino, situated a block or so further down the Strip from Circus Circus. Keen to make some new acquaintances we stopped to talk to several people who were very friendly and during our discussions learnt that it was possible for RV's to stay in the car park of the Frontier for around three days free of charge but it may be possible at this time of year to stay a little longer, all we had to do was to call in and speak to the receptionist in the hotel; so this seemed an ideal way to extend our stay in Vegas without incurring more site fees.

We were also advised that when we resumed our journey that we should keep our eyes open for the 'Flying J Travel Plazas' as they are RV friendly.

Our new acquaintances even gave us a 'Flying J' leaflet that explained that the company has over 160 locations and claims to be North America's premier highway hospitality service provider. The facilities at 'Flying J's' are apparently used and enjoyed by many lorry drivers or should we say 'truckers' as they offer competitively priced fuel, food and trucker shower facilities and much, much more. 'Flying J's' also welcome RV's by providing free overnight parking, often alongside the many trucks, low LPG prices, fresh-water and RV dump-station facilities.

Thursday 8 April – Saturday 10 April

In the morning after disconnecting the Trek from the electricity, fresh water and dump facilities at Circus Circus we said our fond farewells then moved just a mile or so down the Strip towards 'The New Frontier Hotel/Casino' where we planned to stop for a while.

Staying at this venue also meant that we would have a little less walking to do to get right in amongst the action along the Strip, but on arrival the signs at the front of the complex were a little intimidating as they stated 'No RV Parking', but not to be deterred we drove round to the rear of the premises and soon located the dedicated flat tarmac park for RV's. There we noticed that about a dozen other RV's were already parked, but there was still a lot of space left for our little Trek and during the day more vehicles arrived, including a very expensive looking 40 foot or more long American Eagle and an equally large and impressive Damon Escaper that had both come all the way from Quebec in Canada and it transpired that the owners had been on the road since early December 2003 and were now on route to the Grand Canyon.

Although there was no 'hook-up' on this site to provide water or electricity, the hotel did provide large bins for dumping general rubbish or should that be trash?

The New Frontier boasts of having five restaurants, countless slot machines and numerous gaming tables in the 65,000 square feet casino, but unlike Circus Circus is understood to be designed primarily for adults. The venue also provides some exceptionally good evening entertainment in Gilley's saloon that includes live country music with very professional bands and in addition on certain evenings they feature bikini-clad girls who apparently enjoy a spot of mud wrestling and some are also known to participate in a little bull riding (the mechanical version of course).

Linda and I did venture into Gilley's one evening where full Western gear was warn by both male and female, so Stetsons, boots, chequered shirts and belts featuring large flashy buckles were very much in evidence, there was even sawdust on the floor. During the evening we noticed some 'mean dudes' who really added to the fantastic atmosphere, we thought we had gone back in time as we listened to the really excellent sounding six piece live country band and could not resist the occasional look over the coral to see all those dudes and gals enjoying their line dancing, but although the place was extremely crowded everyone appeared polite and well behaved, even those mean dudes!!!

Before long we noticed that Gilley's served super food and we were utterly amazed to see the portion sizes, enough to feed Linda and I for several days, the portions seemed too large even for the Americans as so much quality food seemed to be left on the very generous sized plates.

Although still comparative strangers to Vegas we were soon at home hopping on and off the various 'hotel courtesy buses' to get to new venues without having to walk quite so much in the heat.

During one afternoon we visited the 'Auto Collection' at the Imperial Palace, as we had acquired some complimentary entry tickets from one of the many 'street touts'. Once inside we strolled around some 250 classic cars, including a 1933 Duesberg and marvelled at the craftsmanship that had been lovingly spent on it and all the other classic vehicles so could not help wondering who would be prepared or be able to part with up to $5 million dollars in order to own a piece of automobile history?

To be honest I rather fancied a beautiful green Aston Martin, but at a mere $3 million had to say to the attendant 'sorry but I've left my wallet at home'!!!

We also ventured out as far as the Hard Rock Hotel/Casino and spent some considerable time admiring or should I say drooling over the guitars once owned by the likes of Eric Clapton, David Bowie, Carlos Santana and stared at the outrageous stage costumes of Elton John, Brittany Spears and of course Madonna and also those of many other famous artists.

We frequently wondered how best to summarise our visit to Las Vegas and in the end settled on just one word 'breathtaking', however we did appreciate that Vegas may not be to everyone's liking as it is fast and furious so is certainly 'over the top' in many respects, but in our opinion it most definitely lived up to the apt nickname of 'the entertainment capital of the world'.

Nevertheless we learnt that there is much more to Vegas than just the Strip and Downtown Las Vegas, as the entire valley offers fun and excitement as well as the natural beauty and the breathtaking sight of the surrounding desert. We were amazed to learn that in the year 2003 around 36 million people visited the area and then heard the local radio station stating that a staggering $860 million was spent in the casinos in February 2004 alone!!!!

As may already be appreciated, The Strip is fantastic by day, but it takes on an even more magical theme at nightfall when millions and millions of multi coloured flashing neon lights and displays are switched on, then literally everything becomes even larger than life. It was well worth the visit and would return again in the future if we ever have the opportunity, everyone encountered seemed to be extremely polite, friendly and helpful, especially all the RV owners.

However anyone contemplating a visit would be well advised to prepare accordingly by carrying ample drinking water, as it is all too easy to dehydrate and of course it is essential to wear very comfortable clothing as well as appropriate shoes and be prepared to walk and walk. Yes, there are numerous retail shops and venues oriented specifically towards the mass of tourists, but there are many very up market department stores and retail outlets such as Gucci, Prada and Chanel that would rival the very best to be found in London or Paris, with prices to match.

It is not really necessary to spend a fortune to enjoy Vegas as people watching is free and there are many breathtaking, fabulous buildings to see and there is also an abundance of fee shows to enjoy.

THE VALLEY OF FIRE AND LAKE MEAD

Valley of Fire

Sunday 11 April

We realised that it was Easter Sunday as we stowed our possessions safely away in the Trek and said a really very sad farewell to The New Frontier and headed out of Las Vegas bound for 'The Valley of Fire'.

Fortunately our journey out of Vegas was far easier and quicker than we had anticipated, so it was not long before we were heading North on Interstate 15, but as we were low on diesel and needed to dump our grey and black waste decided to try to find one of the 'Flying J Travel Plazas' near Cheyenne at Exit 46. As we left this exit we noticed a number of large trucks that appeared to be heading towards the same venue or at least we hoped they were, so tagged along behind for the last part of the journey and luckily arrived without any trouble.

With the Trek refreshed and loaded with fuel, all of 31.16 gallons that cost $66.03, we resumed our journey and headed North on Highway 15 until we turned off on to Highway 169, which was just inside the Moapa Indian Reservation, down the narrow winding and undulating road to the 'Valley of Fire' State Park.

Having paid our modest $6 entrance fee we trundled slowly through the valley and were absolutely astounded by the sights of the magnificent sandstone rocks that lay before us as they displayed dazzling hughes of red, pink and grey rising as if by magic out of what in reality was a very barren land. Few words can adequately describe the scene and unfortunately even high quality photographs are hard pressed to accurately capture the picture, it was just magic.

We detoured slightly passing fascinatingly named places such as the 'Beehives' which are very unusual sandstone formations weathered by the ever eroding forces of nature, 'Mouse's Tank' apparently named after a renegade Indian who used the area as a hideout way back in the 1890's, 'Rainbow Vista' a favourite photographic opportunity with breathtaking panoramic views of multi coloured sandstone.

Although it was a Bank Holiday there was very little traffic so our journey was unhurried and very relaxed allowing plenty of time to stop at the designated 'stops' to take many, many photographs.

We then continued our journey along Highway 169 until we came to 'Overton Beach Marina', located on the Northern arm of Lake Mead National Recreational Area and it is an ideal location for boating, water skiing and water boarding with its purpose built slipways and many secluded sandy beaches.

It also boasts of having a good RV park so is an idyllic place to spend the night or even longer and is not that expensive at $19/night, for full hook-up with super uninterrupted views of the surrounding area.

This was one of our more leisurely days, as we covered just seventy eight miles from Vegas to our overnight stop at Overton Beach Marina, so spent much of the afternoon relaxing and walking by the shore admiring enviously many of the expensive motor boats moored on the covered jetty.

Lake Mead

Monday 12 April - Tuesday 13 April

With the Trek refreshed from it's overnight stop at the very tranquil location of Overton Beach Marina, we headed south on the North Shore Road, towards 'Government Wash' where we were told that we could probably dry camp for a number of days without any charge.

As we purred along in the luxury of our RV we were absolutely mesmerised by the scenic views and again encountered very little traffic, on the left we could see glimpses of Lake Mead as we rounded some tight bends and when not in view we could see fantastic multi coloured rock formations, while on the right were the Muddy Valley Mountains rising majestically in the distance.

Naturally we took full advantage of the many photographic opportunities with the camera working overtime as we stopped at quite a few of the designated 'Photo Stops'.

Then after a mere forty four miles or so we pulled off the North Shore Road then followed the signs to Government Wash, where we were greeted by signs indicating that free camping was permitted for up to 15 days at a time on the headland.

The sights as we pulled in were really breathtaking so quickly found a fairly level site on the gravelled surface, but still needed to use our levelling jacks to make the RV occupants feel comfortable. From this vantage point we had panoramic views of the surrounding mountains as well as the stunning Lake Mead and although there were other happy campers dotted about the area, they were in the distance so there were plenty more unoccupied camping spaces so yet again had fortunately found another peaceful and magical location.

We studied the information we had collected and learnt that before Lake Mead was created that this had been a very sparsely populated desert area that had been home to many Native American groups that had been there for at least 10,000 years. Then in the twentieth century modern pioneers built a 726-foot high dam on the Colorado River, higher than any previously constructed dam and it still remains today as the tallest concrete dam in the Western Hemisphere.

The construction is of course the Hoover Dam that calmed the floodwaters of the Colorado River, supplied power for the southwest and changed the nature of the country forever.

Lake Mead is the reservoir created by the Hoover Dam, but the lake only takes a minimum amount of water from the Colorado River itself, nevertheless the lake has created an abundance of water so that each year a specific volume of water is released to supply farms, homes and businesses in Nevada, Arizona, California and Mexico.

However in an average year the amount of water that flows out of Lake Mead is greater than that flowing in, so the water level is going down because the Colorado River runoff in recent years has been below normal so that the water level in Lake Mead is now something like 86 feet lower than it's high of 1,225 feet in mid 1980's.

It is even understood that the historic town of St Thomas, a small western town, that was founded in 1865 can just be seen above the water that covered it for more than thirty years when the Glen Canyon Dam reduced the lake to their current levels.

We were fascinated to learn that Lake Mead is at an elevation of about 1,220 feet and that the reservoir covers roughly 250 square miles and extends about one hundred and ten miles upstream towards the Grand Canyon and about thirty miles up the Virgin River.

The width varies from just several hundred feet in the canyons, up to roughly eight miles and is the largest reservoir in the USA with a shoreline of some five hundred and fifty miles and it was fascinating to learn that the lake was named after Dr Elwood Mead who was the US Reclamation Commissioner between 1924 and 1936.

Geographically the National Recreation Area borders the Mojave desert, The Great Basin and the nearby Sanoran Desert so although Lake Mead occupies less than 13% of the total park area it has 9 marinas, 8 campgrounds and motels as well as 6 RV campgrounds with hook-up and is visited by roughly 7 or 8 million people every year.

Wednesday 14 April

After several peaceful and very relaxing days, we said goodbye to the tranquil and beautiful setting of Government Wash and somewhat reluctantly headed the Trek towards Henderson as we planned to visit the Hoover Dam next and our journey took us along the Lake Mead perimeter Highway 169 then onto Highway 564 along Lake Mead Drive.

Then as we joined Highway 582 we noticed that Camping World had a store just on the other side of the dual carriageway, so decided to do a little retail exploration and pulled in to their car park.

Once inside Camping World it was difficult not to make several purchases and ended up with an RV compass plus a stars and stripes table cloth for some friends, the opportunity was also taken to speak with a member of staff about their range of portable garages and RV covers, although it was soon established that they did not hold such items in stock and that it would be necessary to order by telephone from their head office.

As it was by now reasonably late in the day, enquiries were also made about the feasibility of staying overnight in the Camping World parking area and were told this would be fine, providing the Trek was parked at the rear of the building.

Moving the RV a short distance to the designated area we soon found a very peaceful, tarmac surfaced site that was reasonably level and for a time were the only vehicle there, but eventually as the day drew to a close were joined by one other RV and one Fifth Wheeler, not exactly crowded.

This was one of our shortest daily journeys so far as the Trek registered a total of just twenty miles, however as we had stopped on route to do some essential food shopping at Wal-Mart and another good store called 'Food4Less', the time just seemed to disappear.

Later we walked to a few nearby shops and quickly concluded that walking is not a favourite American pastime, as frequently the pathway or should that be sidewalk would suddenly just stop, never to reappear. To venture further on foot it may then be necessary to 'walk off-road' and proceed on the rough ground adjacent to the road or go through a car park.

Crossing at traffic lights was also a daunting experience as the lights frequently took a long time to change and to signal that it was OK for pedestrians to proceed, however as the roads were very wide it was necessary to move swiftly to even get as far as the centre of the road before the pedestrian lights started to flash signifying they would soon change again, at that point it was necessary to keep an eagle eye out for any vehicles that could emerge from almost nowhere moving rather swiftly.

THE HOOVER DAM AND HISTORIC ROUTE 66

The Hoover Dam

Thursday 15 April

Reasonably early in the morning we rejoined Highway 582 and headed off in the direction of the Hoover Dam, stopping off to do yet more window-shopping and to visit the small street market at Boulder City. With a population just 15,000, Boulder City is an extremely pretty and well-kept environment with beautifully tended green grass, even this early in the year many of the splendid trees that could be seen were already showing vivid green foliage, quite a dramatic contrast to the desert areas that we had grown accustomed to in recent days.

As we approached the Hoover Dam, a number of security personnel were much in evidence and along with all the other vehicles had to pull over for the routine inspection but this was carried out extremely courteously by one of the immaculately dressed guards who wanted to inspect the RV's interior as well as the exterior lockers. After a comparatively swift but thorough examination, the Trek was given the 'all clear', the guard shook my hand, then waved us on our way with the customary phrase of 'have a good day'.

The next phase of the journey involved driving along some very narrow stretches of road with nasty looking Armco barriers that seemed to be very close, at times possibly too close, as we followed the undulating road and also encountered a number of large vehicles as well as trucks coming in the opposite direction. This was a little intimidating to say the least, but we need not really have worried so much as we eventually arrived safely at the perimeter of the dam complex after a journey of some twenty-five miles.

Linda noted as we crossed the road over dam that one side is actually in Nevada and the opposite side is in Arizona but due to heavy traffic we slowly drove the Trek away from the dam and climbed the hill on the Arizona side then parked the Trek in the reasonably large visitors' car park and then walked back to take full advantage of the photographic delights.

What an amazing structure, rising in the air to around 726 feet with a base that is reputed to be some 660 feet thick, a really fantastic feat of engineering that needs to be seen first hand to be fully appreciated.

The dam is actually situated in the Black Canyon on the Colorado River about 30 miles southeast of Las Vegas and is classified as a 'high arch-gravity concrete dam' that is around 1,244 feet in length and about 45 feet wide at the top and as many as 2,000 vehicles a day drive across it.

Informed sources believe that the structure contains around 4.5 million cubic yards of concrete and that during peak electricity demand times, that something like 300,000 gallons of water per second run through the generators; in addition there are 2,700 miles of transmission lines sending electricity from the Hoover Dam to Los Angeles.

Built during the depression the dam surprisingly took less than five years to build and was then the largest dam of it's time and was constructed by on average 3,500 workers, but that total rose to a peak of around 5,200 people and in 1934 the monthly payroll was something like $500,000, a great deal of money in those days.

For the record the pressure at the base of the dam is said to be as much as 45,000lb/square inch a very high pressure indeed.

It is an awesome experience that should not be missed by anyone should they ever get the opportunity to visit the area and it is not surprising that the Hoover Dam is still rated by the American Society of Civil Engineers as one of America's seven modern civil engineering wonders.

As we walked back across the dam we stopped briefly in the centre between the two towers then looked up at the ornaments that rise majestically 40 feet or so above the crest of the pathway and placed one foot in Nevada and one foot in Arizona.

Then to our surprise we were caught off guard by the immense strength of the wind rushing down the valley that suddenly arrived unannounced and almost swept us completely off our feet into the road, luckily no vehicles were passing at the time, we then continued our walk into Arizona retracing our steps up the quite steep hill to the Trek.

Later in the day we continued our journey on Highway 93 Southeast passing the Black Mountains on our right then on to Highway 40 East and off at junction 53, once again the Trek tucked in behind some large trucks that we hoped were also on route to the same the Flying J Travel Plaza at Kingman where we planned to stop overnight.

Fortunately the trucks did go to the same destination, but on our arrival found that the parking area was almost full, so had to park alongside several gigantic trucks so the Trek seemed just so small and vulnerable against all those monsters.

For the record the town of Kingman takes it's name from Lewis Kingman who apparently sited the Santa Fe Railway there in about 1883 and now it has a population of around 33,000 and is situated in Mohave County in the Hualapai Valley so therefore has a very agreeable all the year round climate that is mild in winter but is not too hot in summer and has a rainfall of only about 3 inches per year.

Later we walked to 'Gashas Supermarket' that was conveniently situated just a 'stones throw' down the road and purchased a freshly cooked chicken at $5 and some asparagus that cost only 99 cents/lb, but on our return, the poor little Trek was completely hemmed in by even more juggernauts and before long discovered yet another bonus as we found out that we were parked fairly close to the railway and began to hope they did run many trains at night!!!!

Our hopes were dashed, the trains did run all night and seemed even closer to our RV as the noise obviously appeared more annoying in the middle of the night and early morning, although the real irritation came not from the trains but from the trucks running their noisy air conditioning systems most of the time, a valuable lesson that hopefully we would not forget!!!!

Historic Route 66

Friday 16 April - Sunday 18 April

Waking early due to noise from the trucks as well as the trains we surprisingly felt quite refreshed and raring to go, so after a quick breakfast the Trek was topped up with yet more diesel, 17.62 gallons at $1.99/gallon, plus 10.8 gallons of LPG at 1.69/gallon and we also purchased half a gallon of engine oil for just under $10. The opportunity was also taken to dump the black and grey waste but this took longer than it should largely due to our inexperience and the fact that we had to queue for the various services that were in different locations.

Consulting the map, we had the option to continue our journey to the Grand Canyon via Interstate 40 which was shorter and therefore quicker or to take the more scenic and relaxed route along Historic Route 66, in the end there was no real competition so we naturally chose the latter as it seemed a good opportunity to travel on this legendary highway.

At one stage Route 66 traversed almost half way across the USA and for nearly 50 years was the main highway to the West Coast and over the years achieved a mythical like character and is still spoken about with much affection today. It has almost been immortalised and is frequently celebrated in that very well known song 'Get Your Kicks On Route 66' which was apparently written by the drummer with the Tommy Dorsey Band and has been sung by just about everyone over the years including the great Ray Charles, Chuck Berry and the Rolling Stones.

Before the 2,400 mile long Route 66 was constructed back in the late 1930's it had been extremely difficult and often hazardous to travel from the west to the east and vice versa due to the very rough terrain, deserts and mountains. When built this new highway connected Chicago with Los Angeles, starting at Lake Michigan in Illinois, passing then through Missouri and the edge of Kansas and in Oklahoma it was routed west to Northern Texas, New Mexico, Arizona and then on to California where it ended in Los Angeles.

Local residents around Route 66 soon appreciated that the growing stream of people and traffic using the road needed fuel, food and accommodation, so not surprisingly many hundreds of restaurants, filling stations, bars, grocery outlets and stores were constructed. However around this time the great economic depression gripped the country and if that was not enough, the area was unfortunately devastated by a drought that gripped the Mid-Western region with crops in Oklahoma, Kansas and Missouri failing so that the earth just turned to dust.

Consequently thousands of farmers and many others lost everything including their homes so then headed west in their search for employment in other areas. Eventually Route 66 became yet another victim of progress as it was progressively replaced by a new system of high-speed Interstate roads and so by around the mid 1980's the last remaining section of Route 66 near Williams in Arizona was replaced by a new Interstate road, nevertheless it is still just possible to find sections of the old highway running along the old route.

We were lucky that one of the longest stretches in-fact goes from Kingman through Seligman, then on to Williams where we could then join Highway 84 on our planned journey to the Grand Canyon and that seemed just brilliant.

With great excitement we therefore headed off along Historic Route 66 and drove close to the Mohave County Airport, on through Hackberry, Valentine then Truxton passing the Grand Wash Cliffs and on route went close to the Hualapai Indian Reservation around Peach Springs.

At Nelson we stopped very briefly in the car park at the Grand Canyon Caves, but after a short discussion, decided not to visit the caves on this trip as we still had so much to see that was already planned into our itinerary. Rejoining Historic Route 66 we continued our journey driving close to the Aubrey Cliffs and began to sing the 'Route 66' song, probably totally out of tune, as we trundled along beneath brilliant blue skies, the Trek purred and hummed in cruise control mode, almost as if it was really trying to sing along or in reality was attempting to drown our voices.

In some areas it was a little sad to observe that a significant number of business premises as well as domestic dwellings now lay abandoned or were rapidly falling into disrepair, proof that progress had not helped everyone in that area, as almost all of the traffic that would have would have brought the much needed business to the local communities was now using the Interstates.

Since arriving in the US we had been attracted by the romantic names often given to various locations and rivers so were delighted to pass close to the attractively named 'Singing Mountain School' and both wished that we had been lucky enough to attend such a super sounding school that conjured up thoughts and feelings of good old country values.

Later in the day we learnt that some communities along Route 66, such as the town of Seligman have now become tourist attractions so are apparently doing better than when they relied on just passing trade, therefore it was no real surprise to see quite a number of signs in some of the smaller towns proudly proclaiming that they were on the 'Historic Route 66'.

At one stage we did briefly stop in the town of Seligman that is situated in Yavapai County at the junction of Historic Route 66 and Interstate 40 where we were told that the area was once known as Mint Valley and that it's name was subsequently changed to Prescott Junction and then finally to the name of Seligman after two brothers. The brothers were apparently joint owners of the Aztec Land and Cattle Company and they also owned shares in the Atlantic and Pacific Railroad that originally connected Prescott to the Atlantic and Pacific Mainline, then in the late 1890's this railroad became known as the now famous Santa Fe Railroad.

Later we stopped to purchase some food and beverages in the City of Williams which is apparently often referred to as ' The Gateway To The Grand Canyon' and also visited the

Bill Williams statue in Monument Park erected in honour of the trapper from whom the town takes it's name. While there we managed to see the famous station and learnt that the original railroad was built in about the 1800's, to transport ore from the Anita mines forty five miles north of Williams, but subsequently due to dwindling resources of ore the railroad ran into financial difficulties in around 1900.

However in 1901 the Santa Fe Railroad took over this ailing company then completed laying the one hundred and thirty miles of track to the Grand Canyon and that notable passengers on the first train included Teddy and Franklin Roosevelt, Dwight Eisenhower, Clark Gable as well as the one and only Jimmy Durante.

Nowadays the railway is privately owned by Mr. and Mrs. Max Biegert and employs about 50 staff dedicated to restoring and running the historic steam and diesel locomotives as well as the period carriages so that visitors can have the opportunity to experience first hand the tremendous thrill of riding on one of the old 'Iron Horses'.

As would be expected Williams was once a 'rough and tough' frontier town and glimpses of it's long history can still be seen as many buildings have been carefully restored or recreated in keeping with that image, even today Western Gun Fights are a part of the towns summer entertainment for the locals as well as the many tourists that visit the area.

Our all too brief stop in Williams turned out to be more expensive than originally planned as we encountered a very good Western Outfitters, where the customary white Stetson just had to be purchased; well we did not want to look so out of place did we? A real cowboy was also in the store at the same time and was taking matters very seriously indeed, trying on virtually every hat in the shop; eventually he made his final selection but then asked the assistant if 'Rodeo Straps' could be fitted to his hat, it turned out that these straps, normally made from leather, are used to ensure the hat does not fly off when riding furiously.

While in Williams we also discovered a small music shop so could not resist acquiring a cheap acoustic guitar to serenade us on the rest of the journey.

Before leaving Williams we enquired at the local tourist office regarding RV campsites at the Grand Canyon only to be informed that it was really advisable to telephone to make an advance booking, however as it was already somewhat late in the day decided to find somewhere locally to rest up until after the weekend when the rush at the canyon hopefully should have eased a little.

Leaving Williams on Highway 64 we headed towards the Grand Canyon but luckily just about four or five miles on spotted a sign indicating that there was an RV site at Kaibab Lake, situated in the Kaibab National Forest, so decided this could be an appropriate stop-over and was worthy of investigation.

So after a total journey during the day of two hundred and seven miles stopped the Trek at the site entrance where we were greeted by the rugged and elderly warden who suggested that we select a suitable pitch wherever we liked, he explained that as it was only April there would be no charge, apparently the site opens all the year round but charges are only levied from May until the end of September each year.

As we drove through the site, we were extremely happy to discover that we were in a very beautiful and picturesque pine forest and could not believe our good fortune; the whole area was really peaceful, very attractive and to our amazement was almost empty.

Therefore it did not take us very long to find a really good hard standing pitch very close to the small lake and not only was this very secluded it had a large concrete hard standing area for the Trek, a picnic table with seating for around six people, a Bar-B-Q and open fire place so could not believe that we had found such an absolutely brilliant location.

It was not long before we noticed a friendly Albert Squirrel (slightly larger than the grey squirrel that now lives in the UK) with a very bushy tail and fluffy pointed ears that seemed to be very inquisitive, but all too soon some dark blue very noisy and bossy birds called Stellar Jays joined the party so the squirrel was forced to take cover.

Over next few days we spent much of our leisure time walking by the lake and in the adjacent beautiful forest area where we encountered several friendly people who stopped to chat and we learnt that there were deer, elk and wild turkeys in the area, nevertheless during our time there our luck was just not good enough and although a few elk tracks were noticed near the lake and that seemed to be about as close as we were going to get to any wildlife.

However we did manage to observe some Osprey flying low over the lake and even found a pair of birds that were in the process of building a nest in a tall, but rather well worn old tree, that had seen better days that was not far from our pitch.

Keen to get some decent photographs we discretely visited the location several days running and although the birds were seen in the area they decided not to visit the nest or pose for any photographs, in the end we appreciated that they were probably aware of our presence so were very wary and not wishing to disturb them anymore left them in peace.

Surprisingly even at the weekend the site was not at all busy and although a few additional people arrived to fish in the lake, it always remained peaceful, calm and idyllic.

Some really hardy campers even stayed over the weekend in their tents and cooked their meals over open fires, but this seemed quite surprising really as although the daytime temperatures were acceptable it got very cold at night as the location was at a height of some 6,770 feet above sea level and one night it even snowed reasonably hard so could not help feeling sorry for all those poor souls who were under canvas, as they must have been really freezing!!!!

THE GRAND CANYON PHENOMENON

Monday 19 April

Somewhat reluctantly we left the tranquil setting of Kaibab Lake with the intention of finding another site closer to the Canyon that was just off Highway 64; however on arrival we were not too impressed by the facilities, so continued our journey.

On route, we stopped several times and tried unsuccessfully to telephone to make site reservations with the camping grounds actually within the Grand Canyon park area, but undeterred we continued our journey and at Utahan stopped to purchase a one year National Park Pass.

It costs $50 for two people and it provides unlimited access for a twelve-month period to all the American National Parks so is the most economical way to gain entry particularly if it is the intention to visit several parks.

When we eventually reached the park entrance, the signs outside the rangers' check-in booths indicated that there were spaces available at most of the RV sites that were open on the south side of the canyon but those on the north side of the canyon were still shut due to the weather and even some on the south side were not yet fully operational as it was still very early in the season.

Regrettably the signs were, lets say a little out of date, as we eventually discovered that there were no spaces available when we arrived at Trailer Village, although were told that we could dry camp without electricity at the nearby Mather Camp Ground, so we therefore took the opportunity to book a pitch at Trailer Village for the following two nights as we really wanted an electrical hook-up.

However as the weather was still extremely cold it was decided that ideally we would like to have electricity for the night, so retraced our steps to a site we had noticed just outside of the National Park, called Camper Village. This is a commercially run site, some eight miles south of the canyon at Tusayan, however when we arrived were quoted $36/night for a pitch with an electric hook-up but were a little surprised to find that if a full hook-up with fresh water was required then this would be even more expensive, in addition showers would be yet another further charge!!!!!

As these prices seemed to be exceedingly high and not compatible with our tight budget decided to head back to the Grand Canyon National Park, so after covering seventy one miles during the day we eventually found a really super site in the pine forests at the Mather Campground, that is operated by the National Parks Service and this cost the princely sum of just $15/night without any hook-up facilities.

Considerable caution was however required when driving to the various pitches as the routes were via a tarmac driveway which meandered through the tree lined roads, however judging by the marks left on some of the trees no doubt by RV's, Trailers and Fifth Wheelers, some trees were a little too close to the track. We specifically requested a site that would attract the most sun as we were looking to find some warmth at long last, so were pleased to be allocated one that attracted the sun most of the day.

Mather Campground proved to be a very peaceful location that was within easy walking distance of the Market Plaza that has a few shops selling essential foods, tourist trinkets and two restaurants.

We also discovered that we could catch the free shuttle buses, powered by natural gas, from the Plaza to both the East and West Canyon 'best viewing' points on the South Rim of the Canyon as the North Rim was not scheduled to open until 1May, but that date was dependant on the weather.

It was not long before we 'hopped' on one of the buses and headed for Canyon View Information Centre and were surprised to be greeted by concrete paved walkways and some really excellent tourist facilities that included a good bookshop as well as excellent restrooms. Having conducted a little more research about what to see we walked the short distance to Mather Point across the road that incidentally had solar powered traffic lights and on reaching the Point nothing could really have prepared us for the magnificent sight of the Grand Canyon, although we had seen many pictures and films of the area nothing compared with seeing it first hand, the camera worked overtime.

It is very difficult to adequately describe the canyon in words alone, like many canyons in this part of the country the Grand Canyon is probably the worlds' most spectacular example of the power of erosion. The main agent being water and we understand that the Colorado River played a significant role in bringing the canyon to its present depth, also water that comes from other sources such as rain, snow and the streams that flow into the canyon from either rim play a part, as does the wind. Compared to the actual rocks from which it is carved the Grand Canyon is in geological terms relatively young and is thought to have been formed in the last six million years or so.

Each of the rock layers within the canyon erodes in its own manner, giving it a characteristic stepped pyramid look and the shale's erode to slopes and the sandstone forming cliffs with the dark igneous rocks of the Inner Gorge, that are more resistant to erosion than the softer sedimentary rocks above, produce the steep walled gorge.

Vertical fractures are common and are responsible for the tall pillars as well as the erosional remnants that are so common along the rim itself, of course colour is one of the most remarkable features of the landscape; much of it is apparently due to small amounts of iron and other minerals that stain the surface of the canyon's walls hiding the true colour of the rock.

The size and scale of the canyon is quite difficult to fully comprehend and at the bottom flows the Colorado River some 5,000 feet below the rim and from Lees Ferry to the Grand Wash Cliffs, officially measures 277 miles long and is up to 18 miles wide and occupies an area of more than 1,900 square miles. However in an attempt to put things into perspective a little more it is possible to see from the Yavapai Observation Station a suspension bridge at the base of the canyon near to the Phantom Ranch and from the observation vantage point the bridge looks about the size of matchstick. In reality the bridge is 440 feet long and 5 feet wide or to give other comparisons the Grand Canyon is so large that it is easily distinguishable from space and can be clearly seen from an aircraft flying over it at an altitude of some 40,000 feet.

Via the shuttle buses we visited other viewing points such as South Kaibab Trailhead and Yaki Point to the east on the Blue Route, all yielding truly fantastic and unforgettable sights.

Fairly early one morning Linda walked to the wardens' office on Mather Campground, but came hurrying back after seeing a warning notice advising people that mountain lions had been seen in the area and the notice advised people not to travel alone or to leave young children or pets unattended.

We both went to the wardens' office later that morning to study the mountain lion notice and yes it was just as Linda had said, the advice given was not to travel alone on foot or if a lion were to be encountered then people should stand up-right, look the lion right in the eyes, but if attacked they should put up a strenuous defense, we do not recall reading any instruction about not feinting or calling for help or taking refuge in a vehicle etc.

Later in the day we made full use of the onsite laundry facilities and while there struck-up a friendly conversation with Frank and his wife Judy and in the evening they joined us in the Trek for a snack and a glass or two of wine, but little did we realise that we would encounter them again elsewhere!!!

Tuesday 20 April - Wednesday 21 April

As planned we moved the one mile or so to the adjacent Trailer Village that has 84 RV pitches with full hook-up and parked the Trek on it's allocated 'drive in/drive out' pitch, L83, but when we went to make the electrical hook-up soon discovered that the site only provided a 30 amp supply so needed to use a suitable electrical adaptor with the 50amp connector before it was possible to connect to the on-site power supply.

Unfortunately the whole site complex although adequate did appear somewhat in need of some tender loving care as some of the pitches had overhanging branches that could possibly cause expensive damage to taller vehicles and many of the hard standing pitches themselves were poorly patched with tarmac.

Naturally we continued to make maximum use of the shuttle buses, going to virtually all the viewing stations on the East and West sites on the blue and red bus routes going as far as Yaki Point on the East side and Hermits Rest on the West side, the camera working overtime at each venue.

Thursday 22 April

As there was just so much to see and experience it was decided to extend our stay by moving back to Mather campground as it seemed on reflection to be a better site overall and this time selected pitch 110.

It was truly breathtaking to observe just how many the views as seen from the canyon rim could change as the lighting varied and at times it was almost as if the whole scenery had been changed before our very own eyes, as the sun light and clouds made such dramatic visual alterations to the scenes. The opportunity was also taken to walk along the tarmac path, that is wheelchair friendly, known as the Rim Route at the top of the canyon from Pipe Creek Vista about two miles all the way to Yapavai Observation Station and that walk was just sensational.

Goodbye Grand Canyon and Hello Monument Valley

Friday 23 April - Saturday 24 April

Unfortunately it was trying hard to snow as we departed from a very cold and chilly Grand Canyon and headed off on Highway 64 in the direction of Desert View, on route we stopped to take more pictures of the canyon from numerous vantage points that we had not previously visited. Fortunately the road surface was very good and on each side could see hundreds and hundreds of beautiful green pine trees swaying in the strong wind as if trying to catch the snowflakes and wave goodbye.

When the Trek drew to a halt at the Desert View car park the wind seemed extremely harsh and as we stepped out of the RV, we were caught off guard as it packed a punch just as if delivered by a boxer wearing gloves of ice!! Furthermore those threatening snow laden clouds seemed to have followed us on-route, nevertheless the brief stopover was well worthwhile as the views were outstanding so we naturally took full advantage of the last opportunity to soak up the sights of the notorious Grand Canyon.

To get out of the atrocious weather we climbed the well worn winding stone stairs to the top of the Desert View Observation Tower that overlooks the canyon to marvel at the magnificent views of the canyon itself as well as the surrounding area; later we signed the visitors' book and made the comment 'absolutely stunning and really superb'!!!

Feeling hungry we took the opportunity to acquire a light snack from the little on site restaurant, luckily the hot dog and the hot chilidog were really tasty and extremely good value for money at under $2 each, they were so delicious we will definitely try them again if we are ever in the area. Resuming our journey we passed through some stunning scenery along the undulating pine tree lined road then joined Highway 89 North then stopped at Little Colorado Overlook to take a few pictures of the impressive scenery, some Indian traders were also using the same location to sell some of their wares, so Linda could not resist purchasing a few small bracelets as presents.

As we drove away from the parking area we thought for a moment that we could hear a thunderstorm brewing in the distance, but as the ever-increasing noise seemed to approach extremely rapidly, we began to have doubts. Just as we were about to pull away we noticed some fifty or more Harley Davidson motorcycles as they came majestically roaring into view, all in single line formation, snaking down the twisting road and obviously travelling rapidly judging by the deep rumble of the unique Harley engines. To any bystander this must have seemed almost like the cavalry arriving and to any motorcyclist, ex-motorcyclist or would be motorcyclist, it sounded tremendous and resembled a scene from a movie but all too soon the riders disappeared from our view over the horizon although we could just still hear their engines as they thundered onwards.

We drove on for a while then decided to stop for a break at the Historic Cameron Trading Post and Lodge and there in the car park were all the 'Harley Riders' that had thundered by some while ago.

At first glance they really did look a mean bunch of really tough dudes, dressed in denim and leather, with bandanas in their hair, tattoos on their arms and that was just the girls. To our relief they all seemed very well behaved and ultra polite nothing like the image they portrayed, one accidentally walked in front of Linda and was very quick to apologies saying 'sorry to have walked in front of you m-a-r-m, I hope you will forgive me', not quite what would have been expected!!!

The Harley motorcycles in the car park were also a revelation as without exception, they all looked immaculate, with gleaming paintwork and of course lots of highly polished chromium glinting in the sun and contrary to popular belief there were no visible signs of any oil leaks and were definitely not tied together with wire or string. They were all expensive machines that looked as if they had just been driven out of the showroom so were a real credit to their fairly wealthy owners, who appeared to be 'out playing' and may have been schoolteachers or high-powered executives when back at work.

The Trading Post was extremely interesting and was literally packed with some of the best quality souvenirs seen so far, but for a change we were not tempted to make any purchases.

Shortly after leaving we drove through the aptly named Painted Desert region and were greeted by magnificent pink coloured rocks rising regally on each side of the road and they were truly magnificent and a really breathtaking sight!!!

After some time we turned on to Highway 160 and headed towards Tuba City where a stop was made to fill the Trek with another large quantity of diesel, 23.4 gallons at $1.99/gallon, then with this chore completed, the chance was taken to browse round the rather run down and dusty old shop and while there could not help noticing that a section of the premises was being run as a pawnshop so could see that a number of Western style horse saddles piled high on the floor that had obviously been pawned and thought that it must be a very sad day when you have to pawn your saddle?

Resuming our journey we stopped at a Gashas supermarket, but as it was also rather run down and had obviously seen better days so was not too well stocked, decided to move on.

By now the feeling of tiredness became evident as the road leading to Monument Valley seemed endless with monotonous desert for mile after mile and in the distance we observed some very dark and threatening heavy storm clouds gathering and although rain spots danced over our windscreen a few times, we managed to escape the main storm itself, but could see the lightning.

At Kayenta we joined Highway 163 then soon noticed yet another Gashas supermarket so felt compelled to stop and fortunately this one was well stocked so purchased just a few essential food items.

By now we both hoped that we must be on the final leg of the long journey to the Goulding's Monument Valley Campground, yet the road still seemed to go on and on without end so we both became more than a little worried just incase they were full. Of course there were no public telephones in such a desolate area so had been unable to obtain a mobile telephone signal to make an advanced booking so should the site have been full, wondered if there were alternatives?

Nevertheless undaunted the Trek purred on relentlessly and as we eventually drew close to Monument Valley, possibly one of the most photographed landscapes in America, we were utterly amazed to actually see before our own eyes some of the monoliths and buttes that have been a Hollywood backdrop for so many Western films for eighty years or more. So after one hundred and eighty five miles we pulled slowly and very wearily into Goulding's, the area's first trading post and yes, it was our lucky day, they did have space for us, so breathed a big sigh of relief!!!!!

Following site registration we slowly drove the Trek the short distance to pitch 25 and made the necessary hook-up connections to our RV, this was not a very pleasant experience as the camp had been deluged by the torrential rain, thunder, lightning as well as hail that we had seen in the far distance prior to our arrival, this had made the red earth exceedingly muddy and extremely slippery.

Goulding's has some 66 pitches with full hook-ups of which around 30 are 'drive through' and the facilities are surprisingly good for such a remote location with a laundry, showers, store, cable TV and even a swimming pool. To our surprise we were told that we had again passed into another time zone without realising the fact, so needed to adjust clocks and watches to Mountain Time.

When we walked round the site a little later it was clear to see that we really need not have worried so much as the site was only about half full, but speaking with the site wardens were assured that they do get very busy in the next month or so.

As the location was so magical we decided to stay for two nights that cost $28/night and booked one of the guided tours that would take us through the valley the following day at a cost of $27.50 per person for the basic 21/2hour 17mile trip. From the literature collected we knew that the area was a traditional Navajo homeland that is now accessible by private vehicle, however we appreciated that it was a good idea to join one of the guided tours so as to get to many of the really good locations, as it is necessary to travel over some restricted roads that are just not suitable for an RV anyway.

We were glad that we made this decision, as our male tour guide was from the Navajo tribe, who wore a big smile and a large black Stetson with two eagle feathers tucked in to the hatband. He was of course very knowledgeable and well informed, as he knew the history of the area exceedingly well, had an in-depth appreciation of the Navajo way of life, the culture and of course was on hand to answer questions. During the trip it was easy to appreciate why a robust 4x4 type vehicle was the only sensible way to see the most memorable Monument Valley locations first hand as the terrain was extremely rugged to say the least as much of the journey was really 'off road' and included quite deep rutted and rough sections.

Our guide told us that Monument Valley is a Navajo National Park measuring some 30,000 acres and that it was established in 1958 and is located on the boarder of Arizona and Utah within the 16 million acre Navajo Reservation. Positioned just to the west of the Colorado-New Mexico state line, the park is roughly 5,500 feet above sea level and is accessible all the year round with temperatures that range from the average low 25 degrees Fahrenheit to an average 90 degrees Fahrenheit in the summer and experiences a rainfall of only about 8 inches per year.

Apparently before human existence Monument Valley was a vast lowland basin, for hundreds of millions of years' layer upon layer of eroded sediment from the early Rocky Mountains was deposited in the basin and cemented into the rock that is mainly sandstone and limestone with the presence of iron giving it the very red colour. Then a slow, gentle uplift created by constant pressure from below the surface elevated the horizontal strata so what was once a basin became a plateau of rock 1,000 feet high and over the last fifty million years or so, the subsequent erosion by the wind, rain and temperature gradually cut and peeled away the surface of the plateau. This wearing down of alternate layers of hard and soft rock gradually created the natural wonders of Monument Valley that currently stands at between 400 and 1,200 feet tall.

Incidentally the Goulding family was responsible for establishing the first trading post there and they also marketed the area to the film industry, persuading the likes of John Ford to make some memorable Western movies there, the first was of course the well-known film called 'Stage Coach' featuring the all American cowboy himself John Wayne. Making a movie in this location produced an income for the Navajo's and also helped build a basic infrastructure, as John Ford had to build a road system before he could move his equipment and crew into the area to make the first film.

Nowadays Monument Valley features in a whole range of commercials as well as modern day films and over the years movies such as Kit Carson, Billy the Kid, Fort Apache; She wore a Yellow Ribbon, The Searchers, How the West Was Won and Back to the Future 111 have been made in this very unusual and theatrical location.

During the trip we spent time visiting a 'Hogan', a traditional Navajo dwelling constructed from red cedar wood on the inside that is externally coated with red mud and once inside we were treated to a display of traditional rug making by an elderly Navajo lady.

From there we were taken via the very informative visitor centre into the park itself stopping at numerous locations to take full advantage of the many extremely good photographic opportunities. Our Navajo guide helped to make the whole experience extremely interesting and rewarding by providing snippets of information and pointing out places of interest, so during the trip the camera worked hard in an attempt to capture the majestic and romantically named locations such as El Capitan, Eagle Rock, Bringham's Tomb, the King and his Throne, Big Indian, John Ford's Point, Elephant Butte and many more.

When we returned from the all too brief, but very enjoyable trip, we noticed that adjacent to the Information Centre that there was another RV camping ground where dry camping cost just $10/night, so had Gouldings' been full when we initially arrived there was at least one more site in the area where we could have stayed.

Later in the day Linda soon discovered that Goulding's had a well-stocked grocery and provisions store near to our own site that had good quality produce at quite reasonable prices so felt that it may have been better to stop there rather than at Gashas supermarket on the way to the Valley.

PAGE AND ZION NATIONAL PARK

Page

Sunday 25 April

We waved a very reluctant farewell to Monument Valley and retraced our steps along Highway 163 then joined Highway 160 towards Tuba City, turned right on to Highway 98 heading towards Page that is on the borders Arizona and Utah. On route we unfortunately encountered probably the worst rough road surface since our journey began, it was really terrible and did not improve until we were on the outskirts of Page, the poor old Trek really did not appreciate all the 'shaking, rocking and rolling' and to be honest neither did the occupants.

On the outskirts of Page we stopped at a Shell station to fill the Trek with yet more diesel this time adding 16.8 gallons at $1.99/gallon and while there noticed that they sold LPG and had an RV dump station, but we did not need to use either.

As we drove away from the garage Linda's eagle eye noticed a Wal-Mart on virtually the next block, so with a little economic overnight parking in mind pulled into their quite large parking lot, fortunately there were no other RV's there apart from just one old VW Campervan that looked as if it had been there forever, but after about one hundred and twenty nine miles, many of which were 'bone shaker miles' we were extremely pleased to find a convenient place to stay over.

Just our luck, this particular Wal-Mart sold mainly clothing and general goods but not to be deterred we walked to the very smart and well-stocked Bashas Store that was close by.

We also took the opportunity to stroll across the local golf course to take in some of the sights and delights of The Glen Canyon Dam on Lake Powell, not quite on the scale of the Hoover Dam, but still worth the visit.

In 1957 the Bureau of Reclamation chose the 700 feet high sandstone walls below the seemingly barren mesa as the site where they would construct the Glen Canyon Dam on the Colorado River and brought in many workers as well as masses of equipment to complete the 7 year long project.

At that time the camp was called 'Camp Page' in honour of the former Bureau Commissioner John C Page, however soon the 'Camp' portion of the name was dropped and the town simply became known as Page.

Today, Page is a thriving town of nearly 7,000 residents, visited annually by around 1.5 million people who come to the area to enjoy the amenities that include a super golf course, an excellent marina as well as the beautiful surrounding countryside and scenery.

When we returned to the Trek we noticed that a few more RV's had joined us in the Wal-Mart car park and felt that our RV would be no-doubt be glad of the company!!

During the evening Linda was searching in the cupboard below the sink and discovered that there was some kind of water leak as a few of the items stored there were wet, but fortunately it was not a significant leak and as it was already getting dark, placed a bowl strategically underneath to catch the drips until we could investigate further in the morning.

Zion National Park

Monday 26 April – Wednesday 28 April

After a peaceful overnight rest we tried to discover the source of the mystery leak and managed to trace it to the fitting below the sink that connects the copper tubing from the hot tap to the plastic supply pipe. But even with some additional borrowed tools it proved very difficult and to be honest almost impossible to reach under the sink and attach a spanner to the offending connector, let alone get enough leverage to tighten the joint. At this stage we were concerned that if connector were damaged further then it may leak more or fail completely, then we would be in trouble, so it was better to leave well alone until a new connector could be acquired. As a temporary measure a small cardboard box was lined with plastic then placed under the sink to catch the drips, furthermore we discovered that if the water pump was turned off and the tap opened to release the pressure then the leak stopped.

It was also noted that the Trek's front tyres seemed to be wearing a little unevenly so decided to keep a close eye on the situation and to get the tracking/wheel alignment checked as soon as possible.

While all this was happening Linda went off to Wal-Mart to purchase a pre-paid Telephone Card but had difficulty finding out how many minutes the card would consume if a call were to be made to the UK. To her surprise she could not find any relevant information on the card itself neither could store staff provide an acceptable answer, in the end she had to purchase the card, activate it by rubbing the reverse side to reveal the unique number, then ring AT&T and ask them the question, but luckily the store did agree to refund the card purchase price if Linda could not get a satisfactory answer.

Contacting AT&T proved frustrating as Linda was greeted by a pre-recorded message system that proved to be not terribly user friendly, however eventually she found out that for every minute used while speaking to the UK actually consumed three minutes of the time on the card, in addition the minimum time for any call made to the UK would automatically be charged at a ten-minute rate, a good deal or not?

We also wanted to telephone 'Covercraft', a company that advertised RV covers, but were a little unsure how to dial their number as their advertisement showed it as '1-800-4covers', in the end the telephone operator helped and fortunately the solution turned out to be fairly simple. Just dial 1-800 followed by the numeral on the touch tone telephone dial corresponding to the letter 'c' on the dial, followed by the numeral corresponding to the letter 'o' etc, simple really, but only when the correct procedure is known. In the end Covercraft told us that they did not sell direct to end users and stated that it would be necessary to contact one of their retailers.

At this stage we decided instead to telephone Camping World on their free phone number, indicated by a prefix 1.800 to order a tailor made RV cover as well as a set of tyre covers to keep the Trek snug and warm while stored in Oregon. Ideally we wanted one of their portable garages but found the delivery charge of over $350 on top of the cost of the garage too much for our small budget.

With these chores completed we set off on the last leg of our journey to Zion National Park in Utah driving across the Glen Canyon Dam on Highway 89 then over the state border into Utah.

As we headed towards Kanab, there was very little traffic on the road so could travel at a more acceptable and leisurely pace soaking up the sights of the fabulous scenery.

Eventually we needed a natural break so stopped in a convenient parking area to also take yet more pictures of the countryside only to find that it was also the entrance to the Paria Historic Town Site, where quite a number of Western movies had been made. Regrettably the actual town was still several miles further down a rather dusty unmade track and as the Trek would not have been very happy to take that route decided not to venture any further down that road so resumed our journey along the main highway.

Before long we passed the aptly named Parai Canyon Vermillion Cliffs Wilderness Area, which looked just as if someone had been busy with a paint brush and a very large box of paints filled with only multiple shades of vermilion so it was really quite an astounding sight.

After passing through Kanab we turned on to Highway 9 at Mount Carville Junction, but nearly missed the poorly signed road to begin the last leg of our journey to Zion, numerous times we believed that we must be nearly at our destination, but the road seemed to go on forever and ever. When at last we approached the entrance to Zion National Park we drew to a halt at the Ranger Station then showed our National Park Pass, all was OK so far, but soon learnt that it would be necessary to travel through two tunnels, the first would present no problems, but the second would be a little different!!

The ranger stated that all vehicles over 7 feet 10 inches wide or 11 feet 4 inches in height (and for the record the Trek is 11feet high) must have an escort through the Zion Mount Carmel Tunnel. This means that all oncoming traffic has to be held at the park exit so that large vehicles entering the park can travel through the tunnel safely in the middle of the road and the fee for this service is $10 per vehicle.

Incidentally it transpired that if we had used another entrance on the far side of the park, then it would not have been necessary to drive through any tunnels, but as that entrance was just too may miles away had little choice but to use this route to get into Zion.

In addition we learnt that vehicles over 13 feet 1inch tall, trucks and commercial vehicles or those carrying hazardous material, or those single vehicles of over 40 foot long are not actually permitted to use the tunnels at all, so felt that we were probably lucky not to be driving a large Prevost, Beaver or Monaco or similar sized RV.

Not knowing what to expect we paid the $10 fee and rather gingerly commenced our journey by moving slowly towards the mouth of the first tunnel along the very narrow winding road and as they say 'sailed through' without any problems.

Linda wanted to stop to take advantage of the brilliant photographic opportunities, but we could not do so due to the narrowness of the road and the queue of traffic building up behind the RV.

Eventually we arrived at the entrance of the Mount Carmel Tunnel, this time the tunnel aperture appeared extremely small and as we waited our turn to enter did get quite nervous and wondered if everything would be OK as there were only cars in front and behind us, no other RV's were insight, perhaps they knew something we did not?

The ranger eventually checked our paperwork then asked for our signature on his own documents no doubt absolving the park of any responsibility should we have an incident or accident?

After a short wait the ranger stepped forward again then asked for vehicle lights to be put on and for sunglasses to be removed then waved us towards the entrance. The journey of around one mile went surprisingly without incident but it was nevertheless quite daunting as the light in the tunnel was poor and the narrow twisting road just went on and on, but on occasions bright light could be seen streaming through a few apertures in the tunnel walls.

Pleased that our ordeal was almost over the Trek emerged from the tunnel into the bright and dazzling sunlight where we noticed another ranger, who had stopped the on-coming traffic, literally jump up and down in the air and then give us the 'thumbs up' as we approached, after that the remainder of the journey seemed pretty easy, although the road was narrow and extremely twisty, just like a typical Alpine pass.

We initially tried the Watchman Campground that charges $18/night with electrical hook-up but as pitches are allocated on a first come first served basis we were presented with just three pitch options that on inspection proved not to be really suitable for us or the Trek.

We therefore decided to try another site within the park complex called South Campground and were very pleasantly surprised as this was located in a small wooded area containing cottonwood trees and that proved to be much more secluded. So after one hundred and nineteen miles we drove the Trek sedately in to South Campground and soon found a suitable pitch, number 40, as it fitted our requirements and those of the Trek extremely well.

The pitch cost just $16/night for an RV, Fifth Wheel or Tent and the method of payment is straightforward, just simply take a registration form from the warden's area, tear off the receipt section then place the completed form plus the required fee, cash preferred, into the envelope provided then post it in the warden's mailbox.

Then all that is left to do is to display the receipt section of the form on the numbered marker at the perimeter of the chosen pitch.

South Campground is very well equipped with toilets, fire-grates, picnic tables, fresh water plus an RV dump station and is merely a short stroll away from the excellent visitor centre from where LPG powered Shuttle Buses operate and provide a free service at 7 to 10 minute intervals throughout the day, ferrying visitors to the most popular vantage points and trail walks within the park.

Naturally we took full advantage of this service throughout our stay, as it is an extremely good system that was introduced to combat the growing traffic, parking and pollution problems.

It now runs from April through to October ferrying passengers on either of two loops, one that includes nine stops within the Zion Canyon itself, while the other includes six stops on route to the adjacent town of Springdale.

There is one other campground in the park called The Lava Point Primitive Campground, but this is only open from May until October and has fire grates, tables and toilets but no water, but as there is no pitch fee, is no doubt very popular during the high season.

During our visit we soon discovered that the Zion Lodge offered free Internet access, so naturally took the opportunity to retrieve any personal e-mails and also send a few to advise friends and family of our progress.

Each day we travelled to selected vantage points and did as many of the trail walks as were possible, so during our stay went on the three-hour Canyon Scenic Drive, walked the Weeping Rock Trail and also attempted the steep trail leading to the magnificent views of the tall rocks, known as the Sentinel and the Three Patriarchs.

The Riverside Walk was really fabulous as it presented a good opportunity to chill out and admire the breathtaking views through the forested glens as we meandered along adjacent to the sparkling clear waters of the Virgin River that runs through the floor of the canyon.

Enough energy was mustered to even walk the Kayenta Trail that is rated as a 'moderate one mile one way, 150 foot ascent', but in reality this proved reasonably tough as it led to an unpaved climb on a sandstone ledge that connects 'The Grotto' to the 'Emerald Pools'. If that was not enough we continued on and ventured as far as the 'Middle' and 'Upper Emerald Pools', the latter was a mere 200 foot ascent over sandy, rugged and very rocky terrain, it was possibly a little too far in one morning and our legs confirmed this to be correct. The trek also became very unpleasant and uncomfortable when a fierce wind suddenly sprung up without warning, blowing sand everywhere, so all those hikers in the vicinity were well and truly 'sand blasted'.

During our stay we saw eagles, numerous wild turkeys, mule deer and even a skunk; however we still did not see any signs of any mountain lions that are reputed to reside in the area.

One of the shuttle bus drivers mentioned that there were Sand Beavers actually living in the riverbanks and that the beavers had learnt not to build their hideouts in the river itself as their homes could get frequently washed away in the flash floods.

Unfortunately the beavers still seem to be partial to the odd Cottonwood tree and can cause significant damage to the trees, so much so that the lower sections now have to be protected by wire netting.

Another unforgettable sight was that of some climbers scaling the face of the very high rocks at Big Bend, they looked like tiny, tiny dots clinging rather precariously on the great expanse of rock and we believed that they must have been super fit and tremendously courageous to attempt such a feat.

It is virtually impossible to find words to accurately or adequately describe the sights of Zion National Park, it is a place of wondrous beauty and nobility with the sculptures of the magnificent high and very colourful rocks rising majestically skywards in a land that seems to have escaped the passage of time, a truly awesome experience.

One afternoon we ventured into Springdale on the shuttle bus going as far as the last stop to a location known as Majestic View another apt name as the camera had to work over-time in an attempt to capture the magnificent picture postcard surrounding countryside.

On the advice of the shuttle bus driver we ventured across the road to the Majestic View Lodge and were fascinated when we entered the Wildlife Museum that occupies an area of some 3,000 square feet as inside the displays featured scenes of Moose, Polar Bear, Brown Bear and Buffalo and much, much more, all exceptionally well done and definitely worth the time.

The lodge also had one of the better gift shops featuring spectacular Native American gifts, jewelry, beadwork and artifacts as well as a very ornate horse saddle that had apparently taken the lone Native American craftsman about five years to produce by hand.

To make the return journey back to the park a little more enjoyable and interesting we used the bus part way then leisurely strolled the remainder of the journey so we could enjoy the experience in a more sedate and unhurried manner and on route found a small shop selling ice cream so could not resist purchasing one large cone that had the unforgettable name of Moose Claw. It was absolutely fabulous, probably the very best ice cream that we have ever sampled anywhere in the world and luckily it was more than large enough for two to share!!!

During our walk we stopped at the Zion Canyon Campground, that is situated not far from the park entrance to collect some information about the site but were a little surprised to learn that an RV pitch with full hook-up cost $24/night for a vehicle with two occupants, this did seem expensive compared to the Watchman site that charged only $18/night with electricity and that was actually in a better location as it was in park complex!!!!

On our last evening we travelled on the shuttle bus to Zion Lodge in the hope of sending some E-mails using their Internet facilities, but shortly after our arrival the whole area was plunged into darkness due to a major power failure in the area, so had to return to the Trek without accomplishing our mission.

On to Bryce Canyon and Fruita the oasis in the desert

On to Bryce Canyon

Thursday 29 April –Saturday 1May

Not to be deterred by the previous unsuccessful attempt Linda returned to the Zion Lodge via the shuttle bus to try the e-mail system again and fortunately she was successful this time but while there learnt that the power had been off all night and had only been restored at 3.45am

After replenishing the Trek's fresh water supplies and discharging the grey and black waste at the dump station we left Zion National Park retracing our route through the snaking alpine like Highway 9, through the tunnels on the journey towards Bryce Canyon National Park. The twisting roads lasted for about nine miles and that proved to be quite stressful as we encountered a number of large vehicles coming in the opposite direction, so had to ensure they did not collide with the Trek's protruding wing mirror.

On route the opportunity was taken to stop at a buffalo ranch that had been noticed on the inward journey in the hope of photographing some of the beasts but on this occasion the herd were really too far away happily grazing in their vast pasture.

While there we visited the ranch shop to see if they sold buffalo burgers, but were told that they were only sold in their restaurant as part of a set meal, so curious to find out more ventured in and were surprised to find the little place literally crammed with people enjoying their meals and for a moment were very tempted, but decided that at around $10 each we would not be able to do full justice to these large burgers as we had eaten breakfast a little earlier.

Continuing our journey for around twenty-one miles we eventually turned on to Highway 89 heading north and on route encountered several snow showers and some pretty black looking skies, the temperature dropped considerably from the 70/80 degrees Fahrenheit that had been experienced the day before in Zion. Between the showers it was just possible to see the towering cliffs known as the White and Pink Cliffs, but on this occasion they all looked extremely grey, then at Long Valley Junction we could see on our left the Dixie National Forest and as if by magic the weather suddenly seemed to improve a little, well at least the snow showers stopped!!

Later we joined Highway 12 that is reputed to be one of the most spectacular roads in the country so is often referred to as the 'National Scenic Byway 12' and stretches across the richly varied landscape serving as the main artery through the remote and rugged region of the Colorado Plateau, so the sensational scenery draws people from all over the world to journey through the unforgettable terrain. Heading east we stopped briefly to take more photographs at Red Canyon, yet another unbelievable sight and yes the canyon did look red and really had to be seen first hand to be fully appreciated. Turning on to Highway 63 we noticed Rubys Inn that has an RV Park with full hook-up, a general store and much more, but opposite Rubys, Linda spotted a large garage selling gas, diesel, LPG and noticed a big sign saying that they undertook RV repairs and servicing!!!

We did wonder if they could cure the Trek's water leak and also check the front wheel tracking, so decided to call in and speak with them over the next day or so.

The road leading to the entrance of Bryce Canyon had recently been resurfaced and was a delight to drive on, then at the entry to the park we showed our National Parks Pass then quickly calculated that we had already saved $10 so far by purchasing the pass in advance as opposed to paying $20 at each park visited. The journey to the North Campground with over 100 pitches took just a few minutes so soon located a suitable pitch, number 23, checked the Trek's mileage and noted that we had covered just eighty seven miles since leaving Zion.

Again this was 'a pay and display' site so we walked to the kiosk to deposit the two night fee of $20 in the by now customary envelope then posted it in the box provided, returning to the Trek the receipt was placed on the marker post to confirm that payment had been made.

Later we chatted to the Duty Site Warden who informed us that the Shuttle Buses would not be operating until May and that the other campground called Sunset Campground with more than 100 pitches was also shut until that date.

Luckily we did not want a full hook-up as both campgrounds provided dry camping only but we had hoped to be able to obtain fresh water and also make use of the dump station. It transpired that the water was still turned off and the dump station closed as the weather could still be exceptionally cold at this time of the year, fortunately we could manage without these facilities for a little longer.

During the early afternoon we took a short walk to the rim of Bryce Canyon and on first sight thought that we must have been looking at a very old city rising from the bottom of the canyon as it appeared as if there were gothic columns stretching skywards. In amazement, we rubbed our eyes then looked for a second time and for a moment thought that we could also see an army of ancient warriors standing nearby as if guarding the secrets of the canyon.

The sights were truly remarkable; everywhere we looked challenged our imagination so we wondered if the views were real or not and thought that perhaps we were looking at some form of mirage or alternatively a science fiction film set?

But no, what we could see were 'Hoodoos', the name given to the fantastic array of different shaped brightly coloured orange pillars of sandstone rock that are formed by erosion over many, many thousands of years.

On this occasion we did not stay too long as the wind was extremely cold, but paused long enough to take yet more customary photographs and agreed to return as soon as the weather improved.

Later in the day we drove the RV back to Rubys then called in at the adjacent Fairyland Canyon from where the very spectacular Navajo Mountain could just be seen on the horizon.

On the Friday morning we arose around 8am and looked out from one of the Trek's windows and surprise, surprise, it had snowed overnight so there was about 3/4inch of white virgin snow covering the pine trees and roadways as far as we could see.

Perhaps as it had been so cold and as the elevation was around 8,300 feet above sea level we should not have been so taken aback, especially as snow had been encountered on route to Bryce.

In such cold conditions there was real concern that the diesel powered Trek may not start but in reality need not have worried as the engine burst into life without too much difficulty, furthermore the fresh and waste water systems seemed to be also OK so we both breathed a sigh of relief.

After allowing the engine to warm for a few minutes, the button was pressed to retract Treks' hydraulic levelling jacks and we were very relieved as they slowly began to move; luckily they had not frozen in the extended position.

Very slowly and cautiously we drove the Trek away from the overnight pitch then headed back towards the garage opposite Rubys and observed that a light but attractive quilt of snow also covered all the roadways, but this did not make driving very pleasurable as it would have been all to easy to lose control of such a heavy vehicle on the cambered road.

After about five miles we arrived at the garage and spoke to Mike the foreman, who advised us that they did not undertake any sort of plumbing work so could not help to cure the small water leak, neither did they have the necessary equipment to undertake wheel alignment on RV's, so as we drove away began to question why they displayed a notice board that stated that they service and repair RV's!!!!

Heading back to the North Campground along the snow-covered road we listened to the weather forecast on the radio that stated that the conditions should improve during the afternoon, unfortunately the very dark clouds overhead and in the distance seemed to indicate this forecast might be a little optimistic to say the least!!!

Later in the morning we ventured out on foot in the very cold wind to walk the short distance to a small general store where we both purchased a pair of woolen gloves for the bargain price of under $5 for two pairs. Those gloves seemed to make all the difference and feeling a good deal more comfortable ventured as far as the nearby Bryce Canyon Lodge, where we took shelter for a while and managed to thaw out a little.

Eventually, it was time to return to the RV so we walked along the rim of the canyon and were confronted by around six or more mule deer, who kindly posed for the customary photographs.

For most of the morning the skies remained extremely grey and showed little sign of the promised improvement, but so as not to waste the day and also to help keep warm we walked briskly to the nearby visitor centre to conduct a little research on the area. Fortunately the centre was warm and welcoming so while there watched a really informative and excellent film all about Bryce Canyon. During the film it was explained that as Bryce Canyon has such thin, dry, clean air that on most days it is possible to see almost two hundred miles as far as the Black Mesas in Eastern Arizona and this was quite staggering when compared to most locations where the horizons are a mere twelve miles away!!!

Furthermore as Bryce has very low levels of light pollution, when night falls, it is possible to see as far as Andromeda and that is just over two million light years away!!!!

When the time came to leave the centre and as if by magic, the sun attempted to peep through the clouds and no doubt everyone prayed it was going to get any warmer.

With the vague promise of better weather to come we decided to be brave and walk the Queens Garden route all the way down into the canyon itself returning via the Navajo Loop.

The camera worked overtime as each step taken presented yet another unbelievable photographic opportunity, so it was not long before the digital camera's memory was full, yet the journey had just begun so felt compelled to continue. The sights were absolutely brilliant; the coloured rocks were mesmerizing, as they were still partially covered with snow and were also back-lit by the sun that kept trying to surface from behind the lifting clouds, so we did not want to miss a thing.

The walk took us to the base of the canyon some 320 feet below the rim and although it was not too taxing on the journey down, climbing up was an entirely different matter so the round trip ended up being about five very strenuous miles and so both felt extremely tired by the time the Trek came into view.

Overnight the temperatures again dropped considerably, but luckily this time it did not snow so we awoke the next morning to vivid blue skies and surprisingly much warmer temperatures that soon reached the dizzy heights of around 60 degrees Fahrenheit.

Not wanting to miss out on all of the photographic opportunities that had not been captured on the previous day, we decided to set out to do the whole trek again and on route encountered a couple of real cowboys on horseback who were admiring the breathtaking views from the canyon rim and Linda never one to miss an opportunity and keen to capture them on camera, asked if she could take their photograph and back came the immediate response 'Y-O-O——B-E-T'.

Continuing on our way we chatted about how much the temperatures could change so much at this time of the year between the day and night, as we had been told that the daily temperatures could frequently be in the mid to upper 60's or even lower 70's degrees Fahrenheit, but at night could plummet by around 30 degrees Fahrenheit or even more. With such wide fluctuations it was therefore really amazing to see quite a few people actually camping under canvas at the North Campground and concluded that they all must be very tough.

To summarise therefore, if the Grand Canyon was 'awesome' and Zion 'spectacular' then in our own opinion Bryce can only be described as 'absolutely stunning' as it is a really super, unforgettable and magical location so is an experience that should not really be missed. Nevertheless while April is a very good time to visit the area, as the tourist season has not really started so it is not crowded; the temperature at night can be extremely uncomfortable even in a well-equipped RV.

Fruita the oasis in the desert

Sunday 2 May

We departed from Bryce and noted that the dump station had just been opened but did not make use of this facility as we still had enough capacity to last a few more days, but noted that there was a $2 charge to use the facility.

On our journey out of the park we stopped once more at the garage opposite Rubys to fill the Trek with yet more diesel taking onboard 20.6 gallons at $2.07/gallon and noted that they were charging $5 to fill up with fresh water, luckily this service was not needed on this occasion.

Joining Highway 12 heading east we passed through some very spectacular and almost unbelievable countryside with masses of amazing sandstone rocks and cliffs with vivid colours ranging from the oranges seen at Bryce, to vast areas of different reds, greys and then even blacks.

Our journey took us into the Dixie National Forest which was by contrast very green, then we slowly climbed over Canaan Peak that is 9,296 feet above sea level, then on through Escalante, down the steep descent into Calf Creek, eventually climbing the twisting but traffic free road that still had snow piled high by the verge as we climbed to around 10,000 feet.

To the right were the Henry Mountains and the 11,522-feet high Mount Ellen Peak that looked very picturesque covered in snow and in the valley below could see Capitol Reef and the Waterpocket Fold, a large lake area of brilliant shimmering crystal clear blue water.

We continued on to Torrey then turned east on to Highway 24 for about nine miles towards Capital Reef and were once again stunned by the huge multi-coloured sandstone rocks reaching imposingly into the clear blue sky.

As a matter of interest the Capital Reef National Park lies in the heart of Utah's canyon country almost halfway between Bryce and the Canyonlands National Parks, apparently the Navajo call the area the 'Land of the Sleeping Rainbow' due to the super multi coloured rocks, a very appropriate name as it really does live up to the title.

After one hundred and twenty six miles we arrived at our planned overnight stop at the camping site known as Fruita, the site has 71 pitches with picnic tables, restrooms, fresh water, RV dump but regrettably no electricity.

It was once an old Mormon settlement that dates from the 19th century and is extremely picturesque with several orchards of apple, peach, cherry, pear and apricot trees, without doubt an extremely attractive location and a real oasis in a very barren and unforgiving land. Fruita is very tranquil with friendly deer roaming through the area and it is a very good place to rest for a night or so, or to use as a base to travel along the scenic drive or to walk the trails that are close to hand. The site is open all the year round and daily summer temperatures in the area can reach 90 degrees Fahrenheit, falling to 50 or 60 degrees Fahrenheit at night and fortunately the humidity is low but thunderstorms are common during the summer afternoons.

Winter brings cooler weather and sometimes a little snow, but flash floods can apparently occur at any time of the year but are most likely to occur in late summer or autumn.

Pitches cost just $10/night and are allocated on a first come first served basis, but as they vary in size from small to large, this can mean that sometimes the smaller RV's, Fifth Wheelers, Trailers and cars that arrive first frequently select the more spacious pitches making it very difficult for larger vehicles that pull-in later to fit on to the smaller pitches that are left.

THE LONELIEST ROAD IN AMERICA

Monday 3 May

Fruita was such a relaxing and beautiful location we really would have loved to have stayed a little longer but as we had scheduled in several more locations that ' just had to seen' on the planned journey back to Crooked River Ranch in Oregon, felt it advisable to depart without further delay

When the Trek's engine burst into life we felt somewhat sad to be leaving this super area but drove slowly away on the very dusty road then later joined Highway 24 and stopped at Loa to stock up with a few essential food supplies from Royal's Supermarket.

Continuing through Piute Country we drove by Fish Lake and could see Mount Marvine at 11,610 feet high and Mount Terrel at 11,530 feet high in the distance, before long we reached Sigurd then continued the journey North on Highway 28 to Salina.

On the outskirts of town we stopped at 'Country Ways', a very well stocked agricultural merchant's to spend time looking at their vast array of products, but were very much attracted by their extensive range of Western Wear.

It was not long however before Linda noticed that they stocked a collection of portable fold away fabric dog kennels that she thought would be ideal for our whippets Willow and Tigger as the kennel could be very useful in the RV or in the house. Fortunately Linda had seen similar products before when she attended an event held at Longleat in the UK, but as they were then quite expensive did not acquire one at the time. However in 'Country Ways' the very same kennel manufactured by the same company were to say the least 'extremely good value for money' so believed it to be a bargain so purchased one, hoping that it would fit into one of our suitcases when the time came to fly home.

While in Salina we just could not resist visiting Burns Saddlery, a very large and impressive shop specialising in most things Western that ranged from Stetson's to saddles, a really special venue for anyone interested in looking at real craftsmanship and quality whether to browse or purchase.

As we left the store we were excited and thrilled about the next leg of our journey that would take us along Highway 50 so enthusiastically discussed the opportunities this could reveal as we munched on two rather delicious hot dogs purchased from a nearby takeaway.

For the record Highway 50 is in Nevada's Great Basin Desert and spans the US from Sacramento to California, to Ocean City, Maryland, where the Highway goes through Nevada between South Lake Tahoe on the Western Californian border and Baker on the Eastern Utah border and is often referred to as 'The Loneliest Road In America', foolishly we wondered why?

Prior research revealed that the Pony Express riders blazed trails across the mountains and deserts to deliver mail long before the steel tracks were laid west to east to make way for the railroads that were eventually constructed in the region.

Gold, silver and copper mines opened then closed when new and more lucrative 'finds' were made, numerous settlements were established in places with exotic sounding names such as Eureka and Ely as the miners and others stayed on to inhabit the area.

We learnt that some of the Pony Express stations and trails are still visible so we were keen and anxious to start our long journey or should we say trip back in time, but before doing so thought it wise to ensure the Trek had adequate fuel, so added 16.6 gallons at $2/gallon then headed out of Salina on the famous Highway 50 West.

We passed through Scipio, then drove south for one junction on Interstate 15 to Holden where we rejoined Highway 50 West to Delta then went east onto Highway 125 to Oak City in the Fishlake National Forest.

The scenery was not too interesting so the journey seemed to be endless as it took literally ages and ages to reach the campsite at Oak Creek where a planned overnight stop was scheduled.

However when the site was eventually found and that was not an easy task, we were surprised to find it was absolutely deserted, so somewhat reluctantly concluded that it was really far too isolated to spend the night there safely alone.

This was obviously a major concern as Oak Creek was literally in the wilderness so we needed to locate a suitable alternative venue to spend the night so had to agree that our only real option was to retrace our steps then rejoin Highway 50, from there we could travel in the direction of the Great Basin National Park and hopefully find somewhere suitable to rest for the night once on route. Therefore with heavy hearts and weary bodies we turned the Trek round then headed back along Highway 125 then drove on to Highway 50 West, this decision was not taken lightly as it was appreciated that we possibly had at least another 100 miles or more of barren desert to cross before reaching the Great Basin National Park.

This had been a real set back, but when we reached Delta noticed a small but rather shabby RV campground so pulled in to make some enquiries and when eventually the rather deaf 'old timer' in charge surfaced, he said the charge was $10/night to park with or without electricity. However as the site was extremely close to the Highway we were concerned about the potential noise from the road and also had concerns about personal safety and had visions of the Trek loosing its wheels or something by the next morning.

The decision was therefore taken to move on but could not help thinking that perhaps on reflection that this may have been a rather harsh and possibly biased assessment of that particular site.

On the outskirts of Delta we stopped at the Antelope RV Park, a very smart looking site with hard standing, however the charge seemed quite high at $24/night with or without electricity and for a while we were quite tempted until a locomotive was heard not far away and then it came thundering by almost going through the grounds of the site so soon recalled our restless night at the Flying J Plaza at Kingman!!!!

Somewhat reluctantly we therefore decided to continue our journey, so rejoined Highway 50 then later passed through the outskirts of the Sevier Desert and on our left could see the Black Desert Rock and in the far distance could just make out the Cricket Mountains.

We climbed the Confusion Mountain Range and later passed the beautifully named Wah Wah Mountains on the left, but by now appreciated that it would almost certainly be dark by the time we arrived at our proposed destination, so the tension grew as we knew this would be our first 'after dark' drive since arriving in the US, so naturally felt a little apprehensive.

Highway 50 proved to be an excellent smooth tarmac road, but as expected it was extremely desolate as we encountered very little traffic, so could now fully appreciate why it was aptly named 'The Loneliest Road'.

The earlier section of the journey was tedious to say the least as we headed towards the sunset with the sun almost blocking our field of vision, probably quite a spectacular sight but not while driving, but then all too rapidly darkness began to descend and with many miles still to go the journey turned in to a nightmare as we had to exercise extreme caution as there was a real danger of wild animals or even cows straying onto the highway and on route did pass several unlucky animal carcasses that had been sent on their way to the 'big green pasture in the sky'.

Furthermore it would have been most unwise to venture off the highway for any reason as the terrain looked very hostile and not at all suitable for a reasonably heavy RV, so considerable concentration was required at all times to ensure that the Trek stayed safely on the tarmac.

On route we noticed a sign indicating that there was a camp site on our left, but as it was some seventy miles down what appeared to be a narrow dusty rough road, decided that it would not be wise or appropriate to make a detour that late in the evening so continued the tedious journey on the good old Highway 50.

After what seemed to be far too many hours of driving without encountering hardly any other vehicles we must have crossed the border into Nevada without really appreciating that we had done so. Eventually in the far distance, as if by magic, we could just make out what appeared to be some lights and sincerely hoped that it was the next and only service area we would encounter on this section of the journey. Naturally our spirits were raised, as we believed that our campsite destination should be close to the service station, although it took an inordinate amount of time to get any closer to those distant lights, at least 30 or more minutes.

By now we had a much better appreciation of the vast distances between some locations in the US something that probably really does need to be experienced first hand to be believed, as they can be really awesome.

After ages and ages we drew close to, then at long last, eventually passed the service centre and turned off onto Highway 487, then joined Highway 488 leading into the Great Basin National Park, but the roads seemed fairly narrow or perhaps it was just because there were no street lights so it seemed exceptionally dark so called for maximum concentration.

When we eventually arrived at the site finding a suitable pitch in the darkness was extremely difficult and not one to be recommended, but eventually located the only pitch still left that was large enough for the Trek, but encountered difficulty driving in, as the entrance was very narrow.

The RV could not be reversed in safely as the narrow tree lined entry could not be seen well enough in the darkness, in the end there was little alternative but to enter the pitch front first, so although this was contrary to the site rules was the only viable option. At least we managed to park safely having covered two hundred and eighty nine miles, a far greater distance than had been scheduled for the day!!

That task completed Linda walked back to the site check-in area that was not manned and placed $10 in the envelope provided then posted it the appropriate box to cover the cost of the one night stay on pitch number 9.

Tuesday 4 May

The morning was warm with brilliant cloudless blue skies and looking outside we could see to the rear of the RV the spectacular sight of Wheeler's Peak rising some 13,063 feet in the air with it's snow covered summit.

Nearby many of the white/silver barked Aspen trees were just beginning to show their foliage as if to welcome the beginning of spring while basking in the delights of the warm sun.

As the area is the home of the renowned Lehman Caves we agreed to pay them a visit, but first had to get safely off the pitch and knew that was not going to be easy but fortunately there was little traffic movement on the site, so it was possible to reverse out without too much difficulty and then with Linda leading the way on foot drove the wrong way out of the site, certainly not to be recommended, but this was our only viable route out, if we were not to cause any damage to the Trek.

Once safely back on the road, we drove to the nearby Visitor Centre where the princely sum of just $2 each was handed over to participate in the 1/2hour journey into the Lehman Caves.

While there we were informed that we had unexpectedly crossed into yet another time zone so needed to adjust our clocks and watches, this time turning them back one hour, this meant that we had approximately one hour to spare so decided to eat breakfast at the small, but very picturesque restaurant located within the visitor centre complex.

As we waited the spectacular views that unfolded just outside the window held us both captivated and could still hardly believe that we were actually there, then almost all too soon two delicious breakfasts arrived consisting of ham and eggs plus some toast and the meal was of course thoroughly enjoyed and very filling, so vowed not to eat again until much later in the day.

In due course accompanied by an experienced guide, our party of about six people ventured into the caves and walked in almost total darkness down nearly 1/2 a mile into the bowls of the earth to literally marvel at the stalactites, stalagmites, draperies, shields and helictites that are calcite formations that curve and appear to defy the effects of gravity.

Even in the dim light the photographic opportunities were almost boundless and as usual were exploited to the full, a really fantastic experience and one not to be missed.

Leaving Great Basin National Park we retraced our steps rejoining Highway 50 West and drove through quite mountainous terrain including the Snake Range until we turned right onto Highway 486 to Cave Lake State Park, apparently one of the most scenic mountain parks in Nevada. At a height of some 7,300 feet Cave Lake is situated high in the Schell Creek range just seven miles from Highway 50 and occupies an area of some 1,240 acres and features a spectacular 32 acre blue/green coloured lake.

Pulling into Cave Lake Park after seventy-eight miles we soon located a really gorgeous pitch, number 33 that actually overlooked the lake, then walked to the kiosk and posted the fee of $14 that consisted of the park entrance fee of $4 and the overnight camp fee of $10 in the now familiar post box. Although Cave Lake Park has only 34 pitches it is open all the year round and experiences summer temperatures ranging from about the high 80's/ 90's degrees Fahrenheit down to the low 40's degrees Fahrenheit. During the winter temperatures are often around 30/40 degrees Fahrenheit during the day falling at night to 30 degrees Fahrenheit below zero. The weather can get so cold that the ice on the lake can apparently reach around two feet thick so is therefore often used for ice-skating but at other times of the year the lake offers good fishing opportunities and is home to rainbow trout and other similar species of fish.

Animals including elk, mule deer and predators including bobcat, mountain lion and coyote are reputed to reside in the area as well and we were told that it is also possible to see hawk, eagle, vulture, pinyon jay, magpie as well as a range of waterfowl and songbirds.

This proved to be an exquisite and very tranquil location to spend time recovering from the long and tedious trek across the endless barren desert areas of Highway 50, but is also a good base camp to use for exploring the region.

Wednesday 5 May – Thursday 6 May

Surprisingly Cave Lake State Park camping ground does not have it's own RV dump station so on our way out drove to it's sister park, called Elk Campground, which was not far away to use the facilities there, then continued on to rejoin Highway 50 West.

At Ely in preparation for long journey across yet more desert terrain we filled the Trek with diesel taking onboard 24.4 gallons at $2.19/gallon and according to several RV owners and a few truckers, also filling their vehicles at the same time, this was a very high price to have to pay for fuel, but even so some of the local garages were noticeably more expensive. One trucker was taking on board something like 180 gallons of fuel so we could fully appreciate what that was going to cost, nevertheless we believed that this may be the only opportunity to purchase reasonably priced diesel for many, many miles as it was likely to be even more expensive once on route.

While in Ely the opportunity was taken to replenish our dwindling stocks of food so were fortunate enough to find a Gorman's Market where a selection of essential supplies were acquired along with some 'Buffalo Patties' (burgers).

These patties are made from exceptional good lean buffalo meat and are just 'out of this world' as they melt in the mouth and are really just so delicious and of course very, very tasty.

Resuming our journey we noticed several garages further along the highway that were advertising diesel at the comparatively high price of up to $2.45/gallon, so obviously felt pleased that the decision had been taken to fill the Trek with diesel while in Ely as we hoped that we would have enough fuel on board to get all the way to Fallon where fuel would hopefully be cheaper.

The journey along this section of Highway 50 West was yet again extremely arduous and so very tiring, in addition there were only a few designated stopping locations or services areas on route, so could not always pull-over when and where we wanted.

On route we passed the 7,588 feet high Robinson Summit and on the left noticed signs to the Ruth Copper Pit, one of the worlds largest mining pits then later we climbed over Little Antelope Summit rising to a height of 7,438 feet and then a little later went over Pancake Summit at 6,520 feet high and thought that whoever named these locations probably had a good sense of humour?

We were pleased and relieved that the scenery was reasonably interesting so did not to get as bored as we had been told we would, although some of the terrain was very barren and so a little monotonous.

On occasions we wondered if we were starting to see things, as any vehicles coming in the opposite direction first appeared in the far distance just as if they were a mirage and then it seemed to take forever and a day before it could be ascertained whether they were real or imaginary and it took them literally ages before they passed, often at high speed.

Eventually and not before time we reached Eureka, which proclaimed itself to be the 'Friendliest Town On The Loneliest Road' where we stopped briefly on the roadside for a short but much needed rest.

Continuing our journey we drove close to the Toiyabe National Forest and the Bob Scott Campground situated adjacent to the Simpson Park Mountains then on through the Toiyabe Range to Austin.

However while crossing one of the valleys the Trek suddenly took a very violent turn to the left, swerving dramatically towards the opposite side of the road just as if a herd of stampeding buffalo had hit it in the side. Linda could not help shrieking in terror as we went extremely close to the edge of the other carriageway, where we had an all too good view of the rapidly approaching steep embankment. At one stage it looked as if the Trek was going to get some expensive and unwanted modifications and the occupants likewise, only at the very last minute was control regained and the Trek guided safely over to the correct side of the road, the whole incident happened in just a few seconds but seemed to last forever.

We eventually concluded that we must have been hit by a very, very strong gust of wind racing through the valley that had arrived without any visible signs or prior warning at all, luckily at the time there were no oncoming vehicles passing or trying to overtake, as this would almost certainly have resulted in a very nasty and unavoidable accident.

However had the gust of wind hit the Trek from the drivers and not the passenger side, there surely would have been a serious accident as there was a steep drop on that side of the road and there would not have been sufficient road space or enough time to make the necessary corrections.

After that nasty and quite frightening incident the Trek's speed was reduced from a modest 55mph to around 45mph just incase any more gusts of wind were encountered and on several subsequent occasions we did experience more side winds. However these could often be predicted, as it was sometimes possible to see the tumble weeds dancing on the plains or see the swirls of sand rising from the desert or salt from the dry salt lakes bordering the highway, but luckily these gusts were not anywhere near as fierce as the one that tried to take us off the road.

With the Trek's speed reduced to about 45mph, the journey seemed even more tedious and frustrating, but our spirits lifted when we noticed signs at the side of the highway proclaiming that we were actually travelling along the old 'Pony Express' route.

Eventually we stopped for a short, but much needed break at Cold Springs one of the old staging posts, where we learnt that in June horseback riders were scheduled to travel along the old route once more to celebrate the Pony Express and that they planned to stop off at Cold Springs, just as they would have done in the olden days.

Rejoining Highway 50 the remainder of the journey seemed endless only made tolerable by the sight of a few interesting landmarks that included the Shoshone Mountains, Clan Alpine Mountains and the impressive sight of a few modern jet fighter aircraft flying low into and out of the Fallon Naval Air Base.

On the last section of the journey the highway went through a very desolate area of salt flats where previous travellers had placed stones or rocks near the edge of the road to spell their names or had left some cryptic message to be enjoyed by those that followed, reading a few of them at least helped to remove some of the boredom.

Arriving at the city of Fallon it was readily agreed that was enough driving for one day as we had covered some two hundred and seventy five miles so were exceedingly pleased and relieved to guide the Trek into the large Wal-Mart and Safeway car park.

Nevertheless now we could proclaim that we had successfully driven along a significant stretch of the 'Loneliest Road' in the US and had survived the unforgettable experience.

We began to think and wonder what it must have been like to have been an early pioneer or settler taking a similar route, say on horseback or in a covered wagon, as there would of course not have been any tarmac road nor any proper signs to even show the way.

During the day it would have been necessary to cope with the intolerable dust and searing heat encountered in the vast desert plains and in contrast the extreme cold with possibly freezing temperatures at night.

The journey would certainly have taken a far longer time than just the two days it had taken us in the luxury of our very well equipped RV, in a covered wagon it would have been surprising if they could have managed to travel more than just a few miles or so a day and each mile would no doubt have felt like a marathon and each hill like a mountain.

When the travellers encountered the real mountain ranges they would have been faced with possibly two options, either to detour and go round thus extending their journey or to try and find a suitable, but probably very tortuous route over the mountain. Whichever option they took would have added to their ordeal as well as their journey time so would have been extremely challenging to the people and their animals.

After considering what the early settlers and travellers had achieved and the harsh conditions they would have surely encountered, concluded that in comparison, that our journey was 'a piece of cake'.

With Trek parked safely for the night in the Wal-Mart car park next to a very large 40 foot Beaver Patriot RV and not far from an immaculate Monaco Dynasty, amongst these giants our RV looked and felt the real baby of the bunch.

This particular Wal-Mart had little in the way of food, so consumable supplies were acquired from the adjacent well stocked Safeway, where Linda purchased some asparagus for just 99 cents/lb and along with other purchases the bill came to $28, however as Linda had a US Safeway Club Card and purchased only items on 'special offer' managed to reduce the amount actually handed over to just under $14 and so we both had broad smiles on our faces as we left the store.

Fallon has a population of roughly 6,500 and has beautiful tree shaded sidewalks and is about four hundred and fifty miles from Las Vegas and just about sixty miles from Reno and proved to be a very convenient place to rest after the long journey across that endless desert, so decided to stay for two nights to rest and recuperate.

During our time there we did a little local sight seeing but concluded that apart from the local Naval Airbase, numerous hotels/motels, casinos, a range of shops and some fast food outlets that there was not too much more to see in Fallon itself.

Nevertheless for those willing to travel further, there is a large reservoir to the west of Fallon called Lahontan Lake that is reputed to very good for fishing and to the east is Sand Mountain which is two miles long, one mile wide and over 600 feet high and nearby is a tumbled down site of an original Pony Express station where the riders and horses used to rest.

Later we learnt that a Mike Fallon had built a 'crossroads store' on his ranch back in about the mid 1890's and so the City of Fallon had subsequently been named after him and that it is considered to be a high desert community, we were also told that the area just west of Fallon is renown for its highly productive farmland so is often referred to as 'Cantaloupe Country'.

As we did not wish to venture far time was spent looking round the town where we found a very interesting establishment called Openshaw Saddlery that specialises in the production and repair of Western Saddles and associated equipment, where it was really fascinating to stand and watch their two highly skilled craftsmen working with traditional materials and mainly just hand tools.

Unfortunately the Navy uses a large section of the airspace to the east of Fallon for combat pilot training so this has made the area uninhabitable; furthermore oil and fuel spillages as well as bomb drops have resulted in considerable accumulated environmental damage. This naval air station is the US Navy's Premier Tactical Air Warfare Training Facility and in recent years has expanded its' activities that has resulted in an influx of additional staff with associated economic benefits for the local economy.

During the second evening at Wal-Mart, the Trek was joined by a very large immaculate looking Prevost RV Coach that must have been worth in excess of $1 million, several Monaco RV's and one or two fifth wheeler's and one trailer, all the Trek's friends from the previous night having departed early that morning.

Unfortunately late in the evening a large truck parked nearby and continued to run its loud and thus very disturbing air conditioning system all night, creating considerable annoyance to all the RV owners that were trying to get some all important rest and sleep, ready for the next stage of their own adventure. A similar problem had been also encountered during the earlier phase of Our American Dream when we stayed overnight at Flying J's in Kingman!!!!

CARSON CITY AND ON TO LAKE TAHOE

Carson City

Friday 7 May

We rejoined Highway 50 West on route to Carson City and then stopped at the Fallon Speedway to fill the Trek with more diesel adding 20.4 gallons that cost $2.20/gallon and this proved to be a prudent move as all the other garages in the vicinity appeared to be charging even higher prices.

At the outskirts of Fallon road works were encountered and as some of the heavy earth moving vehicles partially obscured the road direction signs we nearly made a wrong turning and it was only at the last minute did we appreciate that there was more than one Highway 50, one is known as Highway 50 and goes to Carson City, the other is known as the 'Alternative Highway 50' that goes to Reno. Fortunately we managed to just catch a glimpse of the small sign saying 'Carson' in just enough time to turn off, without causing other vehicles any inconvenience, but both laughed as we noticed the road was called 'Bongo Road'.

The journey went smoothly and before too long had passed through Silver Spur, Stage Coach, Dayton and Silver City then noted signs on our right to Virginia City and although we were tempted to make another visit continued on to the outskirts of Carson City where we stopped briefly to look at some gorgeous looking new RV's at McKinnish Camper Corner.

Whilst there we were given a grand tour of a modestly priced 40 foot Itasca Meridian, OK it was only $250,000 and a somewhat cheaper $180,000 34 foot Itasca Meridian by Randy the sales associate who said that he was an ex-sheriff, but was now thoroughly enjoying his time selling RV's. Randy offered a test drive in either vehicle without obligation, but as we were only 'window shopping' declined to take up the kind offer, however we were surprised not to be pressurised to 'do a deal' there and then, as we had been told that US sales people can be very determined to 'make that sale'.

Continuing our journey we drove through the centre of Carson City and luckily it was not too busy at all and then continued onto Highway 395 South heading towards the Wal-Mart on the outskirts of town for another 'economy stopover'.

However we could not resist stopping in the city to take some photographs and to walk along a short section of the route known as the Kit Carson Trail designed specifically to take walkers near the turn of the century buildings and courthouses.

As a matter of interest Carson City is situated close to the eastern foothills of the Sierra Nevada so is about thirty miles south of Reno and is understood to have taken its name from the Carson River, named by John Fremont in honour of his scout Kit Carson in 1844.

In the 1860's Carson City was a station on the Pony Express and the Overland Mail run by Butterfield and Wells Fargo Co and it flourished as a boomtown after the discovery of the nearby Comstock Silver Lode and eventually became state capital in about 1864.

Today Carson City is Nevada's only territorial and state capital whose economy is based on tourism and legalised gambling, but back in 1851 it was a trading post on the route from Salt Lake City to California but now offers a host of nearby attractions ranging from golf in the summer to skiing in winter and is only around 20 minutes drive from Lake Tahoe or Virginia City.

After a very enjoyable time exploring at least some of the City, we continued the short journey to the nearby Wal-Mart and soon noticed that it was fairly full with a significant number of RV's, Fifth Wheelers and Trailers.

As we pulled in Linda noted that the Trek registered just sixty-six miles on the speedometer since commencing this leg of the journey and felt lucky to locate a reasonably level safe site for the RV at the far end of the car park.

During the late afternoon we participated in a little retail therapy purchasing a few necessary food supplies then wandered through some of the new large stores and noted that nearby even more were in various stages of construction. Naturally it was difficult not to compare the vast ranges of goods offered for sale and the relatively low and therefore attractive prices compared to the UK.

On to Lake Tahoe

Saturday 8 May

With customary blue skies overhead and high temperatures outside we moved on from the Carson City Wal-Mart then drove west on Highway 50 on route to Lake Tahoe climbing steeply to some 7,000 feet on alpine like twisty roads with breathtaking views looking back towards the city.

On route we passed a sign on the roadside that stated that this was 'bear country' and thought that sounded a pretty exciting prospect so sincerely hoped that we would be lucky enough to see at least one real live bear!!!! Later we turned on to Highway 28 to commence the journey around Lake Tahoe itself in an anti-clockwise direction and were stunned by the views, they were truly amazing and with the azure coloured water of the lake it would have been possible to convince most people that they were in the Caribbean, probably the only thing out of place were the snow covered mountain peaks in the background.

In North America, Lake Tahoe is regarded as the third deepest lake at 1,645 feet and is located in the Sierra Nevada at a height of around 6,230 feet above sea level and is twelve miles wide by twenty-two miles long and has fantastic crystal clear but cold water at this time of the year.

Nowadays the area has become an all year round recreation destination for activities such as fishing, hiking and boating in the summer with skiing, snowboarding and a whole variety of sports in the winter. Regrettably and as a consequence some areas have been very commercially developed but some others seem to have escaped the 'ravages of progress' so still retain their rustic charm.

The area boasts of having around 19 campgrounds but many did not appear to open fully until the end of May but it was noted that some are only able to accommodate the smaller RV's and not all offer full hook-up facilities.

At the northern section of the lake we crossed from Nevada into California and at Tahoe City joined Highway 89 and it was duly noted that camping charges appeared to vary considerably from the Lake Forest campground charging $15/night to Tahoe Pines where the charges apparently ranged from $28/night to a staggering $60/night.

In the northern area of the lake diesel was priced at a 'heart stopping' $2.65/gallon but we also noticed that in the more popular lake locations that there were very good tarmac cycle ways, so with fuel this costly thought that bicycles would be very useful.

Nevertheless after completing some one hundred and four miles from our previous overnight stop in Carson City, the Trek was carefully driven into Sugar Pine Point State Park, a very secluded and peaceful site set among a beautiful green forest of pines that is only about half a mile from the lake and at the park entrance paid the ranger the overnight price of $12 and were assured that fresh water as well as the RV dump station would open that very day.

The ranger stressed that as we were now in 'bear country' that it was necessary to read and adhere to the rules posted on the notice board at the Ranger Station and again in the camp ground itself.

For the record the notices in big bold letters advised anyone using tents to store all food items in the robust steel 'Hyd-a-meal' cabinets provided and for everyone to dispose of any partially used or unwanted food in the special locked bins on the site so as not to attract the bears.

In the afternoon we took a leisurely walk in the forest following a well signposted nature trail down to the edge of the lake adjacent to the rather magnificent Queen Anne style Ehrman Mansion that is now a splendid nature centre. As on previous occasions the digital camera worked overtime, as there were just so many unbelievable photographic opportunities, but to our great disappointment we still did not see any sign of the elusive bears!!!!

Sunday 9 May

After filling the RV with fresh water an attempt was made to use the RV dump station, but to our dismay found that it was still not operating, so departed from Sugar Pine Point and drove on Highway 89 South. The route took us through countryside that resembled an alpine setting with steep descents, hairpin bends with deep ravines on each side of the road, which was no doubt very spectacular for the passenger, but the driver needed to concentrate on the road ahead to ensure that the RV remained safely on the tarmac.

We stopped at the exceptionally picturesque Emerald Bay to take photographs of the magnificent and very spectacular 500 foot Eagle Falls waterfall then continued on slowly the short distance to Fallen Leaf Campground where the charge without electricity, showers or RV dump was $20/night.

It transpired that anyone wanting to use the RV dump facilities would need to travel to Camp Richardson that is just down the road but would then have to pay $5 to actually use their facilities.

Although the site looked appealing it was almost empty and not really fully operational at this time of the year so we decided to continue our journey to Camp Richardson and that was all of eighteen miles further on from Sugar Pine Point.

On arrival we soon located a nice secluded pitch, number 52, that was situated right in the heart of a beautiful pine forest and then booked in and paid the site fee of just $19/night to dry camp, but that also allowed access to water and free showers, although there was still a charge of $3 to use the RV dump station.

During the day we walked to Lake Tahoe and to the stunning smaller lake called Fallen Leaf Lake where many more photographic opportunities were exploited to the full, as the weather was really good with blue skies overhead and temperatures around 70 degrees Fahrenheit, we foolishly thought that summer had arrived at last.

In the late afternoon we attempted to walk along one of excellent tarmac cycle ways to a shopping area known to the locals a 'The Y', which refers to the junction of Highway 50 and Highway 89, as we had been told that it was only about 2 miles away. However after several hours of brisk walking concluded that it was probably actually further away than we had been led to believe, so decided to return to Camp Richardson before it got dark, just in case any of those elusive bears were perhaps out looking for an evening meal.

Regrettably throughout our time in the area we did not see any evidence of those much spoken about bears, but were assured by the locals that they were around, perhaps somewhere or were they?

Yosemite National Park

Monday 10 May.

Overnight the temperatures must have dropped considerably, as it was snowing quite heavily when we awoke so the surrounding area was completely covered in a beautiful new white coat, however as we planned to travel to Yosemite National Park we did not relish driving what still seemed to be a large RV on unfamiliar slippery roads covered in snow.

Nevertheless with a slight improvement in the weather we left Camp Richardson driving very cautiously and commenced our journey on Highway 89 South stopping to get essential food shopping at 'The Y'.

The skies overhead remained grey and very overcast as we continued our journey and a little later were required to pull into a designated area, where it was necessary to declare to an official from the Californian Agricultural Department if we were carrying any fruit or similar produce and fortunately after a brief inspection were given the 'all clear' and waved on our way.

While at Camp Richardson Linda had carefully planned our intended and hopefully the shortest route to Yosemite, but we did not know at the time that this was going to lead us into big trouble and would involve driving much further than planned.

On route the Trek slowly trundled up the Luther Pass climbing to some 7,740 feet high to reveal picture postcard scenery set against a backdrop of snow-covered mountaintops with the road snaking and undulating just like in the Alps then near the junction of Highway 8, Linda even managed to catch a glimpse a low flying eagle that was probably looking for breakfast.

Continuing south on Highway 89 we eventually came to the junction with Highway 4 and read a bold notice stating that Highway 4 was not recommended for vehicles over 25 foot long, so following that advice continued our journey on Highway 89, later climbing Monitor Pass at 8,314 feet and drove fairly close to the Carson Iceberg Wilderness area.

However on reaching Topaz at the junction of the 89 and 395, to our dismay noticed a large sign stating that Highway 120 West going to Yosemite was in-fact shut and would not reopen until later in the year due to snow!!! This came as a huge surprise, particularly as our journey had already taken us along routes at similar altitudes so had made the mistake of assuming that this route would also be open.

This obviously presented a major problem, as there appeared to be just three options.

a) Abandon the scheduled visit to Yosemite, but this was the least acceptable solution.

b) Travel to the other entrance that was open on the far side of the park, but this would involve a journey of many miles and probably take far too long.

c) Turn round and return to Highway 4 to give that route a try and under the circumstances that seemed to be the most acceptable and appropriate solution.

The whole episode was frustrating, particularly as Linda had telephoned the National Parks Service on their free phone number the previous evening to make our reservations and had specifically enquired if all the roads leading to Yosemite were open and was told 'yes' there were 'no problems'!!!

We returned along Highway 89 in silence, feeling quite depressed and naturally upset as the journey was now going to take much longer than anticipated so this could mean that there may be less time in the park than had been scheduled.

The return journey all the way back to Highway 4 seemed to take forever and ever, but in reality was probably only around twenty five miles or so, then on reaching Highway 4 once more intently studied 'that notice' again.

It stated something along the lines 'This is a narrow, winding and in places steep road that is not recommended for vehicles over 25 feet and that the hazardous stretch of road was about twenty five miles long'.

However, after considerable thought and deliberation believed that as the Trek was 25 feet 9 inches long, that it should just be OK so decided to give it a try.

So very cautiously and slowly we proceeded along Highway 4 and for the first mile on so everything seemed OK, but observed that the road was actually getting narrower and narrower and the incline steeper and steeper and eventually the line in the centre of the road disappeared altogether as the road became ever narrower and much, much steeper.

The scenery was no doubt very beautiful, although this could not be fully appreciated by either the driver or passenger as considerable concentration was required to keep the Trek on what was fast becoming an extremely narrow road with alpine like bends and steep descents on either side with no room for error, even a few inches either way could have spelled disaster.

By now the Trek was fully committed, as it was no longer possible to turn back even if we wanted to, the road was just too narrow and any pull off areas were just not large enough for the RV, so safe progress now required the full attention of the driver and navigator.

Linda had to perch on the front edge of her seat in an attempt to view the road ahead as far as possible, this was particularly helpful when approaching left hand bends as the driver had a very restricted view of any approaching traffic but fortunately the passenger could see the road a little better so could provide feedback on what lay ahead.

We climbed higher and higher the road twisting and turning dramatically and by now had to travel in the centre of the road to negotiate the sharp bends and to avoid the intimidating protruding rocks. The Trek's heater needed to work overtime to keep the inside of the RV warm as the temperature outside was freezing and the snow by the roadside was in places taller than the Trek.

We climbed in an ever-ending spiral upwards and upwards climbing Ebbetts Pass and eventually went over the summit at a height of 8,733 feet, then on and over Pacific Summit at 8,050 feet. Later we passed the frozen Alpine Lake that was covered in brilliant white virgin snow and eventually much to our relief began the descent into Bear Valley the well-known ski and winter sports centre.

In reality we had been most fortunate not to have encountered any other RV or similar sized vehicle coming the other way, nevertheless there had been several 'almost too close for comfort' meetings with around a dozen or so cars and three or four motorcycles, naturally this just had to happen at the most difficult sections imaginable, but eventually arrived safely at the end of this most hazardous section of the journey without any damage to the Trek.

Still on Highway 4 we then encountered road works and were escorted through by a 'pilot vehicle' then at Angels Camp, that is understood to be referred to by the locals as 'Frog Town', purchased more diesel this time taking on board 12 gallons at a cost of $2.5/gallon.

After completing this chore we drove across the road to a small RV park to purchase LPG, as it was significantly cheaper than at the garage and purchased 8.4 gallons of LPG at $1.88/gallon and then resumed our journey along Highway 49.

The countryside resembled the Sussex Downs with beautiful green hills and valleys so was in complete contrast to the snow and ice that had been encountered earlier in the day.

At the spectacular New Melones Lake we pulled over to take photographs of the sparkling deep blue water and while in the area noticed that there were signs mentioning the famous writer Mark Twain and later noticed a sign post showing the way to his old cabin.

On route we drove through the large old town of Sonora then on to the Don Pedro Lake where more photographs were taken then eventually later joined Highway 120 towards Yosemite National Park and ventured into the Stanislaus National Forest region not far from Big Oak Flat.

After a very long drive we stopped at the entrance of Yosemite National Park to show our National Parks Pass to the ranger on duty, once again this saved us paying the $20 park entrance fee and after spending a short time chatting were politely waved off on our way.

However the journey was still far from over as there were at least another twenty-five miles or so to go through the park itself before we would reach our destination at Lower Pines near Curry Village, fortunately the scenery was really spectacular and breathtaking so of course could not resist the temptation to stop wherever possible to take yet more photographs and admire the views.

To our surprise just before reaching our destination we noticed a lone coyote standing at the roadside waiting to cross to the other side, so after quickly checking to see it was safe to do so pulled off the road and took several-hurried photographs, amazingly the coyote did not seem to be in any hurry and graciously posed for several shots before slowly ambling off into the undergrowth, completely un-phased by it all.

Linda's eagle eye had already noted that our destination was adjacent to Curry Village and was eagerly anticipating that she would soon be able to sample the delights of a super Indian meal as she reasoned that with a name like that they must surely have an

Indian restaurant, but later much to her disappointment ascertained that there were not any restaurants of that type in the village.

As we entered Lower Pines the light was starting to fade so it made the search for our already reserved pitch interesting to say the least, as the complex was situated beneath extremely tall pines that stretched skywards and really looked rather ghostly in the fading light. So after such a long and tedious journey it was essential to exercise extreme caution on the way in, as it was necessary drive along a twisty, narrow tarmac road that threaded its way through the tall but far too close for comfort tree trunks.

In one or two places it was only just possible to squeeze through and it was clear to see a significant number of scars on the trees that had been made by previous traffic and we began to wonder just how many of the larger RV's, Fifth Wheeler's or Trailers had actually made physical contact with those menacing trunks and had modified their vehicles in the process?

Even getting on to our pitch, number 50 that cost $18/night with no hook-up, was not particularly easy, especially after such a long and somewhat hazardous journey of about two hundred and forty five miles and that of course included the stressful but unforgettable trek along Highway 4.

Tuesday 11 May

Bright and early but after allowing ourselves the luxury of a little breakfast we strolled the short distance into Curry Village to catch the free shuttle bus to the Visitor Centre and on arrival took the opportunity to watch a dramatic and superbly shot film about the Yosemite National Park and it was so impressive that we ended up buying a DVD copy to remind us of our visit.

It appears that Yosemite Valley is often referred to as the 'Incomparable Valley' as it is understood to be the world's best-known example of a glacier-carved canyon, the impressive scale of the waterfalls, rounded granite peaks', massive monoliths and towering cliffs are truly magnificent and really awesome.

The extensive area proved to be a mosaic of open meadows with attractive wildflowers, shrubs and oak woodlands, mixed green conifer forests with large ponderosa pines, cedar and much, much more.

It is of course home to monarch butterflies, mule deer and of course the famous black bear, which incidentally may be black, brown, cinnamon or even blond in colour.

However each year many unlucky bears are unfortunately killed in Yosemite as well as in other national parks as a result of human carelessness through incorrect food storage and in an attempt to reduce this problem, special 'bear proof' steel food containers are provided for visitors to store their foodstuffs while in the parks and similar bear proof large waste bins are also installed for the safe disposal of any unwanted or used food materials.

The free of charge shuttle bus was used to visit the Yosemite Falls, a truly magnificent waterfall, the highest and probably the most dramatic waterfall in the USA, plunging approximately 2,570 feet from the rim of the Yosemite Valley and apparently May is a good time of the year to see the falls in full flow, as by late summer they become a mere thin string of water that just trickles down the silver rock faces.

Later in the day we made more use of the bus and then walked to such exotic sounding locations as Mirror Lake, Happy Isles as well as the Vernal Fall footbridge and from Mirror Lake exceptionally good views could be seen of Half Dome, a very impressive mountain rising tall in the distance and while at Happy Isles, we went into and spent quite some time in the excellent Nature Centre.

Later in the day the shuttle the bus was again used for the return trip to Yosemite Village where time was taken to leisurely browse in some of the shops, although no purchases were made.

As Yosemite seemed so magical with just so much to see and so much still to experience we tried to extend our stay by one more night but could not do so as all the camping sites in the park were unfortunately fully booked and while chatting to a variety of other visitors learnt that the sites within the park can and frequently do get fully booked as far as five or six months in advance, so in reality stood very little chance of securing a pitch at the last minute.

Although the shuttle bus system was excellent, it would have also been very useful to have some bicycles, as the park provides a myriad of excellent tarmac cycle ways and we could have seen just that little bit more in our limited time there.

However even this early in the year large numbers of visitors were already arriving at the park so the shuttle buses were sometimes quite crowded or completely full and many of the more popular locations were also pretty busy.

MERCED, TURLOCK AND MODESTO

Wednesday 12 May

The shuttle bus was used for one last quick visit to Sentinel Bridge where we planned to take yet more photographs of Half Dome, but while Linda was on the bridge just about to take another shot, she noticed a lone coyote approaching who seemed completely un-phased by our presence, as it came trotting along the road almost directly towards us and was only a matter of feet away, but unfortunately this one did not want to stop or pose to have any pictures taken.

So our attentions were then refocused on photographing the very picturesque and stunning nearby small wooden chapel and noted an adjacent sign indicating that it can on occasions become completely flooded!!!!

Before leaving the park the opportunity was taken to fill the Trek's tank with fresh water and to use the RV dump station at the adjacent Upper Pines Campsite, then with these necessary chores completed we said farewell to the camping grounds then rejoined the road going out of the park, stopping on route to take some photographs at Yosemite Cascades and then exited on to Highway 140 at the Arch Rock entrance/exit.

There we followed the fast flowing Merced River and could not help noticing literally hundreds and hundreds of butterflies in the air and on the road, in-fact they seemed to be everywhere and literally covered the road as well as the surrounding area just like a multi-coloured shimmering carpet. Many of these beautiful creatures had unfortunately already been killed while others were swarming in and were experiencing a similar fate as they encountered passing vehicles, so this was such a tragic and unforgettable sight.

Somewhat saddened by this experience we were relieved to notice some activity on the adjacent river that helped to dim the unpleasant butterfly encounter as we could see quite a number of people really enjoying themselves whitewater rafting or canoeing or even capsizing as they tried to navigate the rapids. They seemed to be having a ball so Linda, being Linda, wanted to stop to take some customary photographs, but as it was almost impossible to locate somewhere safe to park she fired-off a few shots as we went by with varying degrees of success.

Later yet more road works were encountered and this time we were escorted through, however the escort vehicle must have thought it was an Indy Car race as it travelled so fast kicking up so much dust it was difficult to see the road ahead so had to slow down and almost stop.

Once this obstruction was cleared it was possible to resume a more leisurely pace before stopping briefly in Mariposa, which incidentally means butterfly, to browse for a time in some super craft shops and then continued on Highway 40 passing through areas that resembled scenes from Africa with burnt and golden grass that swayed in the gentle breeze and stretched for miles into the distance as far as the eye could see.

Nearing Merced we stopped briefly at a small vineyard called Red Rock Winery and Brewery and could not resist purchasing two cases of Californian Chardonnay for the bargain price of $40.22 in total including tax, so feeling extremely pleased with this acquisition continued the journey to Merced and the Wal-Mart that is located on Loughborough Drive for another economic overnight stay.

Merced proved to be much larger than anticipated and it was not too easy to find the Wal-Mart store so had to stop to ask for directions then in due course and without further trouble followed the excellent advice and a little later arrived safely at our destination after traveling just eighty-five miles from Yosemite where we settled in for another relaxed nights rest. This particular Wal-Mart again did not major on food provisions but as our stocks were in good order this did not present a problem.

Thursday 13 May

Before departing we could not resist treating ourselves to a really excellent 'eat as much as you can' pizza and salad at the Round Table in Merced that cost only about $6 each and following this fabulous meal drove back to Highway 140 without getting lost then joined Interstate 99 North, although it soon it became all too apparent that the road surface on this Interstate was extremely rough and not appreciated by the Trek or the occupants.

Furthermore a great deal of traffic particularly heavy trucks appeared to be hounding the Trek trying to force it to travel beyond a comfortable and safe speed so it was most gratifying to leave this Interstate after nineteen miles to spend the night at the Wal-Mart car park this time at Turlock. As this Wal-Mart specialised mainly in domestic goods we soon located a very good Foodmaxx Store only a short walk away where we stocked-up with a few provisions for the next day at least.

Friday 14 May

With brilliant blue skies overhead the Trek was driven to the adjacent Shell Petrol Station and topped up with a little more diesel, this time taking onboard only 8.34 gallons at $2.41/gallon as it was hoped that fuel prices would be lower further north. Leaving Turlock we rejoined Interstate 99 North to travel to yet another Wal-Mart location this time at Modesto and this turned out to be a real long trip, well OK it was just sixteen miles!!!

At the entrance it was impossible to miss the signs stating 'No RV Parking' and if this were correct we would need to consider an alternative venue but as the Trek drew to a halt Linda noticed a small security vehicle patrolling the Wal-Mart site so promptly went over to speak to the guard about RV parking and the signs. She was told that Wal-Mart use a company called Wakenhut Security to police their premises and surprise, surprise the guard added that it was perfectly OK to park the RV there overnight providing it was not left too close to the store itself. This did seem rather confusing to say the least and we could not help wondering why the store displayed the signs and then still permitted RV's to actually park there, almost certainly the signs had deterred others, as the Trek was the only RV on site.

It did not take long to appreciate that this particular Wal-Mart was very popular as the car park was always very busy, however the parking etiquette of many vehicle owners left a lot to be desired as only a very few managed to park within their allotted space. Furthermore shopping trolleys seemed to be just left all over the place although Wal-Mart staff tried in vain to address the problem by collecting them regularly, yet they just could not do so fast enough so it looked like an ever-ending task.

One shopper returning to his vehicle even rammed his shopping trolley hard against the side of his car at least six times before offloading his purchases and must have caused some damage, but at least it was his car and not one belonging to another person!!!!

Fortunately the Trek was parked as far away as possible from all this frantic action but the situation did cause concern as some careless person could have caused extensive and expensive damage to our vehicle.

Yet again it was necessary to locate another store for food so were lucky enough to find a really super Winco Supermarket nearby that contained excellent produce at very reasonable prices.

As we did not have to pay any camping fees it was decided to treat ourselves to an 'Over Fifties' special priced meal at the nearby Fresh Choice Restaurant where they offered a very extensive choice of mouthwatering salads, pastas and similar 'goodies' on an 'eat as much as you can' basis for the grand price of just $6 each. While eating our meal a considerable amount of activity seemed to be taking place outside, with people gathering a short distance away in the adjacent parking area. Further investigation revealed that a fairly new Sports Utility Vehicle (SUV) was on fire with smoke and flames billowing high into the air, fanned by the strong wind, but fortunately the mobile Wal-Mart security guard had already alerted the police and the fire service so that it was only a matter of a few minutes before they arrived and had things under control.

Later when we ventured closer could see that the SUV was a total wreck and learnt from the firefighters that the blaze had apparently started inside the empty vehicle and not in the engine compartment, but at that stage they did not know what had caused the incident.

The fire had also caused severe damage to several other vehicles that had been parked nearby on the passenger side of the SUV so they were probably 'written off' as well, however the vehicles on the other side of the SUV had escaped without damage as the wind had blown the flames away from them.

The incident caused a considerable amount of interest and commotion as the police and fire service tried to find the respective unlucky vehicle owners' who were no where to be seen so would obviously be in for a very big and unpleasant shock when they did return!!

Fortunately the Trek had been parked quite a number of rows away from the incident so was not in any immediate danger, however the situation had been closely monitored just in-case it had been necessary to move the RV quickly to somewhere safer.

Ripon, Lodi, Rocklin and Yuba City

Saturday 15 May

We rejoined Interstate 99 North then stopped after a few miles at a Flying J's that was just off the Interstate at Jack Tone road in Ripon and on arrival the Trek's fuel tank was filled with 17.63 gallons of diesel at $2.30/gallon and the opportunity was also taken to fill the RV's tank with fresh water and of course made full use of the dump station.

Soon Linda was quick to notice yet another good photographic opportunity when several smart and immaculately prepared American Custom Cars pulled into the garage, en-route to a rally.

Furthermore it was also noted that there were quite a few RV's and several Fifth Wheelers parked in a designated area away from all the very large US trucks and thought to ourselves that it may have been a better overnight stop than the Wal-Mart store in Turlock, hind-sight management is such a brilliant tool!!!!

Rejoining Interstate 99 North we continued the journey to our next planned overnight stop, at you know where, yes yet another Wal-Mart location this time in Lodi that was a mere thirty-nine miles further on and when we arrived were extremely pleased to observe far better 'trolley and parking management'.

While at Wal-Mart and this should come as no surprise by now, indulged in a little necessary local shopping and were still pleasantly surprised at the relatively low prices compared to the UK, so Linda purchased a super pair of fitted jeans for just $7, a leather pair of slip on shoes for 'Ivor the Driver' that cost only $16 and then from Food4less purchased 3lb of bananas for $0.87 together with some really super fresh asparagus for the bargain price of just $0.99/pound.

Sunday 16 May

We left Lodi under the now familiar clear blue skies and rapidly rising temperatures to rejoin Interstate 99 North then drove through areas with large picturesque vineyards on either side of the road.

As we neared Sacramento a series of signs indicated that vehicle speed limits were monitored by aircraft and also saw signage indicating that at peak times only vehicles with two or more occupants were allowed into the fast outer lane of the Interstate and that fines would be imposed for any violation, so we could not help wondering how long it might be before such practices could be adopted in the UK?

As Interstate 99 encircles the city it was necessary to divert to Interstate 80 West, to avoid any unnecessary delays and we said to each other in unison, 'so far so good'. Then a little further on were unlucky enough to take a wrong exit that led to a Shopping Mall in Rocklin and this was in-fact just one junction short of the next scheduled stopover at Camping World that was located in another area of Rocklin.

Nevertheless this opportunity presented a chance to take a little time out and saunter round some of the high quality stores in the area, just to do a 'little window shopping' of course and then after seeking advice from several local people on how best to find Camping World we rejoined the Interstate system for what turned out to be very short journey to our destination.

After a total journey distance of sixty five miles we drove the RV sedately in to the Camping World site on Granite Drive, then parked safely at the rear of the building along with several other larger RV's and were extremely pleased to note that there were no shopping trolleys in sight although the downside was the noise from the adjacent Interstate!!!!

The Rocklin Camping World store was impressive with several large service bays at the rear where RV owners could have the accessories fitted that they had just purchased or perhaps even have an engine oil change.

After browsing in the store for a while we took a short walk to Dan Gamel's RV Centre, that just happened to be conveniently located next door and spent quite a while looking at a few extremely nice 'Fleetwood Revolution' RV's and could not help dreaming about winning that elusive lottery when it might just be possible to return to purchase one particular black and silver 40 foot monster that cost a cool $225,000!!!!

Monday 17 May

While at Dan Gemel's the previous day a Harley Davidson motorcycle shop had been earmarked for a quick visit, so as soon they opened we spent a while drooling over some of the glorious machines where it would have been really easy to 'bend the credit card' in a big way!!!!!

A little later we set off to explore Macy's store in the Roseville Galleria with the aim of purchasing a 'topper' to make the bed in the RV a little more user friendly, however this proved to be far more complicated than anyone could have imagined.

It was not too difficult finding something suitable, but paying for it was an entirely different matter, so although everything seemed to be proceeding well, that is until Linda was asked for her ID and of course produced her UK Photo Card Driving Licence. Regrettably Macy's computer just did not seem to recognise her licence as it was issued outside California, undeterred she then offered her passport as an alternative ID and yes the computer was eventually happy to accept this document. At this point in the transaction, Linda noticed that if she were to open a Macy's account she would be entitled to an additional 10% discount on the her purchase, however the computer system would not allow the transaction, as Linda was not able to provide the store with an American Social Security Number!!!

This did seem somewhat odd, as during the earlier part of the trip she had successfully opened an account with Safeway without having to provide any information of this nature, so after a considerable delay, the transaction was eventually completed via her credit card and we then rapidly departed with the topper tucked under our arms.

Still a little bemused by this experience we rejoined Highway 65 then drove on through to Yuba City and after just forty three miles pulled in to the very large car park outside Sam's Club, a store group similar to Costco where an annual membership is required before discounted goods can be purchased.

As Sam's Club is a division of Wal-Mart they permit RV's to stay overnight providing the vehicle is not parked too close to the store, fortunately this particular Sam's Club was right next to a now familiar Wal-Mart anyway!!

The afternoon was spent browsing round some quite tasty RV's at 'All Seasons RV' where we were particularly attracted to a very nice Damon Intruder, but also took the opportunity look round an Alpenlite Fifth Wheeler and were surprised just how spacious it was inside, but towing such a large unit somehow lacked the appeal of an RV.

On our walk back to our RV we stopped briefly to view a selection of very attractive timber framed single story show homes that had been designed and manufactured in Oregon and were staggered at the spacious interiors and apparent quality but were even more surprised by the comparatively low prices that started at only about $61,000 for a home of 1,280 square feet rising to just under $200,000 for a 2,900 square feet version.

The vendor emphasised that the cost of the land would of course be extra and that about $25,000 should also be allowed for the concrete base and for the erection of the building!!!

So with land being comparatively cheap in some US states it would be perfectly feasible to buy a nice plot then build a really super, comfortable home for the price of a reasonable RV although probably not in California as the land costs are high.

Incidentally during our overnight stop at the Sam's Club site there did not seem to be any mobile security staff patrolling the site as had been seen at previous venues, but noted the familiar security cameras that were operational twenty four hours a day, seven days a week and that was reassuring.

IN TROUBLE WITH THE LAW

Tuesday 18 May

We awoke to find the unusual sight of slightly overcast skies with temperatures probably down in the higher sixties Fahrenheit but felt that was quite acceptable for travelling on the next leg of our journey.

Joining Highway 99 North we went through a spectacular fruit growing region with extensive green orchards stretching for what seemed like miles and miles on each side of the road and on route noticed that there were numerous roadside stalls advertising walnuts, pecan nuts, cherries and strawberries for sale, but regrettably none were open until later in the day.

Some of the road surfaces encountered were rough to say the least, so that combined with the reasonably strong cross winds made it difficult to keep the Trek correctly positioned on the road. However with quite a few large trucks trundling along behind it was necessary to drive at speeds approaching 55/60mph so this was a little uncomfortable at times. Some stretches of the road seemed extremely narrow and this was intimidating when a large truck passed going at high speed in the opposite direction as the poor little Trek was buffeted and thrown off course.

At one stage our RV was stopped by a police patrol car for driving below the speed limit of 65mph and for failing to pull back into the slow lane quickly enough when a stretch of two-lane road was encountered.

We tried to in vain to explain to the officer that a truck had just undertaken us in the slow inside lane and would not let us drop back into that lane any quicker, so that we needed to stay where we were for a while to avoid a nasty accident. It was also stressed that we were driving at a safe speed of around 55 mph taking into account the road surface as well as the prevailing side wind, nevertheless he explained that if we had five or more vehicles following it was necessary to pull over to let them pass, if we did not we would be committing a Californian Driving Offence.

For the record this procedure had been observed and we had been regularly pulling off the road where conditions permitted this to be done safely, but where the incident occurred there was no suitable pull off area, just a steep and very intimidating drop.

Fortunately no ticket or official warning was given, so we were soon dispatched on our way with the instruction 'just drive at 65mph and ignore traffic on the inside lane, just pull over'!!!!

At Red Bluff we pulled into yet another Wal-Mart having covered just eighty-eight miles since leaving Sam's Club, but somehow felt that the journey had been much, much longer!!!

During our brief stay we did not see any patrolling security staff or any notices stating that the site was guarded by security cameras but as this was a very tranquil and peaceful location concluded that they were probably not needed.

Wednesday 19 May

After a very restful night, we awoke to yet more overcast skies but fortunately the temperatures were still in the higher sixties Fahrenheit.

Luckily as we drove the Trek along Interstate 5 North there was not too much traffic so could take a little more time to soak-up the sights of the interesting scenery along the way and at one stage drove close to Castle Craggs State Park that presented good views of Castle Mountain even from the Interstate.

A little later a short stop was made at Dunsmuir for more diesel where we added just 8.23 gallons costing $20 to the Trek's tank then continuing the journey fantastic views could be seen of the extremely large Shasta Lake that looked very inviting with beautiful shimmering blue waters that could be seen stretching into the distance on each side of the Interstate.

The route provided panoramic and picture postcard views of the awesome 14,000-foot high snow covered Mount Shasta in the background rising majestically from the surrounding multi coloured green pine forests.

Later it was possible to see a mountain-sized mound of mining excavation waste that had been extracted from the nearby nickel mine that had been there so long that a large quantity of trees had successfully established themselves on its surface.

At Weed we went north on Highway 97 then a little later stopped at a rest area known as Grass Lake and while there read a notice stating that a number of years ago this had been a conventional lake with an adjacent hotel until a dynamite blast fractured the base of the lake. As a consequence this had unfortunately drained most of the water from the lake and tragically the hotel's appeal waned, so eventually it had to close, however as the area remained very much a marshland it subsequently attracted a considerable amount of wildlife.

Resuming the journey towards Klamath Falls we drove over the state line from California into Oregon then travelled close to the canals bordering both sides of the road where a number of pelicans could be seen that were happily preening themselves on the banks of the waterways.

Arriving at the Wal-Mart store in Klamath, after a journey of one hundred and seventy seven miles, we noticed some signs in the car park stating 'no overnight RV parking', however as this was not the first time such notices had been encountered we ventured into the store to seek clarification and were told by a store supervisor, that the signs had been erected sometime ago by the local council following pressure from one local commercial RV camping site operator.

Much to our relief we were told that as far as Wal-Mart were concerned they would not enforce the 'no overnight' rule and that there should be no problems staying for one or two nights. According to our 'Wal-Mart friend' the store had also experienced a situation sometime ago where a number of people had overstayed their welcome so this apparently prompted action to be taken and for the signs to be erected.

Unfortunately such an act by a few inconsiderate travellers could possibly tempt Wal-Mart to review the whole situation regarding concessionary overnight parking to the detriment of the majority that do not exploit the gesture.

However considerably relieved we made sure that the Trek was carefully tucked away and parked in an area that would cause the least inconvenience to any customers or visitors to the store.

Although the skies were still a brilliant blue it was very noticeable that there was a significant drop in temperature compared to the previous day and soon remembered that this was really to be expected as our route was taking us further and further north.

During the late afternoon Linda telephoned the National Parks office to book a pitch for RV at the nearby Crater Lake only to be told that due to snow, camping would not be possible until around mid June, so while this was a big disappoint we were at least relieved to be told that we would still be able to visit this famous location in the RV during the daytime.

Although we did not require any provisions it would not have been any hardship to walk to the nearest Safeway supermarket that was just a stones throw away.

CRATER LAKE AND DIAMOND LAKE

Thursday 20 May – Friday 21 May

Fairly early in the morning we drove directly to a nearby Shell garage on Washburn Way to partially fill the Trek's fuel tank with yet more diesel taking on board just 8.7 gallons at $2.30/gallon and as we were now in Oregon were pleased to be able to leave this task to the garage attendant.

With this chore completed we drove through Klamath Falls and joined Highway 97 North passing the very spectacular and large Upper Klamath Lake then joined Highway 62 and acting on advice given to us by a local store manager turned off at Modoc Point preferring to take the more leisurely and scenic route alongside the lake itself so as to get a much better view of the extremely green and attractive scenery. On route we observed many contented cows and horses grazing on the extremely lush pasture and could see a number of very attractively designed timber houses that were set in picture postcard locations.

Just before Fort Klamath we rejoined Highway 62 travelling towards Crater Lake and soon encountered a snowstorm then a little further on noticed that the area was still covered in deep snow. On entering the park we showed our National Park Pass and were told by the ranger that only the main road to the visitor centre was open, as during the last day or so around four feet of snow had fallen in the area that had brought boulders the size of a VW cars down on to some of the roads, so they still needed to be cleared.

The ranger explained that in the winter they could get between twenty to sixty feet of snow and that it normally took several teams four months to clear the park roads, he also explained that electronic sensing devices are fitted beneath the road surface to warn the snow clearing crews not to drive their heavy equipment too close to the edge as there was a real danger of them falling into the valley hundreds of feet below.

As we drove towards the visitor centre it was easy to appreciate more fully the vast amounts of snow that still had to be cleared as several of the side roads were under many feet of snow so were completely impassible.

At the visitor centre it was really amazing to see its roof peering out from the many feet of snow still piled up on all sides and it became obvious why it was not yet operational.

Regrettably the photographic opportunities were somewhat limited by the poor weather as it soon started to hail, followed by relentless snow, but it was still possible to appreciate just how stunning the scenic views would have been if the weather had been a little more accommodating.

Nevertheless we braved the elements for a time in an attempt to see as much as possible and noticed that although sections of the lake were still covered in ice and snow some of the thawed areas appeared to be a magnificent dark blue colour that changed to black as the eye peered into the far distance.

Judging by the multitude of footprints in the snow, many visitors had ventured quite close to the rim to get a better look and possibly this was pushing their luck too much as there was a sheer drop of many, many feet directly into the icy waters below, so we kept well back from the edge.

Eventually the weather became so unpleasant that it was necessary to take refuge in the one and only gift shop that was open where we spent time browsing and trying to get a little warmer before finally agreeing that it would be wise to commence the return journey before the area was completely snowed in.

On route a brief stop was made at another visitor centre closer to the park entrance that was open, although it was necessary to use the side entrance as the front door was still completely obscured by a vast amount of snow.

Once inside we watched several interesting videos about the area and learnt that Crater Lake is five or six miles wide and is surrounded by very steep cliffs nearly two thousand feet high and was created almost 8,000 years ago when the remnants of a volcano known as Mount Mazama erupted and then collapsed, subsequent eruptions formed Wizard Island and other volcanic features that are now hidden beneath the cold waters of the lake.

Over time the lake filled with rainwater and melted snow and at 1,943 feet is the deepest lake in the United States and is understood to be one of the deepest lakes in the world and today forests and canyons cover the mountain's outer slopes with a blanket of snow encapsulating the landscape for around eight or nine months of the year and surprisingly it is understood to be Oregon's only National Park so has become extremely popular attracting over half a million visitors a year.

Leaving the park by the south entrance, the only one open, the rain and sleet continued with a vengeance so at times it was very difficult to see the road as the Trek trundled slowly along Highway 62 West, the volcanic legacy often referred to as the Oregon Scenic Byway, to Union Creek.

There we joined Highway 230 North, also referred to as the Rogue Umpqua Scenic Highway and crossed through the Umpqua National Forest on route to Diamond Lake and could see and enjoy the breathtaking views of Mount Thielsan rising in the distance to a height 9,182 feet with it's heavily snow capped summit.

By the time we pulled into the Diamond Lake RV Park the Trek had covered about one hundred and twenty two miles and as it was a peaceful location decided to stay for two nights that cost $27/night for pitch C4 with a full hook-up.

It did not take long to settle-in for the evening basking in the luxury of full site services that meant that we could take a super hot shower as well as undertake some essential laundry duties.

In places snow was still evident on the ground so were very grateful that we could just set the thermostat in the RV to about 70 degrees Fahrenheit and take full advantage of the Trek's heating system after what had proved to be a very chilly day.

The following morning the weather was surprisingly much warmer and as the customary blue skies returned we took a very leisurely stroll along the shores of Diamond Lake to the Diamond Lake Resort, a round trip of about seven miles and once again wished we could have had some bicycles as there was a really good tarmac cycle path encircling the entire lake so we would have been able to see considerably more.

Our walk took us through the Umpqua National Park Camping Grounds and en-route noted that a section of it was already open for the forthcoming season and that the charges for some very good pitches, some right adjacent to the lake, were only $10 to $15/night, but noted that the pitches did not have any hook-up facilities. At one stage we even considered moving there when the time came to leave the Diamond Lake RV Park, but discounted this, as it was likely to be far too cold for our comfort.

Saturday 22 May – Sunday 23 May

Under very cloudy and overcast skies we left Diamond Lake and headed on our homeward journey to Redmond on Highway 139 East towards Bend and as we drove close to the north entrance to Crater Lake could clearly see that it was indeed still blocked with snow.

We drove through the very picturesque Winema National Forest that was also still covered in snow then turned on to Highway 97 North stopping to get more diesel fuel at Chemult purchasing 8.5 gallons for $20.

En-route we could see a whole range of snow covered mountains in the distance and could identify these as South Sister at 10,400 feet high, Mount Jefferson at 10,500 feet high and in the far distance Mount Hood rising to some 11,250 feet in height.

Then after a journey of one hundred and thirty nine miles pulled into the Wal-Mart car park at Bend, but as a local school was holding a boot sale to raise funds and a large area was also allocated to a local company displaying a lot of Fifth Wheelers, Trailers and a few RV's, found it a little too crowded for comfort.

The decision was therefore taken to park the Trek in a nearby Shopping Mall outside car park and return to the Wal-Mart site much later in the evening when more space would hopefully be available. Fortunately this was a correct assumption so when we returned that evening found a reasonably quiet space to spend the evening relaxing and playing cards.

On the Sunday we adopted a similar procedure and drove some five-miles or so to the Bend River Mall where it was easy to park the RV, then we explored some of the excellent retail outlets and returned to Wal-Mart for the overnight stay.

THE BEAVER RV FACTORY AND OUR RETURN TO CROOKED RIVER RANCH

The Beaver Factory

Monday 24 May

During the earlier part of our trip arrangements had been made, via the telephone, to visit the Beaver RV factory in Bend and today was the scheduled day when that was due to happen, so we set off in good time rejoining Highway 97 North and travelled just about ten miles to the factory and showrooms.

When we arrived at the Beaver car park complex, the little Trek was dwarfed by the immense size of all the Beaver RV's and as we pulled alongside several forty-five foot gleaming RVs monsters parked there our poor little Trek looked extremely small and vulnerable.

Once inside the showroom we spent an hour or so drooling over the unbelievable array of very exotic machinery where each and every coach displayed beautifully designed exterior graphics with really eye catching fully painted coachwork that shone and glistened under the showroom lights. We looked closely inside and out at the Beaver Santium that is available in lengths from 36 foot to 40 foot and the similar sized Beaver Monterey powered by a 350 horse power Cummins engine as well as the very impressive Beaver Patriot.

However we were completely bowled over by the really fabulous 525 horse power 45 foot Beaver Marquis that took pride of place and was just stunning! This particular model was from the 'Birds of Paradise' designer range so sported gleaming high gloss paintwork with complementary luxurious interior fabrics that would not have been out of place in Harrods department store or some stately home and in our opinion was a significant and welcome departure from some of the earlier main stream RV's produced for the volume market that historically displayed a somewhat flashy range of interior décor.

The use of exotic hardwoods and the craftsmanship involved, in this instance Natural Cherry with Makori Inlay, just had to be seen to be fully appreciated as they had been exquisitely crafted right down to the last final detail.

The vehicle of course had multiple slide outs and was fitted with just about all the 'goodies' that could ever be wished for, including a six speed automatic transmission with cruise control of course, automatic traction control, anti-locking braking system, rear vision camera with colour monitor, global positioning system, satellite stereo and much, much more.

In summary the design, craftsmanship, attention to detail and choice of really high quality materials made this vehicle look really special, so it was not difficult to understand why this magnificent RV was able to command a premium price running into many thousands and thousands of dollars. Obviously there must be a significant number of people around who are able to afford such fantastic vehicles as we had seen more than a few on our travels and had even seen one or two that were even more expensive!!!

Soon we joined one other couple to embark on the factory tour and were extremely privileged to witness a number of vehicles being lovingly produced by a relatively small team of Beaver craftsmen. Our guide, Tammy, explained that Beaver had originally started in Corvallis in Oregon in 1968 and had moved to Bend two years later where the company produced its first diesel pusher in 1979.

Then in the year 2001 Beaver had been purchased by the Monaco Coach Corporation and at about the same time Monaco also acquired the Safari Motor Coach Company so they now have manufacturing facilities in Bend Oregon as well as in Elkhart and Wakarusa in Indiana.

It was explained that it was the aim of the company to design and produce high quality, high priced RV's primarily targeting the discerning owner who demands the very best and is prepared to pay accordingly.

By adopting modern manufacturing techniques used by Monaco, the Beaver organisation is now able to specifically tailor individual caches to meet the needs of potential lucky owners and in the year 2004 the factory were producing just ten vehicles per week but had plans in hand to increase this to thirteen per week to meet growing demand.

Nowadays all Beaver coaches use the Roadmaster chassis that arrives at the Bend factory complete with engine and drive train already installed and an aluminium-framed superstructure is added and the RV's interior begins to take shape as the vehicle progresses through the production cycle.

Our tour commenced in the joinery shop where most of the machining, assembly and finishing of the various wooden components is undertaken. Sammy explained that currently they were able to produce around one hundred beautifully crafted and finished doors in something like a week. While there we were pleased to see the joinery shop was still using the traditional tongue and groove joints for drawers to ensure durability and long life, it was also fascinating to learn that while some of the high quality veneers were purchased from as far away as Europe, the hard woods were still shipped in from the East Coast of the USA.

Moving on to the actual coach assembly area we saw several coaches in the process of manufacture where everything starts to come together and at one stage we observed genuine ceramic tiles, imported from Italy, being laid on the kitchen floor, nearby another craftsman was fitting a wooden floor while another fitted the luxury carpet. Further along the line, provisions were being made to add the water system that would be plumbed for washer/dryers, whether actually fitted or not, as this would then enable the eventual owner to add equipment at later stage if so desired.

At another stage in the production cycle we noticed a highly complicated looking wiring loom being fitted and were told that it was pre-marked to identify exactly where it should be fitted and how it should interface with the appropriate appliances or equipment.

It was interesting to note that the RV's floor is actually isolated from the chassis and Beaver claim this can reduce road noise by up to as much as eighty to ninety percent, furthermore Tammy explained that Beaver design their coaches so that as much as eighty percent of the weight is kept below floor level as this makes the vehicle much more stable and therefore safer to drive.

Unfortunately for health and safety reason visitors are not permitted to venture into the paint shop, which really was a great disappointment as we were all very anxious to see first hand just how Beaver achieved that fabulous exterior finish on all their coaches.

However Tammy did reveal that each RV receives something like four layers of paint, which amounts to around twenty to twenty five gallons, that is baked between coats for thirty minutes at approximately one hundred and twenty five degrees Fahrenheit and is of course painstakingly and carefully rubbed down between coats.

It was also interesting to learn that all of the fabulous exterior graphics are actually spray-painted and are not just vinyl and if that was not enough, four coats of clear lacquer are then applied over the whole finish to give that deep down sheen.

Later after completion the RV undergoes an external rain style test and is again checked out by staff from the quality assurance department, who then test drive each vehicle for about one hundred miles to ensure it reaches Beaver's high standards.

As our tour came to and end we could appreciate more fully the craftsmanship and care that went into each and every vehicle so wished that we could become a lucky owner, but appreciated that would not be possible without that large elusive lottery win. As we returned to the faithful old Trek we consoled ourselves with the thought that most of these coaches would be a little too challenging or even illegal back home in the UK on our smaller roads anyway!!

Our return to Crooked River Ranch

Monday 24 May - Wednesday 26 May

Following the factory visit we resumed our journey on Highway 97 then headed the Trek in the direction of the Wal-Mart store in Redmond but could not see their full address on our small map so initially missed the turn-off that also happened to go to Redmond Airport as well as the store, so had to continue on until we could back-track taking some of the smaller roads. After just thirty-five miles we pulled into the store's large parking area then selected a very quiet site away from all the other vehicles.

We spent a little time 'window shopping' at the nearby large and very well stocked Big R outlet that specialise in horse, cattle, ranch and outdoor pursuit products and thoroughly enjoyed looking at the super leather Western saddles, cowboy boots, hats, clothing, guns and fishing gear.

Fortunately the over-night temperature remained considerably higher than the 45 degrees Fahrenheit that we had experienced in Bend so had a very relaxed evening.

The following day we stocked-up with a few provisions at the local Safeway store, then rejoined Highway 97 North on the last leg of Our American Dream that would take us back to Crooked River Ranch and shortly after entering the ranch complex stopped briefly at the local outpost to see if they had a copy on RV News and to our surprise were warmly greeted by Jim and Carol who had also just pulled in to collect their mail. After a brief chat we followed them to the ranch and after covering just twenty miles since leaving Redmond parked the Trek adjacent to their large garage.

In the afternoon the Trek was treated to a very good wash to remove all the dirt and road dust that had accumulated over the 3,856 miles since our adventure had started in the USA.

Over the remaining few days a high proportion of the time was spent preparing the Trek for its planned long 'hibernation' until our return to the USA when we plan to continue our American Dream and drive to Baltimore so the vehicle can then be shipped back to the UK.

When time permitted we went for quite a number of relaxing walks in the Crooked River Ranch canyon area and on one occasion were approached by a driver of a 4x4 who pulled alongside for a brief chat. During the ensuing conversation it transpired that driver was from the US, two passengers were from France and two others were from the UK. John from the UK explained that he had been fortunate enough to be employed by a US company so had relocated to the US quite some time ago, so had the necessary documentation to live there permanently. The two people from France were in the US on holiday and had also thoroughly enjoyed their all too brief holiday but planned to return as soon as possible. In due course we said farewell to these 'new friends' and did not expect to encounter them again as they did not actually live in the Crooked River Ranch area.

However the following day a friendly horse grazing in a field of an adjacent neighbour became very agitated, running around as if it was being chased by a swarm of bees and was making a lot of noise. Suddenly overhead there was a fairly loud 'whooshing' sound so looking skywards noticed a Para-glider descending rather rapidly and heading right towards the already very agitated horse. Fortunately at the last minute the Para-glider pilot managed to land on the front lawn not far from the by now even more frisky horse, but the pilot's troubles were not over just yet as the wind made it almost impossible for him to gather-up his chute without being blown into the road. Wishing to be of assistance we ran down the drive and after fighting with the chute for a while eventually managed to get it stowed away safely, however when the pilot removed his helmet and goggles we were shocked to see it was John, the passenger in the 4x4 that we had spoken with the previous day!!!!

Luckily by now the distressed horse started to calm down so no longer looked as of it were going to jump the fence then disappear into the canyon at high speed as it would have been very dangerous for the animal and catching him would have been another problem.

With matters safely under control, John asked us if we had seen anything of George, who had also launched himself off the rim of the canyon with his own Para-glider, initially we did not appreciate that George was in-fact the driver of the 4x4 we had briefly encountered the previous day.

At this stage were completely staggered and for a change lost for words because George was quite a large gentleman who could have played the role of an elderly Mr. Pickwick, without the need for any extra padding.

Surprisingly we never did see the seventy plus year old George again but subsequently learnt that he had flown along the canyon in the opposite direction then landed safe and well, about half a mile further on than his fellow Para-glider friend John.

Preparing for departure

Thursday 27 May -Thursday 3 June

As our departure date clashed with an important fishing competition Jim and Carol planned to attend we drove the Trek to Redmond to reserve a room for the night of Saturday 5 June, at Motel 6 on Highway 97, as from this convenient venue it was only going to be a short journey by taxi to Redmond Airport on the Sunday morning.

While in Redmond the opportunity was also taken to visit some of the local shops and spend time talking with the many friendly people who all seemed to want to stop and chat, so the time just seemed to fly by.

On the return journey to Crooked River Ranch we stopped for the last time at the garage at Terrebonne to fill the Trek with diesel taking on board 31.27 gallons at $2.24/gallon and while there made enquiries about the RV's fuel cap that we believed may have been left there on 1 April.

The attendant disappeared for a while then to our surprise came back with not just one fuel cap, but presented us with three to choose from, however it was not obvious which was the correct one for the Trek as they all actually fitted. Eventually after some deliberation we selected one that appeared the most appropriate, then resumed our journey but could not help wondering if this particular garage made a habit of collecting fuel caps?

The remainder of time was taken up preparing the Trek for its scheduled long 'hibernation' while stored on the ranch awaiting our scheduled return in the not too distant future.

On our vacation we had noticed several specialist small companies such as 'Oil Can Henry's' that carry out oil/filter changes for most vehicles including RV's and at one stage were tempted to have the Trek's oil changed but in the end opted to undertake the work personally. Luckily this task proved be a much simpler operation than first envisaged so would certainly consider undertaking the job again next time, later a special additive was poured into a full tank of diesel to ensure that it does not deteriorate while the Trek is 'in store'.

The domestic water system including the water heater was completely drained with all taps left open, then with all taps closed, one set was opened at a time while relatively low air pressure, about 30lb/square inch, delivered from a small compressor, was blown through the appropriate section of the holding tank to remove any water that may still have been trapped in the system. Once this had been successfully accomplished within the kitchen, bathroom and of course not forgetting the shower-head, a small quantity of special potable anti-freeze was poured into the drains of the respective sinks as well as the shower tray drain to prevent any residue that may have still been trapped in the pipe-work system from freezing.

Both black and grey waste holding tanks were completely drained and then thoroughly flushed using a high-pressure water hose.

The Trek was given one last short run to circulate the new engine oil and to ensure that the diesel additive was dispersed throughout the system, the vehicle was then driven on to a hard standing parking area where the new wheel covers were fitted.

The refrigerator and freezer were of course turned off and the contents were removed and either given to Carol or thrown away, then the units were then de-iced and cleaned, the doors were left slightly ajar to reduce the possibility of mould growth.

All valves on the LPG tank were closed and the 'ElectroMajic' bed lowered slightly from the ceiling and all interior storage cupboard doors were left slightly open to permit air circulation

These tasks were not difficult, just extremely time consuming, however fitting the tailor made cover proved more frustrating and much more difficult than we had been anticipated, mainly due to the high wind.

At one stage a strong gust of wind managed to lift the cover high into the air and everyone had visions of it being blown down the canyon with myself grimly trying to hold onto it.

Eventually and after a considerable amount of effort and hard work, with Carol on the ground hanging onto one corner of the cover, Linda and Jim on tall step ladders on each side of the vehicle and myself on the roof, we did manage to adorn the Trek with its new cover.

Once in position the cover did not look too bad, although we were all somewhat disappointed that it did seem to be on the generous side and so had a tendency to flap around in the high wind.

Completely exhausted we retreated with fingers crossed and hoped that the cover will actually keep the Trek well protected from the elements and that it will not damage the vehicles immaculate paintwork, but as they say 'time will tell'.

THE SMITH ROCK STATE PARK

Friday 4 June

Literally at the crack of dawn, before even the birds were awake, we joined Jim and Carol in their new 4x4 for one last great adventure, a short excursion to The Smith Rock State Park that is situated on the Oregon desert plateau just off Highway 97 near Terrebonne.

The park was named after John Smith who was once sheriff of Linn County and occupies an area of about 650 acres, where the major rock faces were formed some 25 to 30 million years ago from compressed volcanic ash. It now rises majestically up to 550 feet into the clear blue skies and the park attracts climbers as well as hikers from all over the world who wish to take-up the challenge to reach the summit by a wide variety of different routes, as some of the cliff faces include a selection of the toughest routes available and so challenge even the most experienced climbers.

When we arrived, dawn was just breaking but it was surprising just how cold it was and at this stage no doubt all secretly wished that we had put on some warmer clothing.

Needless to say we chose one of the easier yet still very demanding tracks and on route encountered a group of professional photographers, plus male and female models dressed in climbing gear. They really did look the part with climbing ropes over their shoulders but the star attraction was a really magnificent gleaming new 4x4 with headlights blazing that was being photographed for a forthcoming advertising campaign. To our surprise several members of their team were extremely friendly and only too happy to stop and chat to explain what they were doing and it transpired that they had arrived around 4.30am when it was even colder and had been on a grueling two-day shoot but this was their last day.

As the sun began to rise it was necessary to say goodbye and continue the arduous trek towards our ultimate destination as we planned to get to the top of Smith's Rock before the temperature climbed considerably making the going even harder.

This was one tough climb due to the very steep incline and the loose gravel under foot so we needed to stop numerous times to rest and to drink cold bottled water and when looking down could see the Crooked River snaking its way through the valley far below and of course it appeared smaller and smaller as we relentlessly climbed higher and higher.

The track really did get steeper and steeper and the path narrower and narrower as we approached or should that be crawled towards the summit of Misery Ridge and all this time Linda was becoming more concerned about our eventual journey down as it became increasingly difficult to stay upright and not slip over.

After what seemed to be a very strenuous climb we all reached the summit where the views were magnificent and under brilliant blue cloudless skies could see for miles and miles, a perfect 'picture postcard' setting and well worth all the energy it took to get there.

While at the top we picked our way through the rocks to get a good view of Monkey Face, a very large rock monolith some 350 foot high situated close to the river on the west side and in profile the rock certainly did resemble the face of one very large monkey and we were a little surprised to learn that it was possible to stand upright in the monkey's mouth.

The roads and houses below looked positively miniscule as we scoured the sky in the hope of seeing a Golden Eagle, but as normal were out of luck.

As we continued our walk it was possible to see with the aid of binoculars, a very select new housing development of two or three very large mansions, where it is rumoured that the land alone costs in excess of one million dollars so again secretly wished for that elusive lottery win.

During our descent we encountered about half a dozen young men, resembling Himalayan Sherpas carrying heavy loads of sacking and it was somewhat disconcerting to watch them casually walking up as if they were out for a casual stroll and not climbing a very steep hazardous narrow path.

They said that they were going to use the packs of material carried on their backs to repair some of the pathways near the top of the rock and mentioned that they often made the climb to the summit, so were extremely fit.

Linda had been correct as the return journey did prove more difficult and it must have be very amusing for anyone that could see us, sometimes on our hands and knees as we inched our way down, but somehow Jim and Carol did not seem to experience the same difficulties.

The temperature increased noticeable during the descent and Jim explained that it could reach 100 plus degrees Fahrenheit in summer, so we readily appreciated why it had been necessary to start out so early in the morning before it was just too hot to attempt such a strenuous climb.

As we neared the car park at the base of Smith Rock we encountered a handful of walkers who were just starting out and really did not envy them at all to be trekking in the searing heat.

On the journey home we stopped to take some customary photographs and were very fortunate to find a herd of buffalo with their young grazing in their large pasture and the animals were kind enough to stand and pose.

HOMEWARD BOUND WITH FOND MEMORIES

Saturday 5 June - Sunday 6 June

All too soon the time came to leave Crooked River Ranch and sadness descended as Jim accompanied by Carol drove us to the Motel 6 near to Redmond Airport.

As their 4x4 drew away we felt sad that it was time for us to go and wished over and over again that we could just press a button so that Our American Dream could be replayed and by way of compensation in the evening walked a mile or so down the highway to enjoy a superb meal at a family run Mazatlan Mexican restaurant and for a while it did lift our spirits, but appreciated that we were really homeward bound.

In the morning the skies were extremely black and very overcast as we rode in the taxi the short distance to Redmond Airport with probably far too many bags and two very full two suitcases.

Then as we waited to check-in for the first flight we read a notice that indicated that there was a size restriction on the hand luggage permitted on the aircraft and at this point panic set-in as we could not see how the portable dog kennel we were carrying as hand luggage could possibly fall within the prescribed size limit. Furthermore all our other hand luggage, including the camera and laptop computer exceeded the number of pieces allowed on the flight, nevertheless to our amazement, a brief but polite word with the air hostess at the check-in fortunately saved the day, the dog kennel was tagged as fragile and sent off with the luggage, then we were permitted to carry all our other hand luggage on to the small turbo-prop aeroplane with us.

As we left Redmond airport lightning could be seen and it started to rain exceptionally hard as menacing black clouds closed in from all directions so could not help wondering how Jim and Carol would be fairing at their fishing tournament in their boat somewhere in the middle of a large lake?

Despite the atrocious weather the flight passed without incident but we were a little surprised to learn just how many people were flying down to San Francisco on business for the day and discovered that quite a few folk did this on a very regular, if not daily basis.

Once we landed at San Francisco airport it was only two or three hours before we were able to board our flight back to the UK, so spent much of the time browsing in a few of the shops and reflecting on Our American Dream.

Had we been very bold or some may possibly say a little reckless, flying half way across the world to buy an American RV, sight unseen as they say?

Well OK, we had sourced the coach via the Internet but had completed a tremendous amount of prior homework that had enabled us to select the most appropriate RV to meet our own needs, so were confident about the make and model of RV chosen. Furthermore when we commenced our search for a suitable vehicle we had been unable to locate one in the UK that met our high standards, so the opportunity was taken to explore a much wider market place and after searching for a while found a Trek that matched our criteria that was located in Oregon, so as we wanted to tour the USA this seemed a chance that was really just too good to miss and decided 'to go for it' as they say.

We had been extremely lucky in locating the vehicle we desired but equally important we had found the owners Jim and Carol to be most honorable, sincere, trustworthy and extremely helpful so quickly developed a very good relationship and rapport with them so were confident that everything would be OK.

The memories of all the fantastic US states we visited, such as Oregon, Nevada. Arizona, California and Utah are no longer just areas on the American map, they are real and we had been fortunate enough to explore and sample them first hand.

The places visited including Las Vegas, the Valley of Fire, the Hoover Dam, the Grand Canyon, Bryce Canyon, Zion and Yosemite National Parks and all the others will remain indelibly etched on our memories for the rest of our lives.

Along the way we encountered some incredibly kind and helpful people, who were open and friendly, many were real characters and hopefully they will never be forgotten.

The Trek lived up to our expectations, well that is apart from the road holding which is not brilliant but understand that this is a an acknowledged Trek characteristic, but believe that the problem can be resolved by several US companies that specialise in suspension solutions.

Then apart from the small water leak that occurred below the sink and not forgetting of course the missing fuel cap incident that happened not far from Reno, we believe that the Trek acquitted itself admirably and proved to be very reliable.

By the end of the trip we had covered 3,893 miles, consumed some 298.35 gallons of diesel that cost a total of 636.43 dollars so calculated that the Trek had averaged 13.04 miles per US gallon (equating to 15.85 miles per Imperial gallon). At first sight the fuel consumption figures were somewhat disappointing until it was remembered that a high proportion of the journey was made over quite mountainous terrain and that it was often necessary to maintain relatively high speeds in-order to cover the vast distances involved.

Of course with 'hind-sight management' we would have done things a little differentially and funds permitting would have liked to have stayed in the US much longer and taken more time to do the trip and would have loved to have seen other states, visit other interesting locations and encounter more interesting American characters.

Soon our thoughts drifted as we began to appreciate that although this part of Our American Dream was drawing to a close, it would be necessary to return to the US the following year to drive the Trek all the way from Oregon on the west coast to Baltimore on the east coast and then ship it back to the UK, but that is another story and another American Dream.

All in all, we had had a fantastic dream that we were fortunate enough to make come true and can hear you ask, would we do it all again?

Well as they tend to say in the USA - - - - 'Y—O—U   B—E—T'

PHOTOGRAPHIC GALLERY

The following selection of original photographs have been carefully chosen from a large portfolio of digital originals taken exclusively by Linda and David Goodsell that were shot while at the various spectacular locations during 'Our American Dream' adventure.

They record just some of the many fantastic, breathtaking and awesome scenes that can be found in the United States of America so it is sincerely hoped that they capture at least some of the actual magic portrayed by the original subject matter.

Although it must appreciated that even with very high specification and quality photographic equipment it can still prove extremely difficult to adequately capture the real authentic magic and atmosphere of the original scene.

Nevertheless we would like to stress that none of the photographs have been digitally enhanced or altered and that the technically minded may like to know that each photograph was taken using a 'Fiji Film' 'FinePix S2Pro' camera fitted with a 28-105mm 'AF Nikkor' lens with a 'Hoya Skylight filter'.

The historic town of Williams in Arizona on 'Historic US 66'

The idyllic setting in Kaibab National Forest Arizona

The picture clearly identifies the location

Despite temperatures in the seventies Fahrenheit note the snow capped mountains

110

Another captivating view of the Las Vegas Strip

The Las Vegas Strip at night

The smiling Circus Circus clown is waiting to welcome you to Las Vegas

The fountains at the Bellagio hotel in Vegas with the Eiffel Tower in the background

The Valley of Fire in Nevada showing views of the spectacular 'Beehives'

The size of the sandstone rocks dwarf the Trek in the foreground

114

A dramatic shot of the famous Hoover Dam situated on the borders of Nevada and Arizona

The magnificent and truly awesome sight of the Grand Canyon in Arizona

The Grand Canyon from another spectacular vantage point

One of the Iron Horses captured on camera close to the Grand Canyon

The Trek basking beside the hot shore of Lake Mead at Government Wash in Nevada

The Trek taking time out to admire the stunning scenery

One of the LPG buses in Zion National Park in Utah

Making full use of the 'RV Dump Station' at Zion National Park

Welcome to the earth shattering sights of Bryce Canyon National Park in Utah

The spectacular 'Hoodoos' in the stunning Bryce Canyon National Park

Monument Valley bordering Utah and Arizona one of the most photographed locations in the US

The very tranquil Fallen Leaf Lake in California

Spectacular Lake Tahoe located in the High Sierras of California

The fantastic and awesome falls in Yosemite National Park in California

A fabulous waterside setting in Yosemite

An immaculate 'All American Truck'

122

White Water Rafting near Yosemite

Crater Lake in Oregon in late April

Just a few of the magnificent new RV'S outside the Beaver Factory

The beautiful golf course at Crooked River Ranch near Redmond in Oregon

ESSENTIAL CONSIDERATIONS

Purchasing a pre-owned RV in America

Purchasing an American RV is without doubt a major decision and one that can prove very costly if the wrong choice is made, so it cannot be stressed too strongly that any prospective purchaser must really do their homework if that risk is to be minimised and of course the ultimate decision is very much a personal matter that will to a certain extent be dependent on a number of factors including personal needs, lifestyle and of course the available budget.

However it is sincerely hoped that the following review, although somewhat personal, may be of some practical assistance and help to anyone contemplating the purchase or hire an American Recreational Vehicle, so at the very least some form of checklist can be prepared, with this to hand it should then be a little easier to define, quantify and prioritise the most important and not so important features, facilities and accessories that are really needed.

Finally it is worth bearing in mind that an RV purchased in the USA could have a different specification to that of a similar make and model that has been produced specifically for the European market.

RV Types

'A' Class

The 'A' Class bus like RV is probably one of the most popular versions that is constructed around the chassis, engine and running gear of a large commercial vehicle with specially designed and constructed coachwork. So this freedom allows the vehicle designer the opportunity to use his design flair without undue constraints and to create an aesthetically pleasing RV that at the same time maximises the use of the available space.

Furthermore the efficient and clever use of this space together with the addition of quality furniture and fitments should provide a layout that is practical, user friendly and provides a high degree of luxury and comfort for the occupants. In addition the introduction of wide body RV's coupled with multiple slide-out configurations gives even greater opportunity and scope for the designer to meet the needs of today's discerning market

Finally the 'A' Class concept allows the driver and passenger a good field of vision due to the height of the vehicle and the fact that the windscreen is often made from just one section of glass, with no central column to obscure the view. In addition as more space is available within the cab area the seating tends be of a generous size and as both seats can normally be rotated to face the living quarters thus increasing the space available for relaxing and lounging.

'C' Class

'C' Class RV's are constructed around an existing cab, engine and chassis configuration with the coachwork designed to integrate with those parameters, which means that the overall design is to a degree compromised.

In the UK this type would be referred to as a 'coach-built' vehicle and as a general rule they tend to be smaller than their 'A' Class cousins, but can be none the less luxurious, very well equipped, but probably not quite so expensive to purchase with typical prices from say $50,000 to $150,000.

Entry and exit to the cab area is generally easier with this style of vehicle as it will have both driver and passenger doors, furthermore repairs and servicing may be slightly easier and perhaps more economical as most vehicles will be based on Chevrolet, Dodge or Ford components, so garages and mechanics may be more familiar and so happier to work on them.

Furthermore the 'C' Class RV may not seem to be quite as bulky and cumbersome as the 'A' Class models partially due to its narrower cab width and smaller size.

Space over the cab may be designed for sleeping or for additional storage and this may therefore mean that the headroom in the cab is a little limited so may be too restrictive for some potential owners. For health and safety reasons the space over the cab should not be used to store heavy items as they could alter the vehicles centre of gravity and so change the RV's handling, furthermore if the items were to fall, they could unfortunately cause injury.

'B' Class or Van Versions

These are conversions that are generally based on commercially available panel vans and despite their relatively small size are normally very well equipped, however due to their size and design constraints not all vehicles will allow the occupiers to stand at full height unless a suitably designed higher roof or dropped floor has been incorporated.

A typical 'B' Class RV can cost say around $30,000 to $65,000 and can sleep up to four people and includes models such as the Sportmobile that is based on a VW bus, Roadtrek, Chinook and the Rialto from Winnebago that is engineered from the ground up again using a VW. Furthermore due to their comparative small size they are easier to park, manoeuvre so can be driven on narrower roads and are of course more fuel-efficient.

Choice of Manufacturer

In the UK there is a tendency for the public at large to use the name of Winnebago when referring to almost any large American motorhome, whether the vehicle referred to just happens to be say, a Fleetwood, Damon, Gulf Stream or Georgie Boy, a very similar situation to when the Hoover brand name is used to refer to a variety of vacuum cleaners produced by other well known manufacturers. Nevertheless the informed owner, potential owner or RV enthusiast will already appreciate that in addition to the above that there are already a significant number of other American RV's in this country with names such as Thor, Coachman, Dynamax, R-Vision, Newmar, Holiday Rambler, Allegro, Rexhall, Trail-Lite and Monaco/Safari. Naturally these manufacturers and their UK dealers are all keen to obtain a share of the UK market and therefore offer a range of vehicles that should satisfy varying levels of quality, sophistication and price.

Furthermore as the Americans love to pursue an active outdoor lifestyle they also love their RV's so it is easy to understand why the American RV market is vast, with roughly

7.5 to 8.5 million vehicles in existence and has a greater number of manufacturers than just those mentioned above.

In reality those highlighted above represent just a small selection of RV's that are available in the US, but have yet to land on our shores, so there are numerous vehicles that range from the small economy models all the way up to the extremely luxurious ones.

Those falling into the latter category really have to be seen first hand to be believed and are ably represented by manufacturers that include Country Coach, Prevost, Newell, MCI, FMC, Travel Supreme, American Coach and Beaver to mention just a few. These vehicles can cost in excess of half a million dollars and RV's such as the Prevost and Country Coach can actually cost over one million dollars, where a large lottery win would probably be required just to fill the fuel tank. However some of these monsters will probably never find their way to the UK as they would be considered a little too large for our small road system and due to their size could no doubt be classified as illegal anyway.

When researching the market it was interesting to learn that around fifty percent of all the Recreational Vehicles produced in America are actually manufactured in the State of Indiana, nevertheless there is an extensive dealer network for most makes of RV throughout the various US states and of course there is an abundance of vehicles offered for sale privately in numerous locations within the country.

So with funds available and with just a little help from the dealer's enthusiastic salesperson it is probably all to easy to fall head over heals in love with one of the new or pre-owned shiny RV's that can be seen in the vast US showrooms and to be tempted to make a down payment there and then of course a very similar situation can easily be encountered if intending to buy privately as again it can be tempting to let the heart rule the wallet.

However before ever signing on the dotted line, it is important to consider the purchase very carefully so as to be as certain as possible, that the selected vehicle actually ticks all the right boxes for the right reasons. It is also worth remembering that not all US Recreational Vehicle manufactures have a dealer network in the UK so this could have an impact on the resale value of such an RV when the time comes to sell or exchange the vehicle at a later stage as the perceived value could be lower than that of similar vehicles where there is UK representation.

In addition, owning an RV from a manufacturer without a UK dealer network may mean that it could be more difficult to purchase essential spare components when needed, although this of course is not intended to imply that spares cannot be obtained, but it is likely that they may be more difficult and possibly more expensive to acquire. It may therefore be prudent to re-evaluate the situation and select a manufacturer that is already represented in this country by an established dealer network as repairs and spares will be needed at some period in time.

On the other-hand actually getting such a vehicle serviced in the UK may not present a big problem, as most RV manufacturers' tend to standardise where they can so use similar or familiar mechanical components such as the engines, gearboxes and possibly even the chassis, as well as consumables such as filters etc.

However it may be a little more complex when it comes to body panels, trim and interior appliances, but much will depend on the expertise, skills, knowledge and co-operation of the service organisation that is asked to look after the vehicle, although they will obviously still need to be able to obtain the necessary spares.

It is therefore worthwhile contacting a few UK dealers and specialist servicing organisations to at least get an idea about the cost and availability of spares as well as likely vehicle servicing costs.

Once all the homework has been completed the ultimate choice of vehicle is down to the potential, by then well-informed owner to select a manufacturer, model and vehicle specification that will best meet their needs, budget and expectations.

Diesel or Petrol

Modern diesel engines have improved considerably so have become quieter in the last few years but their initial purchase price still tends to be relatively high although they do however have more torque at lower revs but can still be somewhat sluggish on hills.

The modern diesel engine should have a long life span providing they are regularly serviced and kept in good condition and are given regular oil changes.

Incidentally many of the larger luxurious RV's tend to be powered by extremely large, 8 litre or more, powerful diesel engines so if engine noise is considered to be a real issue there is always the option to consider a 'Pusher' style RV, where the engine is located at the rear of the vehicle, so that any noise from that area is reduced considerably and should therefore be confined to that location so may for all practical purposes be eliminated altogether from the RV's cab.

By contrast petrol (gas) powered vehicles have a more rapid response, are more flexible and quieter than their diesel counterpart, their service intervals are longer and the engines should be less expensive to repair. However as a general rule they tend to be thirstier than their diesel competitors, although the fuel efficiency of the modern petrol engine has improved considerably, nevertheless there is of course always the option to have the petrol engine converted to run on LPG, but this can be relatively expensive and the conversion should only be entrusted to specialist approved engineers.

Size and Weight

The trend with American RV's seems to be for larger and larger vehicles with multiple slide-outs complete with extremely lavish layouts that consequently add considerably to the vehicles size and weight. Frequently it is possible to see RV's in America such as Alpine Coach, American Dream, MCI, Beaver, Allegro and Country Coach that are 40 feet or even longer travelling at high speed towing a sizeable car behind.

Furthermore many RV's are now being constructed with 'wide bodies' that may be around 102 inches wide and of course tend to have a gross vehicle weight consistent with their immense size. To the best of our knowledge the quoted vehicle width does not normally include any allowance for any accessories such as an awning and furthermore when the essential pair of large wing mirrors is fitted the vehicle width is obviously even greater.

According to one American RV web site (www.rvorg) this does seem to be a potential legal nightmare even for RV owners in the USA, as the site reports that wide body RV's are illegal on American highways if an awning causes the overall width of the vehicle to exceed the maximum permissible 102 inches, however the article goes on to state that in the year 2004 that the law enforcement agencies did not appear to be issuing citations at that point in time.

Other sources suggest that wide body RV's have been able to drive on at least some four-lane and even some two-lane roads in most states, however in some states such as Arizona, Florida, Kentucky and Michigan that the 102 inch wide vehicles are permitted on Interstate and designated roads only. It does appear that the most stringent restrictions apply to eastern states where the road system was constructed many years ago and therefore is not so accommodating to the larger vehicles.

The whole matter does appear confusing and very complex as many manufactures produce wide body RV's of 102 inches and then frequently add awnings as standard!!!!

Even in America with their generous roads and associated facilities the larger vehicles can on occasions be a little difficult to manoeuvre on some of the narrower roads and sometimes they cannot gain access to all camp grounds. Nevertheless some potential owners may wish to purchase a reasonably large RV, use it to tour some of US then place it in storage while they return to the UK or go elsewhere, then return to the USA at a later date to recommence their travels.

However should it be the intention to import the RV into the UK careful consideration needs to be given to the vehicles physical size and weight, as the very large RV's may prove a little difficult or even illegal on our congested roads!!! This may also be an important factor if it is intended to take the vehicle to the Continent where the cost of crossing the channel may also be a consideration, as could the constraints of the sometimes very narrow and winding roads. Careful thought must also be given to the class of driving licence needed to legally drive an American RV in this country, as

No-doubt it will already be appreciated that in the UK, a C1 car driving licence permits vehicles only up to 7,500kg maximum authorised mass, frequently referred to as the 'gross vehicle weight', to be driven on this type of licence.

However the matter is further complicated by the UK law introduced in January 1997 that states that drivers that qualified after 1 January 1997 are limited to vehicles with a maximum authorised mass of only 3,500kg and are restricted when towing. Drivers that qualified before the 1997 January date can drive vehicles up to 7,500kg but are restricted when towing to 8,250kg maximum train weight, in addition on reaching the age of seventy, drivers are restricted to vehicles of 3,500kg maximum authorised mass unless they are fit enough to pass a medical. As these vehicle weights would easily be exceeded by many of the larger RV's, a higher weight limit driving licence would of course be needed in-order to comply with the current UK driving legislation.

Furthermore the maximum permissible vehicle width in the UK is understood to be 2.55 metres (that is just under 100.5 inches) and that is less than quite a few of the wide body American RV's.

It is sad to recall a reported case of a couple that are reputed to have purchased their RV from one of the smaller UK dealer's, only to find out subsequently that the vehicle was actually wider than the permissible maximum width for use in the UK. Unfortunately it is believed that the RV became virtually valueless in this country and surprisingly the couple lost a lot of money taking unsuccessful legal action against the dealer. It is therefore probably worthwhile actually taking a tape measure to physically measure the width and length of any chosen RV, as the actual dimensions may be slightly different to those used in the vehicle's normal description. For example some owners, dealers and insurance companies refer to our Trek as being a 24 feet long RV (probably in keeping with the vehicle's model number of 2430) but in reality it actually measures 25 feet 9 inches in length and yes we did measure the dimensions to be absolutely sure of its size.

If the RV is to be ultimately imported into the UK careful consideration needs to be given to where and how it is going to be stored when not in use and with the ever increasing cost of fuel, insurance, spares and repairs, the actual cost of ownership should not be overlooked.

The Chassis

Hidden beneath the gleaming bodywork is the all important, but possibly often overlooked chassis that plays a significant role in ensuring that the RV is enjoyable to drive and handles safely under a variety of road conditions.

Furthermore the chassis has a direct influence on the 'maximum gross vehicle weight' sometimes referred to as the 'maximum authorized mass' or may sometimes even be called the 'permissible maximum weight'. In addition it also has an impact on the payload the vehicle is legally permitted to carry and the reasons for this will be explained later.

However even with a well-designed chassis that has been produced by a reputable manufacturer using quality materials much will still be dependant on the skill and expertise of the RV designer to ensure that the chassis design is not compromised when planning the RV's floor plan and associated distribution of weight.

Regrettably aesthetic and practical interior layout configurations may lead to a design that could conceivably compromise the optimum chassis handling considerations, consequently some RV designs that permit the rear of the body to overhang the rear wheels by a significant amount may adversely affect the handling of the vehicle so the associated weight distribution could make the RV's steering feel light and in extreme conditions could contribute to an unfortunate incident or even an accident if the driver were to react excessively.

Therefore when constructing a long vehicle many well-engineered designs will incorporate a carefully redesigned, stretched and modified chassis that actually extends the original wheelbase of the chassis to introduce greater stability.

Most 'C' Class RV's are understood to feature mainly heavy duty van style chassis primarily from the stables of say Dodge, Ford or Chevrolet, however the range of 'A' Class chassis is somewhat broader and includes names such as Workhorse, Spartan, Roadmaster, Freightliner, Oshkosh and Ford.

The actual chassis selected by the 'A' Class RV manufacturer for a particular vehicle model will be influenced by a number of factors including whether a gas or diesel engine is to be used and whether this will be located in the front or rear of the vehicle, therefore it is hoped that the following brief synopsis will serve to provide at least a little more information about just a few of the RV chassis that are used frequently within the industry.

Workhorse Chassis
Workhorse Custom Chassis is a specialist chassis manufacturer that was formed in 1998 to produce a range of 'A' Class RV, commercial van, school bus and European motorhome chassis.

It is understood that Workhorse took over the diesel motorhome chassis business from General Motors the manufacturers of the well-known Chevrolet 'P' Series Chassis some years ago.

They now claim to have the largest chassis manufacturing facility in the world with production facilities in Union City Indiana, administrative offices in Chicago and service offices in Detroit

However at the time of writing some sources have reported that the Navistar International Corporation have announced that its operating company International Truck and Engine Corporation has entered into an agreement to acquire Workhorse Custom Chassis?

Historically Workhorse Custom Chassis have produced a range of chassis specifically for an array of popular RV's as highlighted below.

The 'P' Series Chassis
This chassis has been designed for vehicles up to 18,000lb GVWR and tends to feature the 8.1litre GM Vortec engine. It has anti-lock brakes plus four-speed auto transmission. The 'P' Series Chassis is used by numerous RV manufacturers including, Airstream, Damon, Fleetwood, Safari, R-Vision, Georgie Boy, Winnebago and Holiday Rambler.

The 'W' Series Chassis
According to Workhorse this chassis is a gas chassis that acts more like a diesel and is for vehicles of over 18,000lb GVWR. It features the 8.1litre gas engine and has five-speed auto transmission with overdrive. All electrical cables, brake cables and fuel lines are routed inside the frame rails for safety and reliability. RV manufacturers such as Damon, Georgie Boy, Gulf Stream, Holiday Rambler, Monaco and Winnebago use the 'W' series chassis.

The 'New W24' Chassis
The 'New W24 Chassis' is designed for vehicles with a maximum capacity of 24,000lb GVWR and is claimed by Workhorse to be aimed specifically for use on the largest and best-equipped coaches. It features an Allison microprocessor controlled auto

transmission as well as ABS brakes. RV manufacturers including Damon, Georgie Boy, Gulf Stream, Monaco and Winnebago use the 'New W24' Series chassis.

The 'R' Series Chassis

According to Workhorse the 'R' Series is a diesel chassis that is built from the ground up and features the option of four Cummins diesel engines with horsepower ratings ranging from 330HP to 700HP. The chassis incorporates a six speed Allison auto transmission and is used by RV manufacturers such as Damon, Fourwinds, Rexhall and Winnebago.

Freightliner Chassis

The Freightliner Group is a leading North American truck and specialist vehicle manufacturer that was started in 1929 and is now a Daimler Chrysler Company. They manufacture vehicle chassis for 'A' Class RV's as well as shuttle buses, school buses and commercial delivery vans and are based in Gaffney in South Carolina. Freightliner, currently manufacture a range of RV chassis for Airstream, Fleetwood as well as Winnebago and have been used on the Fleetwood diesel 'Bounder' and 'Discovery' as well as the 'Expedition' models since around 1995.

From August 2005 Freightliner will be providing the chassis for the Fleetwood 'Providence', 'Excursion' and 'Revolution' models.

Roadmaster Chassis

Roadmaster is understood to be a division of the Monaco Coach Corporation with production premises in Oregon and Indiana with service facilities throughout the United States of America and Canada. The company state that every chassis is custom engineered to meet the needs of each specific model and RV floor plan to guarantee that everything works successfully together. Their chassis range of about seven different models includes the R4R that is used by Holiday Rambler on its Neptune model and the Monaco Cayman, the RR4R that is featured on the Safari Cheetah all the way up to the S-Series chassis that is used on the larger coaches from Holiday Rambler namely the Navigator as well as the Dynasty, Executive and the Signature series by Monaco, the Safari Panther and Beaver Marquis Patriot and Patriot Thunder.

Spartan Motor Chassis

Spartan Motor Chassis claim to be world leaders in the design and production of high performance custom chassis for 'A' Class RV's as well as Fire Trucks. They sold their first Fire Truck in 1976 then started to build RV chassis in the 1980's. The company has facilities that are located in Michigan, South Dakota, Alabama, Minnesota and South Carolina and employ over 750 staff

Payload

As may already be appreciated the payload of a vehicle defines how much weight it is legally permitted to carry and the good news is that most American RV's have a more generous load carrying capacity than motorhomes manufactured in Europe.

So unless it is the intention to carry onboard a herd of elephants as well as the kitchen sink almost any of the 'A' class American RV's should be more than adequate for most conventional needs and should ensure that the vehicle stays within the legal limits.

But just for the record, the payload as well as the gross vehicle weight (that is the total maximum weight that can be carried by the RV's chassis) should be printed in the manufacture's specification documentation and/or stamped on the vehicle's VIN plate.

However it should be fairly easy to calculate the payload by subtracting the kerbside weight from the gross vehicle weight, where the kerbside weight, that should shown in the vehicle documentation, is defined as the unloaded weight of the vehicle or in other words the weight of the vehicle as it leaves factory with all the 'as designed and manufactured equipment' already installed. This normally also includes fuel, engine oil and coolant but does not include cargo, LPG, or the occupants and as far as can be ascertained excludes any allowance for fresh water or grey/black waste.

However a few words of caution, as any additional equipment and/or accessories added at a later stage after the vehicle leaves the factory will obviously take the vehicle above the 'as designed and manufactured' kerbside weight.

Furthermore if the grey/black tanks were full this would add to the overall weight carried by the vehicle particularly when it is remembered that a UK gallon of water weighs in at roughly ten pounds. Therefore it is not difficult to appreciate just how easy it is to literally eat into and quickly diminish the permissible payload, so should there be any doubt or confusion it may be wise to seek professional guidance and/or even have the vehicle weighed in the 'loaded up and ready to move mode'.

Vehicle Prices

This is a particularly difficult area and in-depth research of the market is strongly recommended before agreeing to purchase any RV in America, fortunately with the aid of the Internet it is not too difficult to peruse a number of the American Web sites that offer many pre-owned RV's and new vehicles for sale by private sellers and dealers. This will enable the prospective purchaser to at least determine a price range applicable to the make, model, mileage, specification and age of the chosen or preferred vehicle.

Furthermore by using the Internet it is also possible to obtain a free of charge NADA (the largest independent publisher of used vehicle values) guide price for the vehicle in question. As will probably be already appreciated by anyone that owns a car that unfortunately most vehicles do tend to depreciate quite significantly over the first few years of their life so it will therefore not be a major surprise to learn that this also applies to the RV, so that a typical vehicle may depreciate by up to say about 20% in the first year.

Consequently purchasing a pre-owned RV that is in excellent condition and has been well maintained can prove to be extremely good value for money acquisition as the subsequent purchaser can save large sums in comparison to the vehicle's new price. Often such vehicles have hardly seen any use and so can be in 'as new' condition having covered just a few thousand miles and may have been used by the original owner on just one or two occasions.

Nevertheless as the typical US journey can be something like three to four times that of the average UK journey, finding a very low mileage vehicle may take a little more time and perseverance, but rest assured that they are available.

At first sight the price of an RV in America tends to look very attractive compared to the price in the UK and as a very rough guide in the year 2004, the price of an RV in dollars was around the price that would have to be paid in sterling in this country. However it is important not to forget that if the vehicle is to be imported into the UK then there will be quite considerable additional costs incurred, such as shipping, insurance, car tax, VAT and of course the cost of all the necessary modifications to the vehicle etc. At the end of the day the price advantage of purchasing an RV in the USA may not actually be as significant as it first appears and there are also considerable risks and difficulties to be overcome.

However having completed enough research to appreciate the perceived price that will probably have to be paid for the preferred make and model of RV it is recommended that a budget be set, if not already done so, that reflects the price of the vehicle and all the additional cost likely to be incurred such as flights, insurance, vehicle freight charges, currency exchange, import duties, essential modifications to the vehicle for use in the UK etc.

Naturally the temptation may occur where the ideal RV is located but it is just over budget, then the very difficult decision has to be made as the whether to walk away or increase the original budget. In such a situation, in may still be worth at least putting in an offer in keeping within the original budget and be prepared to walk away if that is not acceptable to the seller and perhaps if the vehicle remains unsold it still may be possible to reach an amicable settlement at a later date when the owner may be prepared to renegotiate and be more prepared to accept a lower price.

If the budget is actually exceeded and funds are very tight then naturally all the implications of going over budget have to be carefully considered and evaluated as it is all too easy to run out of funds as the true costs soon begin to escalate. For those that possess very good negotiation skills it should be possible to obtain some form of price discount and as a guide, discounts on vehicles selling for $100,000 could be as much as about 15 to 25% and on lower priced vehicles it may be possible to negotiate say 10 to15%, although much obviously depends on the make, model and condition of the RV in question and how much the owner/dealer wishes to sell the RV. As with most vehicles some brands are manufactured to a higher specification and quality level than others and tend to show less wear and tear so attract a higher resale price.

Whatever happens get everything in writing so that there can be no mistakes or misrepresentation and obtain a written quotation that can be taken away and studied at leisure along with any others that may already have been obtained. To safeguard the interests of the purchaser, it is strongly recommended that any tentative price agreed should be conditional on the buyer or his representative evaluating and approving the vehicle first hand before parting with any large chunks of hard earned money.

Consequently purchasing an RV in America may not be the appropriate route for the faint hearted, although it does present a fantastic opportunity for any prospective owner who would like to purchase an RV in the US then use it to sample the lifestyle and at the same time explore some of that fantastic country before importing the vehicle into this country or possibly the Continent or even to store it in the USA ready for the next trip.

Vehicle Insurance

This is likely to be a complex area for most people visiting the US, so it is important to appreciate that prior research and perseverance will probably be necessary before suitable cover at a reasonable cost can be obtained. Many insurance companies will probably need to be assured that the applicant has a permanent or at least contactable address in America and it may be possible to therefore use the address of friends or relatives, but for those without this luxury it may just be possible that the insurance company may be prepared to accept an address that is say 'care of 'The Family Motor Coach Association or The Good Sam Club and of course anyone attempting to secure insurance with the help and assistance of a UK dealer may find the route a little easier?

In addition most insurers prefer that the applicant is in possession of a full American Driving Licence as opposed to an International Driving Permit and it is important to remember that the latter is only valid for a twelve-month period.

So if the make, model and year of the RV can be defined it is strongly recommended that contact be made with several US insurance companies to obtain a definitive quotation, but even if the precise details of the RV cannot be established at an early stage it still may be worth approaching several potential insurers to establish the necessary insurance rules, regulations and likely costs as this should minimise the chance of possibly receiving some last minute unpleasant shocks when actually in the United States.

Furthermore based on our own experience, a good UK driving record even if it can be substantiated in writing does not necessarily mean that the US insurance companies will take this into account when assessing risk and setting the premium, consequently the cost of good cover can be expensive.

As in the UK it is probably best to select several specialist insurance companies that fully appreciate and understand the broad range of cover that is required and needed by the RV owner and it may therefore be worthwhile contacting companies such as Progressive Insurance, The Foremost Insurance Group and of course GMAC Insurance that is available via the Good Sam Club.

However it is important to obtain the very best cover possible that not only looks after the vehicle but the occupants as well.

Total Loss/Total Replacement

This is the most comprehensive level of coverage available and compensates the owner in full for the damage or total loss so this type of policy is believed to pay out the full price of a sparkling new RV of the same make, model and description if the insured vehicle is destroyed or even stolen and not recovered providing the RV is up to five years old or with some policies it may be up to ten years old.

This may be a standard policy feature or may be an optional extra with other insurers where an additional premium is required but this 'super cover' could be restricted to American Citizens only?

Personal Belongings

This provides a set level of financial reimbursement for the loss of personal belongings and effects

Roadside Assistance

This provides for roadside breakdown assistance that often includes wheel changing, delivery of fuel as well as towing the RV and possibly any vehicle that is being towed to the nearest appropriate garage.

Medical Cover

This covers the reimbursement of specified medical expenses.

Emergency Expenses

This covers compensation for living expenses.

Suspension of Cover

With some insurers it may be possible to make substantial savings when the RV is taken off the road and stored safely during the off- season. For example in the middle of the year 2005, the Good Sam Club were offering discounts of up to 65% for vehicles that were stored in this manner with their VIP Insurance Policy.

Full-Timer Cover

Because many people in the US travel in their RV's for lengthy periods that can run into several years or even longer, the insurance industry appreciates the need to provide cover for those travellers that live and travel in their vehicle on a full-time basis, so this form of cover is readily available.

No Claims Discounts

A good UK driving record even if it can be substantiated in writing does not necessarily mean that the US insurance companies will take this into account when assessing risk and setting the premium.

Insurance Costs

Be prepared as the cost of good cover can be expensive and may be much more costly than in the UK and probably significantly higher than the average American citizen would have to pay with a similar vehicle and similar driving record, however select the best available cover that can be afforded.

RV FACILITIES, FEATURES AND GOODIES

Modern American RV's are literally crammed with so many features, facilities and goodies to ensure that life on the road is extremely comfortable, so much so, that a high number of coaches are so luxurious and very well equipped that it is frequently said that they are 'almost like home from home'. Although some RV's may come 'fully loaded' as standard with almost everything that could be wished for and more, even those that could be described as having a more modest specification are still reasonably well equipped compared to many of their European competitors, nonetheless even the latter have also been improved significantly in recent years.

Therefore some potential RV owners may not consider it necessary to change the 'as manufactured specification' too much, if at all. Nevertheless anyone in the process of formulating their own requirements and even for those that already have a pretty good idea of what they really require, it is probably just worthwhile reviewing some of the important aspects prior to finalising that all important definitive 'wish list'.

To simplify matters, the following assessment has been divided into two possibly very subjective and broad categories namely 'highly desirable', indicating almost essential and 'desirable' meaning not quite so important and may or may not warrant the cost involved, however at the end of the day the ultimate decision of course remains with the prospective owner.

Even for those fortunate enough to be in a position to be able to purchase a new RV, it is still a good idea to ensure that all the desired 'whistles and bells' are carefully considered beforehand and are specified and if possible fitted to the vehicle before it leaves the factory or the dealer, as it may be more costly or possibly difficult if not impossible to have some of them fitted to the vehicle at a later stage.

Furthermore when purchasing a pre-owned 'fully loaded' or very high specification vehicle it is worth remembering that the first owner will possibly have initially paid a high and possibly even list price for all the 'bells and whistles', while the price actually paid by the subsequent purchaser will probably be much lower and will not necessarily reflect the original true cost.

Highly Desirable

Spacious Interior
American RV's are fortunately normally sufficiently large enough to provide a spacious interior with plenty of room to lounge/relax, sleep, eat, prepare, wash and cook food etc. As many RV manufacturers tend to offer at least a limited range of interior layouts, it is a matter of personal preference to select one that will best meet the lifestyle of the owners but as with most things in life some compromise may be necessary.

The Cab and Cab Area
The cab area needs to be comfortable and spacious enough to permit easy entry/exit

and some vehicles may have a separate drivers door, while in other RV's it may be necessary to enter the cab area from the interior of the vehicle.

Adjustable, comfortable cab seating, with moveable arms, for both driver and passenger are essential and it is a matter of personal choice whether to select either fabric upholstery that is fortunately now available in a range of subtle colours or to go for the leather option and fortunately most RV seats, even those fitted as standard, tend to be of very generous proportions, well upholstered and are consequently extremely comfortable.

Seat belts are of course a compulsory safety feature, but it seems that the American RV market has been, lets say a 'little slow' in fitting the lap and diagonal style belts as standard. As a consequence only fairly recently manufactured RV's tend to have this style of belt fitted as standard equipment. This therefore means that many of the older vehicles were fitted with only lap style seat belts, so unfortunately to change from the older style belt to the latest version may or may not be possible and could involve a relatively high cost. For example, according to Monaco, the parent company of Safari, manufactures' of the Safari Trek, to change over from the lap style seat belts to the lap and diagonal system using factory supplied components, actually involves removing the old seats and fitting the newer versions as the seat belts are an integral feature of the seat, an expensive process!!!

Adjustable/Tilting Steering Wheel

As not all drivers will be the same physical shape or size it is important that when they are in the driver's seat that they feel comfortable, relaxed, totally at home and in the best possible position to see and manoeuvre the RV smoothly and safely. Being able to adjust the steering wheel to the optimum position for each driver is therefore a bonus and with a tilting wheel it can be locked in the desired driving position but also permits easier entry and exit to and from the driver's seat.

Power Steering

With a large coach, power steering is really an essential feature and is luckily fitted as standard by most manufacturers of North American RV's.

Automatic Transmission with Cruise Control

Fortunately almost without exception, all American RV's are equipped with automatic transmission and it does make driving considerably less tiring and permits the pilot more time to fully concentrate on the road and the traffic conditions. Driving with a good automatic gearbox that makes both upward and downward changes smoothly can be an absolute delight and ensures that the journey is a pleasure as opposed to a chore. Cruise control can also ease the burden on the driver when long stretches of clear road are encountered, although the driver still needs to exercise due care and attention, particularly when approaching other vehicles from behind, so as to avoid any nasty moments. Fortunately most cruise control systems disengage as soon as the vehicle's brakes are lightly touched or the cruise control disengage switch is activated. Unfortunately some RV's only have three forward gears and an overdrive, so on undulating roads or on some hills there is a tendency for the system to want to change gear quite frequently and this can sometimes be a little stressful.

Fortunately many of the newer and/or larger vehicles tend to have up to six forward gears with highly efficient and powerful engines that provide greater low down torque so this can significantly reduce or even eliminate this possible drawback.

Electrically Operated and Heated Wing Mirrors
Good rearward visibility is essential when piloting a large American RV so can significantly help reduce the possibility of an incident or even an accident.

Fortunately most American RV's are equipped with large two-part mirrors with the upper section providing the general rearward view and the smaller lower convex section giving a lower view of the vehicle and the road behind.

Care is needed to ensure that the mirrors are set in the optimum position each time there is a driver change and before the RV ventures on to the highway and fortunately with electrically operated mirrors 'set-up' should be both quick and easy so both mirrors obviously need to be adjusted to provide the best possible rearward vision and at the same time minimise the inevitable 'blind spots'. It is well worthwhile spending time getting used to judging how far vehicles approaching from behind appear in the mirrors compared to their actual distance, as it is often all to easy to make an error of judgment unless this is done.

Should difficult driving situations be encountered it still may be necessary to ask the co-pilot for some feed-back as they may be able to see something from their vantage point that the driver just cannot see at all.

In view of the RV's large size and relatively modest acceleration capabilities, particular care and attention is needed when overtaking so the rear view mirrors really need to be checked and double checked to ensure that it is safe to complete the manoeuvre. Caution should also be exercised when turning at say a junction or roundabout as it is all too easy to cut the corner off and this could result in an unpleasant experience, so it is important to keep glancing in the mirrors to ensure that everything is alright throughout the manoeuvre and in wet or icy conditions heated mirrors soon disperse the rain or ice to provide a clear vision.

The Trek's mirrors were used extensively when making tight turns in car parks, RV parks etc and were used for almost all reversing activities, the rear view camera although quite good was not actually used very much at all.

Large Sun Visors
Large sun visors are essential for both driver and passenger for occasions when travelling in very sunny areas, particularly when the sun is low in the sky so ideally the visors need to be fitted to the front as well as to the side windows in cab area.

Electrically Operated Dash-Board Mounted Fans
These are useful for providing a gentle cooling breeze when driving in hot climates and where it is not really hot enough to warrant the use of the air conditioning system, nevertheless if desired the fans can of course be used if required in conjunction with the RV's air conditioning system.

Powerful Air Horns

Loud and powerful audible warning notification to other road users of the RV's approach may help reduce the possibility of an accident or incident.

RDS Style Radio/Cassette/CD System and More

Many drivers and passengers will appreciate listening to music, current affairs, news and the all important traffic updates so should therefore find a good radio an invaluable companion.

However due to the vast size of the USA and the remoteness of many locations, good radio reception cannot always be obtained, hence it is good idea to also have a cassette and/or a CD or even an MP3 player system to ensure that appropriate entertainment can be obtained as and when desired, whether on the move or whether parked safely for the night in some backwoods area.

Vehicle Compass

A good vehicle compass is extremely useful, as it is all too easy to become disorientated when driving in unfamiliar territory and especially useful if a GPS Satellite Navigation system is not fitted. However when selecting a particular model it is important to ensure that it is designed for use in a vehicle and that it will not provide a false reading caused by the influence of the metallic objects surrounding it, in this case the RV itself. Some compasses may be self-compensating, while others incorporate some form of adjustment that can be made when the unit is installed in the vehicle. A comprehensive set of instructions should therefore be provided with the compass to ensure that the device can be correctly set-up.

Lounge and Dining Area

The lounge will almost certainly incorporate comfortable seating with generously sized armchairs and possibly a large settee as well and should be just right for relaxing after a long drive with perhaps a glass of chilled wine in one hand and a favourite book in the other.

Most vehicles will also have an integral or separate dining area with a table and some chairs.

Bedroom
Comfortable Bed(s)

After a very lengthy and tiring journey, nothing is worse than trying to get some well earned rest only to find that it is just a mere 'dream', as the bed is not comfortable. As will be appreciated people are different in size and weight so will have differing opinions as to what is comfortable and what is not. It is therefore fairly difficult, no impossible, for the manufacturers to design and produce bed(s) that will meet the needs of every customer. The potential purchaser therefore has to make a very difficult choice, as often the only way to evaluate the bed is to try the one fitted to the RV for just a few minutes, while under the watchful eye of the RV sales person, not an ideal situation, but at the end of the day, a choice has to be made without an adequate trial run based on the all too brief encounter with the RV's bed. Of course if purchasing a new vehicle there may be the option to select another grade of mattress, but again without evaluating one for a reasonable period of time, it is still going to be a difficult choice.

Fortunately all may not be totally lost if the bed subsequently does not provide the level of comfort required, as it is possible to purchase some form of 'mattress topper' if the bed is too hard and this may prove to be a reasonably economic solution to the problem. The alternative and obviously the more expensive option would be to purchase another standard mattress grade or to have one specially made. Fortunately should there be more than two occupants almost all 'A' Class RV's will also have a settee that can quickly and easily be converted into another bed.

Bedroom Storage

Most American RVs will almost certainly provide adequate, if not ample drawer, cupboard and wardrobe storage.

Bathroom

A generous sized bathroom ideally with washbasin, toilet, shower and good storage, consisting of drawers and wardrobes, will undoubtedly feature fairly highly on the list of priorities of almost every prospective purchaser and fortunately most American RV's provide many if not all of these features as standard. Luckily most manufacturers fit marine style toilets that are really quite simple and convenient to use as they have two pedals at the front, one that flushes the system with water and the other that opens the blade or aperture to allow the contents to be dumped directly in to the RV's ample large black holding tanks.

A fairly high-powered extractor fan, fitted probably in the roof of the shower room, should be incorporated to effectively remove moisture from the area when that facility is being used otherwise everything tends to end up getting very damp.

Interior and Exterior Storage

It is surprising just how much space can be taken-up by all those items that are often considered as 'essential' to have on board so it is therefore important to ensure that the vehicle has good interior and exterior storage and fortunately most American RV's are designed and manufactured with this aspect in mind and as a general rule provide extremely good storage facilities.

Interior cupboards and drawer units for food, consumables, cooking utensils and clothing should be well designed and conveniently positioned within the coach to enable convenient, efficient storage and safe operation. It is also worthwhile just double-checking to ensure that all storage cupboard doors, those of the appliances and any drawer units are held firmly in position when they are closed and that they will prevent any contents from shooting all over the floor the first time the RV changes direction.

External basement style storage is confined to several areas below the RV's living space and is also used to house the vehicles storage tanks, heater system and generator and access to these outside lockers is normally gained via lockable doors built discretely into the exterior coachwork of the vehicle. Sometimes the size of the locker door aperture may restrict the size of the items that can be passed through them and will therefore have a bearing on the items that ultimately can be carried within that compartment.

With some RV designs the storage extends all the way across from one side of the vehicle to the other and is therefore very useful for storing long items such a skies and as anyone who has struggled at night will probably confirm, it is extremely useful to have lighting in all the exterior lockers, so that if necessary items can be located and retrieved even when dark.

While it is tempting to try to store items for every conceivable occasion it is wise to restrict the items taken on board to 'just the essentials' as it is all too easy to try to carry excess and unnecessary weight with goods that may not be needed or used, therefore a heavily laden vehicle will adversely affect the fuel consumption and of course the vehicle's handling and braking efficiency. When storing items it is strongly advised that their weight be evenly distributed throughout the vehicle so as not to adversely alter the vehicles balance and handling, as a badly distributed payload will undoubtedly make the RV unpleasant to drive safely and will probably contribute to driver fatigue and of course could be regarded as negligent or even illegal should an accident occur where it could be proven that the payload was the cause or a significant contributory factor. Regrettably not all RV basement storage compartments are totally efficient at preventing water ingress while the vehicle is being driven on rain soaked roads so any belongings that could be damaged should be carried inside the vehicle if at all possible or adequately wrapped and packaged prior to being stored in the outside lockers.

Heated Exterior Storage Compartments
When traveling in very cold climates it is very important to ensure that the exterior compartments or lockers are heated to ensure that any items stored as well as the fresh water, the grey and black water tanks do not freeze. This may be either a standard or optional feature on the RV, but is well worth having to ensure total peace of mind, after all should the water system freeze, it could mean considerable inconvenience and possibly a very costly repair.

The Kitchen
For some the kitchen area may or may not be an important factor and to a large degree will depend on whether the area will be used for serious cooking or just for the preparation of snacks or drinks and for those that like to travel with a well-stocked supply of food that is sufficient for several days or more, adequate wall and floor storage cupboards are essential.

For the chef in the party it is desirable to have reasonably generous work-surface areas on which to prepare food and conveniently 'park' any utensils, pots and pans that will be needed. It is also important to ensure that the work surfaces and appliances are arranged in a configuration that the chef will find easy to work with efficiently and at the same time allow sufficient room to manoeuvre without endangering themselves or anyone else that happen to be in or needing to pass through the same area. When it comes to that all too frequent chore of having to do the washing-up, the sink really needs to be of reasonable proportions so that the items to be cleaned can actually be fully immersed in the water, although for those opting for one of the very luxurious larger RV's, it may be just the case of popping the dirty dishes into the dishwasher and letting the machine do all the work.

However for most owners it is probably going to be one of compromise, because at the end of the day, due to constraints of space available within most RV's, it is then a case of selecting the best available option.

Large Refrigerator
A large dual fuel-electric/gas refrigerator say of 8 Cubic feet or more capacity with an integral freezer is highly desirable and should enable stocks of food and beverages to be stored safely for several days or more.

Convection Microwave
A good quality Combination Microwave ensures that food and hot drinks can be prepared quickly and with the minimum of effort, however if the RV is not connected to a suitable mains power supply it may be necessary to run the generator before the microwave can be used.

Cooker and Hob Top
With good facilities on board it will come as no surprise that really super meals can be prepared and cooked, that are 'just like those enjoyed at home', so it is therefore worthwhile spending some time considering and evaluating whether the equipment actually fitted to the vehicle actually meets the individual needs of the prospective owner. Some RV manufacturers for example may fit a LPG powered cooker as a standard item while others may offer one as an optional extra, so for the serious chef it is therefore probably worthwhile selecting both a good-sized oven, possibly with a grill and at least a three-burner LPG hob top.

Kitchen Extractor Fan(s)
As will be appreciated cooking in a relatively confined space can soon generate considerable heat, moisture and lingering aromas, so one or more conveniently located reasonably powerful extractor fan(s) are essential. Ideally at least one fan should be capable of running from the vehicles 12-volt house batteries and at least one should be mains powered.

Adequate Electrical Power Points
Generally speaking most American RV's are pretty well equipped with a reasonable number of power outlet sockets strategically placed throughout the coach to provide either 115/120 mains voltage or 12 a volt supply from the vehicles house batteries.

It is therefore a matter of personal choice as to whether those 'as fitted' meet individual needs and requirements or whether additional ones are needed. Obviously when and if the vehicle is imported in to the UK, an additional 230 volt 13 amp system will need to be fitted to the vehicle if it is desired to use a conventional electrical mains hook-up in this country.

Inverter
As will probably be already be appreciated the Inverter is a 'smart' electronic device that provides a mains style power supply of some 115/120 volts, in the case of a standard

American RV, from just the 12-volt batteries of the coach and should provide enough power to operate some of the coaches facilities and appliances.

However the Inverter needs to be used with discretion, as it may not be adequate to provide enough power for some of the appliances or to run some of the RV's facilities, such as a powerful microwave or the air-conditioning.

It is therefore essential to consult the appropriate manufacturers brochure and/or manual that should provide comprehensive operational guidelines, furthermore it is also wise to remember that appliances with high power demands or even if the Inverter is used for extended periods of time that this could result in a flat battery, so it is therefore important to switch the Inverter off when it is not actually being used and to keep an eye on the battery condition at frequent intervals.

Generator

Most generators fitted to American RV's tend to be either petrol (remember the Americans say gas) or LPG powered and ideally should have sufficient capacity to provide enough power to run all the electrical appliances fitted to the vehicle just as if they were connected directly to the mains electricity supply. However if at any time additional electrical gadgets are added that will rely on the generator for power, then it is important to ensure that the generator capacity is sufficient to run them and in some cases it may be necessary to be selective and only use certain appliances at the same time so as to prevent the generator from becoming overloaded. Fortunately generators are normally fitted in fairly well sound insulated compartments below the living quarters of the RV and are therefore far quieter than the many portable units often seen in the UK. However they can still be reasonably noisy and can be heard inside the vehicle as well as by anyone outside, so consideration needs to be given to those that may be disturbed by the noise. Some campsites place restrictions on generator use and rely on people using them during specified sociable daylight hours only. Finally it is worth remembering to start the generator and allow it to warm up before expecting it to power an appliance and to switch off all appliances allowing the generator to run for a short while before switching it off.

Day and Night Window Shades

Most RV's are fitted with 'two part' pull down style 'day and night shades' to provide a high degree of privacy for the occupants and normally most designs allow the shades to be lowered individually or even together so it is very easy and simple to lower the blind(s) in a matter of seconds.

The 'day blinds' do block out some light and should enable the occupants to see out but prevent those outside from looking in, whereas the 'night shades' should be capable of blocking out the light during the day, especially useful in helping to keep the interior of the RV cool and when the interior coach lights are illuminated at night to prevent anyone outside seeing in. Good quality pull round blinds should also be fitted to the cab area to provide privacy from the windscreen as well as driver and passenger side windows.

Unfortunately those frequently fitted as standard can often be a little 'fiddly' to operate, as it is often necessary to stretch over the extensive dashboard then pull the blinds along tracks threading them around any dashboard-mounted accessories that just happen to be in the way. However some of the very high specification coaches may even be fitted with electronically operated blinds that can be controlled separately by the 'pilot' or 'co-pilot'.

With a more modest budget in mind the alternative of course is to fit separate external or internal shades that fit over the front windscreen and also cover the drivers and passengers side windows as well. However fitting external shades may or may not be a one-person activity and could also mean that a small ladder has to be used in-order to fit them successfully and this may not be a pleasant task after a long journey, particularly if it is raining or very windy. Some designs of outside windshield covers act like one-way glass, allowing the occupants to see out while preventing anyone outside from seeing into the coach interior, while others block out most of the light altogether. The alternative is of course to fit separate interior shades that are easy and quick to put up and take down and attach to the front as well as the side windows either with a hook and loop tabs or suction cups that attach to the glass, so either of these interior options then eliminate the unpleasant task of having to deal with wet and dirty covers should it rain or snow.

A good effective set of blinds also helps to keep the coach interior temperatures cooler and in strong sunlight go a long way to prevent fading of the vehicle's interior. Finally it is worth looking at the ranges of blinds and windscreen cover options available from some of the 'after market' suppliers that are available through companies such as 'Camping World'.

Fly Screens
When parked in a hot climate it will probably be desirable to leave some windows as well as the main entrance door open to encourage a fresh flow of cooling air to enter the vehicle.

However in such conditions it is highly likely that many small bugs, flies and other air-bourn insects may well be encountered and for some reason they seem to have a strong homing instinct that encourages them to enter the RV often on mass, which is not at all desirable for the vehicle's occupants. Fortunately most RV's have a fine mesh style fly or anti-bug blind system fitted to opening windows in the living area, bedrooms, bathroom, kitchen and of course the main entrance door, that should considerably reduce, if not totally eliminate this type of problem.

Central Control Panel
A central control panel is normally provided within the RV so that most of the services can be monitored and/or operated from within the vehicle via the panel and from the panel it should be possible to at least check such items as battery condition, fresh water availability, grey and black water tank contents, it should also be possible to start and run the generator, operate the retractable exterior step, to turn on the various water pumps and to control some of the interior lighting etc.

Fresh Water Heater
Dual fuel gas/electric water heaters normally provide adequate hot water for household chores and for showering.

Solar Panel

Solar panels are becoming increasingly popular and amongst other uses can be very useful to operate a solar charging system to help keep the RV's house batteries fully charged.

Heating and Air Conditioning

When journeying in cold climates or where it may be freezing at night or may be exceptionally hot during the day, a good heating and air conditioning system is essential to ensure that the occupants remain comfortable, irrespective of the conditions outside.

Ideally the system should cover the interior of the coach including the driver and passenger areas and ideally it should be possible to select and control each area separately.

Carbon Dioxide Detector/Alarm

A carbon dioxide detector/alarm is an essential safety device that should be fitted close to the sleeping areas and needs to be tested regularly to ensure that it is still working effectively. For the record carbon dioxide is an odorless and colourless gas that can result from the incomplete combustion of carbon containing fuels and can be emitted from furnaces, gas stoves and similar appliances. The gas can impede coordination and produce symptoms such as nausea, dizziness, headaches and fatigue so in certain situations can prove fatal and should the symptoms persist it is important to seek medical assistance. If a leak is suspected get into the fresh air as soon as possible, open doors and windows and of course turn off all combustible appliances.

Smoke Detector/Alarm

A smoke detector/alarm is an essential safety device that should be regularly tested to ensure that it is still working effectively.

LPG Detector/Alarm

Liquefied Petroleum Gas is colourless, odourless and heavier than air, so will gravitate to floor level and on contact with a naked flame or even just a spark can explode with devastating consequences. Fortunately most LPG producers add a chemical to give the gas some form of odour, but it can still sometimes be quite difficult for a human to detect an actual leak, particularly if the leak occurs while they are sleeping, so a good detector/alarm system is absolutely essential and fortunately most RV's are equipped with a detector, but if not, one should be fitted as a top priority. Of course the detector should be tested at regular intervals, possibly once a day or at least once a week and of course prior to any trip to ensure that it is working correctly.

Should a leak ever be suspected or detected by the alarm, that should ideally give an audible as well as a visual warning, all flames should be immediately extinguished, including appliance pilot lights then the RV should be evacuated rather rapidly. Once outside it is strongly advised to turn the LPG supply valve off and retreat to a safe distance leaving the door to the RV open to dispel the gas but if the leak appears to be persistent or significant then it is probably wise to call in professional help and assistance.

Fire Extinguisher

Yet another essential safety appliance that could help minimise the extent of any damage or personal injury should a fire accidentally occur.

However attempts to extinguish the fire should only be made if it does not endanger life and the person using the extinguisher is confident that they can handle the situation and have the correct type of extinguisher to extinguish the fire.

Otherwise it is best to summon professional help, although it is fully appreciated that in many remote locations this just may not be practical or even possible.

Fire Blanket

In certain situations a fire blanket may prove to be a more appropriate solution than the fire extinguisher and could of course be used in addition to the fire extinguisher.

Retractable TV Antenna

A high performance fully rotational and retractable antenna is essential if good quality TV pictures are to be obtained, however in the many remote areas of the USA it is frequently extremely difficult to get a good signal or any signal at all.

As the majority of antennas can be raised and lowered either mechanically or electrically or even rotated (to get the best signal) from the interior of the coach it is always worthwhile going outside of the vehicle to physically check to make absolutely certain that it has been lowered and correctly secured before driving away.

TV/Video Recorder/CD Player

A good entertainment system should help to keep the RV's occupants' of almost any age entertained, particularly when the coach is parked and perhaps the weather may not be at its best or it is dark and chilly outside so a relaxing evening inside the RV is on the cards.

As would be expected, the choice of equipment is very extensive and if purchasing a pre-owned RV a suitable system may already be fitted to the vehicle so may be perfectly acceptable to the new owner.

However if purchasing a new vehicle or upgrading existing or purchasing additional equipment there will probably be a whole array of options to consider and the ultimate choice will of course be very much influenced by personal preference, lifestyle, the space available and of course the all important budget. Although it is vital to remember that as most American produced electrical equipment will probably have been designed specifically for the American market that it may therefore not work successfully in the UK and/or Europe, due to the difference in the basic operating systems, the voltage and the mains frequency etc. As most people will appreciate even when purchasing a simple video tape for use on a UK video recorder that it is important to select the PAL format version as opposed to those readily available in the USA that use NTSC cassettes. Therefore before making such a major and potentially costly decision it is strongly recommended that detailed research be carried out to determine if the selected equipment will actually meet current and future needs.

Looking ahead it is hoped that modern advances in technology will enable these inherent differences to be resolved and that in the coming years these apparent problems can be successfully overcome, in-fact even now there are video machines that will accept both PAL and NTSC tapes.

Hydraulic Levelling Jacks

If all RV sites, parks and camping grounds were flat and level, like a billiard table, the need for levelling jacks would surely diminish, however as so many are not, the jacks are invaluable and ensure that the RV can be set up quickly and easily.

Vehicle levelling is important as it helps to ensure that the occupants feel comfortable, after all trying to sleep in a titling vehicle can seem very strange and may mean that they are prevented from getting a good nights rest. It is also important as a level vehicle will ensure that the appliances particularly the refrigerator will operate efficiently, although it is understood that the latest RV refrigerators have been designed to be a little more tolerant so should still work efficiently if not absolutely level. Hydraulically operated jacks controlled from the luxury of the vehicle's interior are particularly appreciated after arriving on site following a long hard drive or when the weather is not very pleasant outside. At the press of a button and with the minimum of inconvenience the RV's jacks can be safely lowered and the vehicle levelled with the aid of a spirit level placed say on the dashboard or even on the refrigerator itself, by adjusting each jack as necessary until the RV is level and stable. In fairness this initially does take a little practice and patience, but it is a skill that can soon be mastered, however with the most recent systems it is not even necessary for the operator to manually control the levelling process as the system does it all on it's own, once it has been activated. Nevertheless on soft surfaces and even on tarmac it is advisable to place some form of support such as a stout block of wood beneath each jack before it is lowered so as to spread the weight and reduce the possibility of the jack sinking into the ground, with possibly unpleasant results. Nevertheless the levelling jacks are not really able to cope with very steep gradients therefore discretion and care are still needed when selecting a site, so with safety in mind it is advisable to ensure that all the RV's wheels remain in contact with the ground and that the jacks are not over-extended to such a point that the vehicle looks or feels unstable. The real benefit of the hydraulic jack levelling system can really be appreciated after witnessing several owners attempting to level their vehicles without them. Obviously before moving off the jacks need to be fully retracted so it is really worthwhile just stepping outside the vehicle and walking round to double check that all the jacks have actually been retracted as the indicator in the cab may just be a little too optimistic and indicate that the jacks have been retracted when they have not, as the consequences of driving off with the jacks not fully retracted could be extremely dangerous and of course potentially quite expensive.

Anti-Lock Disc Brakes

Anti-Lock Disc Brakes are really good and a very worthwhile safety feature that should probably be fitted as standard to the majority of RV's, particularly the larger ones, but unfortunately this may not always be the case and in some instances anti-lock disc brakes may only be available as an optional extra and with some manufactures it may not even be an option. Fortunately anti-lock disc brakes are standard on the Safari Trek!

Bicycle Rack/Tow Bar

Reasonably priced bicycle racks are available in the USA that fit into the tow bar retainer that is normally fitted as standard to most RV's and with some designs this may mean that the actual tow bar itself has to be removed and left off so that the cycle rack can be fitted, but fortunately some designs incorporate both a bicycle rack and tow bar combination, so that both options can be used at the same time.

Good Interior/Exterior Lighting

Adequate lighting in the vehicle and in the exterior under floor storage areas is highly desirable and makes for easy and safe living so ideally inside the RV it should incorporate a suitable combination of both mains powered and 12volt vehicle powered lighting, also some form of directional lighting is very useful for reading purposes.

Electrically Operated Entry Step

When the step is extended it enables easy entry and exit to and from the RV so is really useful as the entrance to most vehicles is quite a distance from the ground. For safety reasons the step needs to retract automatically once the vehicle's ignition system is activated, so that the step folds away neatly and does not become a hazard to others. Also when folded away it can make it just a little more difficult for un-authorised people to see inside or gain access to the RV.

Dual Pane Windows

Dual pane windows have several important roles to play and provide useful thermal and sound insulation as well as a little extra security.

Good Vehicle Locks

Strong and robust locks on external entry/exit door(s) and storage compartments are deemed essential not only for the protection of the vehicle, personal belongings and of course the safety of the occupants.

Vehicle Immobiliser

Many people aspire to owning a luxurious RV and so are prepared to save for many years in-order to purchase one, but regrettably there are a few unscrupulous individuals that prefer to acquire one by depriving the current and legal owner of their vehicle. So fitting a good effective anti-theft device such as an immobiliser, should help reduce the possibility of the vehicle falling into the wrong hands and this should afford the rightful owner a fairly high degree of protection and provide at least some peace of mind.

Fog Lights

Front and rear fog lights should help in situations where fog impairs visibility and should assist the driver to see forward a little better and should enable any vehicle approaching from behind to see and avoid the RV.

Porch Lights

Useful for occasions when returning late at night when the RV is parked in a dark location and where there is little or no other lighting.

Mud Flaps

A good set of mud flaps can significantly reduce the amount of road dirt being thrown onto the RV and can also help reduce the risk of debris and dirt bombarding any vehicle that is being towed or any vehicles that happens to be following behind.

Desirable but not essential

Electrically Operated Driver and Passenger Seats

These are a very nice option to have especially if there is a need to make fairly frequent seat adjustments.

Corian Style Worktops

These look smart are hardwearing and easy to keep clean.

Double Bowl Sink

A Double Bowl Sink provides additional space for draining dishes and other utensils without having to use and then clean worktops.

Ice-maker

An Ice-Maker is a very useful accessory that will be especially appreciated when in hot regions when iced drinks will almost certainly be the order of the day or for when entertaining guests etc.

Slide-Out Compartments

Slide-Out Compartments can dramatically increase the useable floor area and make living more comfortable so are becoming increasingly popular even with the smaller American RV's.

Unfortunately it is understood that on occasions some of the older units were prone to misbehaving and cases of owners experiencing problems extending or retracting the slide-outs are not completely unknown. Also some slide-outs were reportedly prone to leaking at the joints where the unit interfaced with the main RV or Fifth Wheeler structure. It is also understood that it was critical to ensure that the vehicle was carefully levelled before using the slide-outs as this hopefully would minimise the chances of these type of problems occurring, some slide-outs apparently even needed to be supported when fully extended.

However based on conversations with a number of US dealers and quite a few owners of RV's it seems that many of those earlier problems have now been successfully resolved on the newer coaches so hopefully they should be much more reliable and durable so should no longer cause such problems. Incidentally modern slide-outs may be operated, manually, electrically or even electro-hydraulically.

Reversing Camera

A reversing camera can make difficult reversing manoeuvres much safer and easier, in addition it should also reduce or even eliminate the need for any passenger to leave the vehicle in-order to give directions to the driver from outside of the RV, this will obviously please the potential "vehicle director" particularly when bad weather is encountered.

Reversing cameras are obviously very useful for those extremely large RV's where rearward visibility may leave a lot to be desired and nowadays monitors are available in either black and white or colour and some systems also emit an audible warning to alert pedestrians and others that the vehicle is in the process of reversing.

GPS/Satellite Navigation System

A GPS/Satellite Navigation System is a very popular and useful user-friendly device that gives both visual and verbal directions from point to point guided by GPS satellites in a geosynchronous orbit around the earth. The systems are extremely beneficial when travelling in large towns or cities or if making long journeys over unfamiliar territory as they provide turn-by-turn routing and even if a turn is missed the system re-routes to get the vehicle back on the right track.

Various model options are currently available including dash-top or in-dash systems as well as those that interface with the popular laptop computer or there are others that can be hand-held and incorporate a quick release dashboard mounting system. In the USA systems are available that also include thousands of campgrounds and RV parks and in addition show points of interest while on route, furthermore it is possible to obtain systems that cover both the US and Canada with just one CD.

In-depth research is strongly recommended before actually making any purchase and it is essential to determine if a system purchased in the USA will or will not operate successfully in the UK or Europe, however as technology continues to advance at an ever-alarming pace this hopefully may not be a problem for future generations of the GPS Satellite Navigation Systems!!!

Satellite TV System

A Satellite TV System is desirable if an extensive range of entertainment channels is required or for when signals are too weak for conventional television reception, which may often be the case in the USA and even in the UK.

CB Radio

Useful for communication with other road users and could be invaluable in the case of a breakdown or emergency.

Home Theatre System

Possibly regarded almost as a 'must' for lovers of good music or cinema and would probably be most appropriate for the larger RV

Keyless Entry

Lost or misplaced keys could be a thing of the past with a keypad operated personal number entry system that should also afford extra protection and peace of mind.

Window Awning(s)

Very useful to provide shade within the vehicle and would be ideal when parked in very hot sunny locations when natural shade is at a premium.

Vehicle Alarm/Tracker System

A vehicle as valuable as an American RV really should at least be fitted with a good quality immobiliser, but for real peace of mind and to significantly improve the chances of the vehicle being recovered if ever it were stolen, a 'Tracker' style system is strongly recommended. At first sight the cost of the Tracker System may appear relatively expensive, as there is normally an initial fee to purchase the system plus an additional fitting cost plus the annual operational fee.

A more economical alternative is to fit a conventional alarm system that covers the vehicle interior, doors and windows and when triggered emits a laud audible warning and also shows some from of visual indication such as a bright flashing light that if set off so should alert anyone nearby, the alarm system could of course also incorporate a vehicle immobiliser as well.

Washer/Dryer

A useful device to have but as there are a significant number of launderettes around it is not a major problem not having one especially if space is at a premium. A washer/dryer may therefore appeal mostly to those with larger RV's who like to travel in style with maximum convenience.

Wall Clock(s)

A wall clock is obviously very useful for monitoring the time but sometimes when travelling in the US it is very difficult to keep a proper check on the local time, as it is all too easy to pass from one time zone into another without realising the fact.

Fresh Water Filtration System

A fresh water filtration system may be desirable for those that are discerning about their drinking water, however as not all of the water sources found on some of the camping sites are totally safe to use without first boiling the water, caution needs to be exercised at all times. Even though some water supplies are designated as 'potable', experience indicates that in some instances this may be a little optimistic.

Exterior Shower

Extremely useful for anyone that likes swimming, water sports or any other activity, such as quad biking, motocross or mountain biking, where there may be a need to 'clean-up' before entering the RV

Map Reading Lights

Naturally when travelling in un-familiar territory at night there may be a need to refer to a map or directions of some kind, so a map reading light strategically located on the passenger side of the vehicle could prove handy. For those fortunate enough to have full satellite navigation the lamp may of course not be necessary.

Rear Ladder

As the majority of ' A' and 'C ' Class American RV's are fairly tall, a rear mounted vehicle ladder may be one of the only viable ways to gain access to the roof and all the items fitted on to it, such as the TV antenna or the air conditioning unit.

Some RV's have a rear ladder fitted as standard but on some vehicles this may be an optional extra, however it is debatable as to whether a fixed ladder may look like an invitation for unauthorised people to climb on to the roof and possibly cause damage to themselves or the vehicle; it may therefore be a good idea to acquire some form of rigid cover that fits over the ladder to prevent this from happening.

The alternative option is of course to carry a suitable stepladder or small ladder that can then be stored in an appropriate suitable vehicle locker, this then gives a high degree of flexibility as it can be moved round the RV to allow access to other areas of the coach that could not be reached from the ground.

Spare Wheel

Not all RV's are supplied with a spare wheel as standard so it may be necessary to purchase a wheel separately if one is required. As a matter of interest the Safari Trek does not have a spare wheel provided as standard equipment and there are few places on the vehicle that are suitable for mounting one. Nevertheless some owners do purchase a spare wheel and have it fitted to the RV's roof although it must be incredibly difficult getting the wheel up there and somewhat hazardous getting it down safely, others have modified the exterior rear storage compartment to accept the spare wheel.

Furthermore as American RV's are large and heavy, their wheels are sizeable and are therefore also very weighty so it is open to debate whether any owner should actually get involved in the process of changing wheels. Even when appropriate tools are available extreme caution must be taken to ensure that the whole operation is conducted with due consideration to the many and very important health and safety issues. It is therefore a task that probably is better left to the professionals who are experienced in the process and have the necessary tools and equipment, so it is worthwhile investing in a good roadside breakdown insurance service.

Leather Seating

The option of leather versus fabric seating is very much one of personal choice and preference and good quality well-made seating in either material should not only look good but should also last for a considerable time. However for many people leather tends to imply that extra quality, luxury and comfort, nevertheless in hot climates it has a tendency to stick to any exposed areas of skin and when the temperature drops significantly may initially feel cold to the touch.

To keep the leather in pristine condition it will almost certainly be necessary to periodically treat it with special leather preservatives and polishes, in addition it should not be exposed to direct sun light for long periods of time or it may suffer damage. Luckily there is another alternative as most RV manufacturers' offer what they call 'UltraLeather' and this is a man made alternative to real leather that really does look and feel just like the real thing.

Duel Fuel Fillers

Quite a number of the newer RV's are now being fitted with 'duel fuel filler points' on the driver and passenger sides of the coach to enable fuel to be taken on board more conveniently without having to worry which side the vehicle's filler point is when entering a fuel station.

Aluminum Wheels

A good, well-designed set of aluminum wheels can certainly enhance the appearance of the vehicle, but unless they are already fitted, acquiring a set may prove to be fairly costly.

The 'alloys' are also somewhat vulnerable if the RV just happens to touch a curb or similar obstacle a little too hard and with a large vehicle this can happen all too easily.

They may also attract the attention of another 'potential owner' who would prefer to acquire them from their rightful RV owner as opposed to buying a set in the conventional manner. The less costly option of course is a set of stainless steel wheel trims that can look almost as attractive as a set of alloys but cost a good deal less.

Nose Bag or Bra

The front coachwork of an 'A' Class RV is more than a little prone to damage from flying debris thrown up from passing vehicles or from those travelling in-front, so many owners keen to protect their vehicle fit a protective shield to this vulnerable area. This may be in the form of a clear plastic 3M style of film that is applied to the front surface of the vehicle to provide a degree of protection from light stones. The film looks almost invisible to the naked eye and seems to be gaining in popularity with some manufacturers fitting the film to their new vehicles before they leave the factory. An alternative is to fit a 'nosebag' or 'bra' that is made from tough black water resistant material that is fastened and clipped tightly over the front of the vehicle and although they are very effective at reducing damage to the vehicle, they do alter the RV's aesthetic appearance so therefore may or may not be acceptable to the owner. However when selecting a 'nose-bag' it is important to choose one specifically designed for vehicle, particularly if the engine in the front, so that it will not restrict the airflow to the engine compartment otherwise overheating may occur.

Another alternative sometimes seen, is a clear relatively thick Perspex screen mounted on a framework attached to the front of the RV, some even incorporate a hinged section to allow access to the engine compartment. If the system is well designed and manufactured to a high standard it is surprising just how well it can blend in with the vehicle and not look too out of place, furthermore it should offer a very good degree of frontal protection from those flying stones.

Full Body Paint Finishes

Nowadays many RV manufacturers tend to offer coaches with very attractive full body paint finishes that are extremely eye catching and are becoming increasingly popular in the US, therefore maybe the days of vehicles featuring largely white exteriors with possibly just a few stripes to add interest may no longer be fashionable.

Some manufacturers offer full body paint as a standard package or as an optional extra allowing the owner to select from a range of colour coordinated finishes and if that is not enough there is sometimes the opportunity to select a really dazzling custom paint finish, but of course that is likely to be fairly expensive.

The good news is that most manufacturers now use modern hardwearing polyurethane paint protected with possibly several coats of clear polyurethane to provide a brilliant highly polished finish that not only looks very eye catching and attractive should also prove to be hardwearing and relatively easy to keep clean. Furthermore for that extra special look it is possible to have fantastic customised airbrush style murals featured on the rear and/or the sides of the coach that really can look exceptionally stunning.

Air Brakes

As will be appreciated air-brakes are extremely powerful and can be invaluable in bringing large lorries or should that be trucks to a safe halt so tend to be fitted to the larger RV's for good reason.

Tyre Covers

Tyre covers are designed to protect the RV's expensive tyres when the vehicle is parked in hot climates by reflecting heat and light, incidentally they should also be capable of repelling water. Unfortunately they can be a little difficult to fit particularly to some RV's with low wheel arches, but it is worth all the effort when parking for a lengthy period in very sunny locations, as the sun can degrade and damage the tyres reasonably quickly.

Tyre Valve Extenders

Anyone who may have tried and struggled to check the tyre pressure on a vehicle fitted with duel wheels will appreciate just how difficult it is to measure the pressure of the inner wheel as it is almost impossible to get a pressure gauge on to the valve and it is just as difficult to connect an air line. One possible answer is to fit a good quality set of stainless valve extenders that are easy to install and simplify the whole tyre inflation and checking process. Alternatively there is another device called a 'dual tyre equalization tool' that makes the operation even simpler as once fitted it equalises the pressure in both tyres and also has extenders to make the connection easier.

Small Compressor

Small air compressors can be obtained that plug into the cigarette lighter that are powerful enough to inflate RV tyres and could prove to be an invaluable tool in an emergency.

Tyre Pressure Gauge

Tyre pressure gauges suitable for RV's are readily available in the USA and there is normally the choice of either the conventional analogue or digital version.

Warning Triangle

As in the UK, it is advisable to carry an officially approved warning triangle made from fluorescent material for use in a roadside emergency where it is essential to alert other road users to the potential hazard.

Awnings

Most American RV's tend to be fitted with awnings, although it would be very interesting to know whether they are used enough to justify their purchase price?

Of course they can provide useful shade from strong sunshine or even shelter from the rain and it is even feasible with some designs to attach vertical side and front panels to provide an additional enclosed living space that can also be used to house say tables and chairs if staying in one place for more than a day or so.

Nevertheless it should not be forgotten that awnings can suffer badly and also inflict severe damage on the RV should they be attacked by high winds and/or a storm, therefore to minimise the chances of any unwanted mishaps they really do need to be used with caution and ideally held down by appropriate 'tie-down' straps that can be purchased from most good RV stores.

When it rains it is also advisable to tilt one end of the awning to allow the water to drain away so that it does not accumulate on the surface of it and thus add undue weight to the system that as a result could cause damage.

Even if leaving the RV for a reasonable period of time or at night it may be prudent to retract the awning just in case an unexpected storm or strong wind should occur so as they say 'it is better to be safe than sorry'.

Awnings may be manually or electrically operated and in the case of the latter all that needs to be done to either open or retract the awning is to press the appropriate control button and just let the system take over!!!

Small window awnings positioned above selected side-windows are extremely useful as they can be effectively used to provide shade within the RV and at the same time help keep the temperature down within the vehicle

Of course awnings should not be stored away when wet, as they can soon become mildewed, but sometimes this is unavoidable so the awning should therefore be rolled out again as soon as possible and then allowed to thoroughly dry before being stored away again.

When stowing an awning it is important to ensure that the retaining catches are fully engaged and securely locked before driving away, also if awning ties are used on the arms of the structure make sure they are firmly attached.

Other Useful Items

There are of course a few other items that might prove useful to have onboard and they include a mobile telephone, laptop computer, binoculars, digital camera, torch, slow cooker, electric kettle, toaster, coffee maker, box of matches, vacuum cleaner, dust pan and brush, dusters, barbeque, folding chairs, ground sheet and bicycles.

LOCATING THE DESIRED RV IN AMERICA

Despite the considerable distance between the UK and the USA it may not be as difficult as possibly first imagined locating that much sought after vehicle, although it may be necessary to use a variety of means to achieve the desired objective.

For example should the prospective owner be looking to purchase a new RV it may be worth contacting one or more of the UK dealers that specialise in marketing and selling the preferred make of American RV in this country, as it may be feasible for the UK dealer to place an order directly with the US factory and then for arrangements to be made for the new owner to collect the vehicle from the factory or perhaps a US RV dealer or from another agreed source during their pre-arranged visit to the USA.

Should this prove to be a viable option then the UK dealer would no doubt be prepared to offer the necessary help and assistance regarding the subsequent export/import of the vehicle and the necessary modifications needed before the vehicle can be used legally in this country.

The UK dealer may also be able to provide invaluable guidance on the matter on vehicle insurance and also assist with any other matters or queries that may arise.

However it is advisable to seek clarification from them as to how the matter of the vehicle's warranty will be handled and if work were to be needed while the RV remains in the US, how this would be handled and by whom. Furthermore it would be a good idea to also ascertain whether the UK dealer would be prepared to honour any balance of the warranty once the vehicle has been shipped back into the UK.

Even if a pre-owned vehicle is required it still may be feasible that the UK based dealer route may still prove invaluable, as the dealer through their established contacts in the US may be able to assist the purchaser locate a suitable RV and then help with the vehicle's export/import etc.

Whether purchasing new or pre-owned through a UK based dealer it still may be possible for the buyer to successfully negotiation a financial deal that may give the purchaser some saving over the price that would normally have to be paid in this country.

It may then be feasible to pay the dealer for the RV and the subsequent shipping costs in pounds sterling, thus eliminating the need to arrange the purchase and transfer of large amounts of American dollars.

In addition it is suggested that it would almost certainly be worthwhile joining and then seeking the help and guidance from the specialist American RV clubs and organisations based in this country such as the ARVE or the American RV Club, as some of their members will probably have considerable knowledge and experience that they would be willing to share with a new member and prospective RV owner, they may even know one or two contacts in America that could possibly offer further guidance and/or assistance.

Also do try to make the maximum use of the networking process by speaking to friends, family and any business colleagues that may be visiting the USA and ask them to contact or even visit any US dealers they may happen to encounter or to talk to any RVers that they may meet. While in America they could also acquire one or two specialist RV publications such as the weekly publication entitled 'RV Trader' or the monthly publication called 'MotorHome' as both contain advertisement from manufacturers, dealers and classified advertisements of private RV sales.

For some it may just be the case of getting on an aeroplane and doing some searching while actually in the USA and the visit could form part of a holiday, business trip or for the fortunate few just a speculative trip to source the desired RV.

Nevertheless in to-days high-speed world, possibly one of quickest and easiest methods is of course to make maximum use of the Internet to source a suitable vehicle, as it is possible to surf the world from the comfort of your own home and to assist with this method of approach numerous very useful web sites, but not necessarily exhaustive, have therefore been included later that could prove invaluable in the search for the ideal vehicle.

In using this medium it is essential to exercise due caution as it is difficult to ascertain at an early stage in the search process the precise condition of any RV that may be of interest, as descriptions such as 'immaculate condition', 'excellent condition' or 'good condition' are very much open to personal interpretation and the description used by the seller may not meet the expectations of the buyer.

Although photographs are obviously helpful when included with any RV advertisement, it is still not easy to be certain as to the vehicle's actual condition, it is therefore very much the case of **'buyer beware'** and is particularly important if it is intended to make a private purchase as it will be unlikely that any from of reliable warranty will be offered with the vehicle so once the money is handed over it may prove almost impossible to recover it or get the problems resolved should any defects be subsequently found with the RV. Therefore once one or two vehicles of interest have been located it is important for the buyer and seller to establish and build a relationship where trust sincerity and confidence on both sides can be established and it may be possible to achieve this through regular correspondence, via e-mail, letter and/or the telephone. If this proves at all difficult and 'alarm bells start to ring', then it may be wise to forget that particular RV and continue the search.

Do not be afraid to ask searching questions about the vehicle and request supporting documentation plus any additional photographs required, then if everything appears to be in-order it may be appropriate to enlist the services of an independent engineer based in the US to prepare a report on the RV before proceeding further. Armed with all this information it is then in the hands of the purchaser to commence negotiations with the vehicle's owner and to obtain the best possible deal.

However should any form of finance be needed, it is likely to be far easier to organise this in this country rather than in the USA and the UK bank, building society or preferred lender should be able to help with this matter.

Although most US dealers are very pleasant, attentive and helpful it is important to exercise restraint and due caution if contemplating purchasing directly from one, as they have a reputation for being determined and extremely keen to make a sale.

They naturally pull out all the stops to get that 'all important' signature on the dotted line, before the prospect leaves their premises, so the phrase 'what can we do to make you buy today' will often be uttered by many dealer sales staff, as they are extremely keen and possibly often too keen to move yet another RV. They may even try to tempt the prospective purchaser by saying the vehicle is special or that there will not be another like it available, so 'sign on the dotted line now, before it is too late'. Whatever tempting offers are made it is wise not to make any rash decisions and to take some time to evaluate and consider whether to proceed or not.

ALL THAT GLISTENS IS NOT GOLD

Perceived Quality

There is a well known and often quoted saying that 'all that glistens is not gold' and that statement holds true for the RV market, so the potential buyer is therefore advised to undertake a little research of their own to determine how well their chosen RV is designed and constructed and to use their judgment as to whether the level of quality achieved is acceptable or not.

Hopefully any prospective purchaser will already appreciate and acknowledge that quality is really linked to three important and interrelated parameters and they are 'the quality of design', 'the quality of materials' and of course 'the quality of manufacture'.

Consequently the designer is the first step in the chain and has a responsibility to use his skills and expertise to design a vehicle that will meet the needs of the target market and at the same time address the appropriate design standards and specifications. In addition his input will also influence the choice of materials selected as well as the methods of manufacture used for the vehicle but at the same time he will need to meet the price/quality relationship brief of the respective manufacturer.

For example some of the volume produced RV's tend to rely on a wooden framework with an outer layer of fiberglass to form the superstructure of the vehicle and in principle there is nothing inherently wrong with this method of construction although a great deal does depend on the actual design, the materials specified as well as the methods and techniques employed in the actual construction process.

In contrast quite a number of medium to high priced RV's are constructed using a welded metal mainly aluminium framework that is light, inherently strong and is not adversely affected by attack from moisture so in the longer term should prove more durable. In addition the production methods employed during the construction process are somewhat more sophisticated than those employed with the wooden frame design so more specialist tools, jigs as well as skills and expertise are needed to produce a good sound structure and of course if top quality materials are used then they are going to be relatively expensive.

Even coaches produced in this way may still use fiberglass or even aluminium outer side-walls, but most designs will nevertheless rely on fiberglass to form the front and rear sections of the vehicle so skill and expertise is needed to successfully blend these different materials together to form a sound integral long lasting structure.

In general roofs tend to be produced from fiberglass or aluminium although some manufacturers may use what is referred to as EPDM rubber that is said to offer good resistance to the elements but can suffer damage if attacked by say a low-level tree branch.

Interior cabinetry is often produced from particleboard, vinyl clad wafer style board, plywood or even solid wood and each material will of course have its own corresponding cost and so the material actually selected tends to be reflected in the price of the RV.

To assist in the evaluation process it is worthwhile removing some drawers to see how well they have been constructed and look to see if they incorporate just butted and glued joints or if they have been produced in that time-honoured but more expensive way by using tongue and grooved joints. Assess the way the cabinetry carcass has been assembled and ascertain whether there are any signs to indicate a poor standard of workmanship, also evaluate just how well doors and drawers operate and when they are fully shut whether their alignment with the carcass is acceptable.

Take time to look at the electrical wiring as well as the plumbing to gauge how well the work has been installed and whether grommets have been used to shield the wiring looms/pipes where they pass through wood or metal surfaces.

Double check to make sure that there are no exposed staples, screws, bundles of cabling or even debris left under cabinets or seating and it is even worth looking closely at the upholstered items to determine the quality of materials used and just how well they have been produced and finished. Also review the range of appliances and associated equipment so as to form some sort of assessment about their quality, fitness for purpose and how long they may last before it will be necessary to obtain replacements. Make an assessment of how well the cab has been laid out and whether or not it will be easy to see and use the appropriate controls and instruments while on the move. Do look in the engine compartment to determine how easy it will be to carry out all the necessary routine vehicle checks that would of course include monitoring engine oil, radiator fluid, windscreen washer fluid etc.

Take time to thoroughly examine the exterior of the vehicle to see just how well or badly it has been assembled and whether the manufacturer has used excessive amounts of mastic to hide poorly fitting body or roof panels. Look at the paintwork to see if there are tell tail signs that indicate a general lack of care and attention such as an orange peel rough surface, signs of paint runs or even signs of the undercoat showing through the top coat and whether exposed screws as well as other fixings have be properly treated to minimise the chance of rust. Of course the list of items to check and double check is as extensive as the prospective owner wishes it to be but it up to the individual to determine if the level of perceived quality does or does not meet their expectations, although as a general rule it is worthwhile remembering that there is a good correlation between price and quality, so in most cases 'you get the quality you are prepared to pay for'.

Inspecting a Pre-Owned RV prior to Purchase

It is imperative to ensure that a vehicle as complex as an American RV is in good mechanical and bodily condition and that everything including all the appliances, air-conditioning, heating etc. does actually function correctly, as spares and repairs can be expensive.

Check to see if there are any obvious signs of accident damage, look carefully at the paintwork, any graphics and body panels to see if these areas reveal any hint of a previous incident, check the tyres for signs of damage and if problems can be seen it would be then be wise to check more thoroughly. Should any major accident damage be discovered it is imperative to ensure that the damage has been properly repaired, but should this not be possible, it may be better not to pursue the purchase of that particular RV.

One problem that unfortunately tends to occur all too frequently with some RV's is that of the outer walls of the vehicle 'delaminate', this is where the outer wall starts to separate from the inside structure and can be seen by the appearance of bubbles or ripples on the external surface or that the wall actually moves and indents slightly when touched. This problem should not be difficult to detect and often signifies that moisture has penetrated the outer skin from say a leak in the roof or perhaps a badly sealed window frame.

Although with the naked eye, it still may be difficult to actually pinpoint the damp area from inside the vehicle, it may then be necessary to enlist specialist help to locate the problem.

Unfortunately delamination and the ingress of moisture are not only serious, they are costly to rectify and if left unattended will continue to percolate through the vehicle causing even more costly damage, so should any vehicle show any signs of delamination it would probably be wise to leave it well alone and look for another RV.

It is also worthwhile getting into a pair of overalls and taking a good look on the underside of the coach, look for signs of damage, neglect as well as oil leaks and of course the dreaded rust bug.

Inspect the service records of the RV to ensure that it has been regularly serviced, in addition it may be wise to double check them by discreetly contacting the actual service provider(s) to ensure that the records are in order, furthermore if the garage or dealer is co-operative and helpful this can also be a useful way of obtaining a little more vehicle history.

If the RV is being sold privately double check to ensure that the seller is actually the owner and that the title to the vehicle can be assigned to the potential new owner and one way to check the vehicle's history is to use the web site known as Carfax (see later for details) and via this site it is possible to obtain a vehicle history report that checks ownership as well as the vehicle's accident records. Currently the preliminary report is free of charge, but is a little basic so should more information be required it may prove worthwhile to pay the required fee to obtain a more comprehensive analysis.

Whether buying privately or through a dealer it is strongly recommended that personal contact be made with the respective vehicle registration authority, the Driver and Motor Vehicle Services (DMV) if this has not already been done to determine the rules and regulations related to the transfer of the vehicle's title before entering into any contract to purchase the chosen vehicle.

Check to make certain that all the operational manuals for the RV as well as all the appliances are intact and are available with the vehicle and it is well worthwhile spending time reading and studying them so any questions or queries that may arise can be raised with the dealer or owner.

Ensure that the equivalent of the vehicles VIN plate is intact and actually applies to the vehicle being examined, in terms of description, specification, weight and physical dimensions and if necessary get an independent engineer to thoroughly inspect the vehicle and provide a detailed written report.

Where possible evaluate and test drive a number of RV's before making a final decision and insist on a fairly lengthy test so that the vehicle can be thoroughly evaluated over varying terrain and road conditions, but do not attempt to take a test drive until an appropriate driving licence and suitable insurance has been arranged as the consequences of breaking the American laws can be far reaching.

However if purchasing from a dealer some of them may be a little reluctant to let a prospective purchaser conduct a test drive on the highway until they have seen the person's driving licence so the dealer may or may not be happy with an International Driving Licence but may insist that a USA version is produced before the vehicle can be driven. In addition the dealer may want to see that the potential customer has adequate vehicle insurance, although it is likely the dealer's own insurance should cover this situation, but this needs be clarified before the vehicle is taken on to the highway.

If this should prove to be a problem that cannot easily be resolved and the chosen RV appears to be 'the one' and just too good to miss then it may be appropriate to get an independent third party to evaluate the vehicle. As a last resort the prospective purchaser may be able to at least drive the vehicle on suitable private land so that a good appreciation of how it performs can be reasonably established.

Nevertheless it is important to be aware that sometimes some US dealers may want to photocopy the customer's driving licence before allowing a test drive and it is not unknown for some them to then run an unauthorised credit check without informing the owner of the licence, this is despite the fact that there is apparently a maximum fine of $2,500 for doing this without the owner's consent!!

It is therefore very important to fully appreciate the implications of the US credit check system as it can have a significant and negative impact on the actual financial credit rating of the person concerned. Informed sources suggest that when about five or six credit searches have been made the applicant may be automatically rejected from the system with a low or zero rating even if no credit has actually been taken out.

In reality however unless the person concerned has an American Bank Account, an American National Insurance Number, an American driving licence and possibly a permanent US address they may be judged as having an extremely low or even zero credit rating anyway.

Again if buying from a dealer, do insist on driving the actual vehicle itself, not just the demonstration vehicle that happens to be available.

Whether buying privately or through a dealer ensure that any problems that are identified are fully documented in writing and do make it a condition of sale that any and all problems must be rectified before the deal is concluded as this should minimise any future disagreements.

Finally inspect the vehicle thoroughly before actually taking delivery to ensure that it is still in good condition and to ensure that all remedial work has been carried out to an acceptable standard.

SHIPPING, DOCUMENTATION AND VEHICLE MODIFICATIONS

Shipping

Although many shipping agents should be able to arrange vehicle transportation as well as the associated export/import documentation, it is probably worthwhile to at least contact one or more of the specialist American RV dealers based in the UK as they regularly ship RV's from the US to the UK and so have extensive relevant experience and knowledge, so hopefully most should be prepared to help for a reasonable fee although experience suggests some will be more cooperative than others.

It is of course necessary to establish the likely freight costs and timescales involved as well as when and in what currency payment has to be made after determining the preferred shipping port in USA and arrival port in UK

There are of course a number of ports that can be used in the USA to export the RV and a number in the UK to import the vehicle in to, so the actual costs and time scales will depend on those actually selected and the two that seem to be the most favoured are Baltimore in the US and Southampton in the UK

As may already be appreciated the volume of the vehicle, in cubic feet or cubic metres, as well as its weight will be used to determine the actual freight cost, furthermore as a general rule of thumb the journey should take in the order of two weeks.

It is of course important to discuss and agree with the shipping agent and/or the UK based dealer what documentation needs to be raised in the USA and UK as well as whether they can and whether they will arrange some or all of this.

In conjunction with the agent/dealer it will be helpful to agree an outline of the wording to be used on the Bill of Sale or Invoice for the vehicle as this should help to reduce the possibility of any problems arising at the Export and Import stages of the process.

The Bill of Sale for the Safari Trek for example confirms the vehicle's registration number, VIN number, the names of the joint former owners, their Oregon drivers licence numbers, a statement from them confirming that that up until the sale, that they were the sole legal owners and that the vehicle was not subject to any finance liability or claims of ownership by any third party. The document also clearly shows their telephone number, the price actually paid, our names, as new owners and our address in the UK.

The document also confirms that as new owners that we intend to export the vehicle from the US to the UK and in addition it also shows a copy of both sides of the prior owners' photo style driving licences that contains their address, telephone number etc. etc.

The document was also signed and dated by both previous owners and was then officially stamped by an Oregon Notary Public.

The original documents have to be made available for the various authorities and any company involved in the shipping process, but take copies for personal reference anyway.

With regard to the actual shipping of the vehicle informed sources recommend that the RV should not be taken to the appointed docks more than two days prior to the sailing date as this should minimise the chances of any potential incidents occurring that may lead to the vehicle being damaged or to the loss of any contents.

Valuables should of course be removed from the RV prior to shipment, although it may be necessary to leave some personal belongings such as clothing and/or say cooking utensils or similar items that have been used during the time in the USA, so in theory such items should be OK if stored within the locked vehicle or placed in the locked exterior storage compartments, a full set of vehicle keys will of course have to be left with the agents/shippers so that customs officials can inspect the vehicle as and when necessary.

Some owners have even been known to remove the TV then either give it away to say a charity or leave on the floor of the RV so that if someone takes a liking to it then at least they should not damage the vehicle when they try and remove it from its housing, this of course may still mean that other items that cannot be so easily removed are still potentially vulnerable, but hopefully they will not attract too much un-authorised attention.

As a matter of course the grey and black tanks should be emptied, thoroughly rinsed and the valves shut and the freshwater tank should be treated in a similar manner.

However opinion seems to vary regarding what procedure should be adopted regarding the vehicle's fuel, be it diesel or gas, as some sources suggest that it is OK to leave the tank full while others take the opposing view and say the tank should be left almost empty. A similar range of views seem to be held about supplies of LPG therefore it may be worthwhile seeking clarification from the selected agent/shipper in the hope of clarifying the situation prior to arrival at the dockside.

It is also the responsibility of the vehicle owner to decide whether or not to pay for insurance cover for the vehicle while it is in transit on the high seas, although it is understood that cover is not cheap and that a claim may only be successful if the ship were to sink, so it may be difficult if not impossible to successfully make a claim for the repair of a dent or scratch that occurred while in the hands of the shipping company. Having spoken to quite a number of UK based RV dealers some do not insure the vehicles that they import as they are confident in the level of care taken by their agents/shippers and reason that if an RV is damaged in transit they will bear the costs themselves as the repair cost is likely to be lower than the premium that they would have to pay in relation to the number of RV's they ship in on an annual basis, so they are prepared to take a calculated risk.

However in-order to give peace of mind the Trek will be insured for its forthcoming trip to the UK and photographs will be taken before it leaves the USA and again when it arrives in the UK.

Finally just one last piece of advice, ideally an American RV should only be shipped by a 'Roll-On Roll-Off' vessel, as it is probably unwise to attempt to lift such a large, heavy vehicle.

US Customs

From April 1999 the US Customs are understood to require either the original title or certified copy of the title and the certification of that title can only be made by a government issuing authority such as the DMV and notarised copies of the title are no longer acceptable, furthermore if there is a lien holder on the vehicle a letter from the lien holder must also be provided. These documents are required for US Customs clearance for export and all original and certified copies are returned on clearance. Consequently this is possibly a complex mine field and the best advice that can be given is to seek specialist help and assistance from the professionals who should be familiar with and have sufficient knowledge and expertise to deal with the situation and so be able to resolve any problems or hitches without undue delay and unforeseen cost.

UK Customs

Again this appears to be another complex area and anyone contemplating personally importing any RV from the US is strongly recommended to make direct contact with the respective Customs and Excise Department to determine the rules and regulations. However be prepared to pay Vehicle Tax (currently 10%) and VAT (currently 17.5%) based on the Vehicle Price plus Shipping and Insurance. Possibly some form of concessions may be allowed depending on the vehicles age, mileage and the time the RV has been owned at the time of importation and how long the owners can prove that they have been away from the UK/EEC.

Vehicle Modifications

As will probably already be appreciated certain work will be necessary to ensure that any American RV imported into the UK meets current UK vehicle legislation if it is to be used legally in this country in the longer term. It is therefore recommended that contact be made with one or more UK dealers or RV companies that specialise in RV repairs, servicing and conversion work to determine what exactly needs to be done and what costs are likely to be incurred for the specific vehicle in question.

Almost certainly the conversion will need to include modifications to the vehicle's lighting system to ensure that the front lights dip to the left and not the right, the rear lights may also need to be changed should the rear direction indicators be housed in a red and not an amber glass enclosure. Incidentally in Oregon for example, the front indicator lights may be amber or white and the rear ones red, amber or even yellow.

Furthermore the American TV supplied with the vehicle will almost certainly have to be changed for a UK version, as the US supplied TV is not currently compatible with the UK TV operating system.

However if the American TV originally formed part of the reversing camera system it may still be possible to retain it as a monitor, although it may be more appropriate to have a new independent, dedicated screen fitted specifically for that purpose that is situated in a more convenient and user friendly position for the driver.

It is also understood that sometimes the reversing camera may also need to be changed and this could be a good opportunity to acquire a colour monitor and also select a system that gives an audible reversing warning, if one is not already fitted that can be retained.

Should a 240volt power supply be required for the vehicle including a number of 13amp sockets outlets installed within the RV then this will entail the fitting of a good quality transformer. The conversion will need to well engineered as it will have to supply 240 volt 13 amp at 50 cycles as well as providing a 115/120 volt 60 cycle supply to run all of the American made appliances originally fitted to the vehicle, such as the microwave and refrigerator etc, nevertheless do be aware that a cheap conversion could lead to damage to the expensive appliances and so could prove ultimately more expensive.

In addition as will be appreciated the vehicle will need to be registered, taxed, insured and fitted with UK number plates and if over three years old will also need to pass the appropriate MOT.

VISAS AND DRIVING LICENCES

Visas

Citizens of the UK and other countries that are eligible under the Visa waiver programme do not currently need a Visa to travel in the USA for a period of under 90 days. Although if a traveller does not:

a) Possess a machine-readable passport.

b) Wish to travel in the US for more than 90 days.

c) Wish to travel for a purpose other than leisure or business or

d) Is not eligible under the Visa waiver programme then a valid Visa is required.

The Visas are issued by the US Embassy or Consulate and entitle the holder to travel to the USA and apply for admission; however possession of a Visa does no guarantee entry as the immigration inspector at the port of entry actually determines the eligibility for admission.

Therefore due to the continually changing situation in the world today it is strongly recommended that contact be made with the US Embassy, Consulate and/or a reliable travel agent to determine the visas requirements applicable at the time of proposed visit so as to avoid disappointment and stress, obviously this should be done well in advance of the scheduled travel date.

Driving Licences

If intending to drive in the United States for up to one year, an International Driving Licence should be acceptable, but in addition it may also be helpful to carry a UK Photo-card Driving Licence.

In certain situations both documents, in addition to or possibly as an alternative to a Passport, may be useful should proof of identity ever be required.

Anyone intending to stay and drive in the US for over 12 months will probably have to take and pass a US Driving Test and this normally takes the from of a written Driving Knowledge Test as well as a Safe Driving Practical/Skill Test and the test requirements are understood to vary from State to State so prior research is strongly advised.

In general a visitor to the USA is restricted to driving the same class or category of vehicle that applies to them in the UK so it is understood that in some US States a conventional car licence will probably not be an acceptable grade of licence to legally drive the larger 40 feet or longer RV's or those that exceed a certain weight limit.

During our visit we did attempt to discuss and clarify this situation with various RV dealers in several different states and in our experience many of them tended to go a little quiet when theses issues were raised, so we were still left unsure.

However referring to the Oregon Drivers Manuel, the section devoted to recreational Vehicles does clearly state the 'drivers of recreational vehicles (RV's) used for personal, non commercial purposes need only have an Operator Class C and that is understood to be roughly equivalent to the UK C1 licence.

Within the manual there is mention of a weight limit of some 26,000 pounds and it is assumed that although they mention cars and single vehicles this may also apply to Recreational Vehicles, but it is not that clear.

As this is a complex and important matter, particularly with respect to legally driving the larger/heavier vehicles, it is recommended that the driving licence requirements should be clarified with the US Embassy and/or State(s) to be visited prior to departure as rules and regulations can and do change.

PRECAUTIONS

Safety and Welfare

It is a very sobering thought to consider for a moment that each year America's roads claim the lives of around 5,000 pedestrians that are killed in traffic accidents, some 17,000 die in alcohol related accidents and some 13,000 meet a similar fate in speed related accidents and that more than half of these accidents happen on rural two lane individual highways!!!!!

So it is vitally important to ensure that all people travelling are adequately covered by a very good and comprehensive Health, Medical and Accident Insurance, it is also of course important to carry a comprehensive Medical and First Aid Kit.

Therefore it is wise to observer at least the following guidelines:

a) Read and learn US driving rules and regulations but be aware that they can vary from state to state and also adhere strictly to the speed limits particularly in built up areas and when near schools.

b) Don't drink and drive and always use seat belts when the vehicle is being driven on the roads and adhere to designated signed routes and don't wander off in desert or forest regions etc.

c) Don't attempt to change an RV wheel, unless in an absolute emergency, this should be left to the professionals as most RV wheels are large and heavy, furthermore specialist lifting gear is necessary to raise the RV to a sufficient height before the wheel can be removed and replaced by a spare that is if one is even fitted. Damage could be caused to the RV if the jacks are not correctly positioned and last but not least serious injury or worse could result should the vehicle fall.

d) In the event of a vehicle breakdown stay with the RV and summon help with the aid of a mobile telephone, but if in areas where reception is poor or non existent, place prominent signs on the vehicle to attract the attention of passing vehicles, aircraft and/or helicopters.

e) Watch out for domestic and wild animals or even people straying on to the roads.

f) At night do not forget to lock the vehicle or even in daylight when the RV is left unattended, it is also good practice to set the vehicle alarm system when necessary.

g) Keep valuables and money out of sight and do not leave valuables on display in vehicles and also endeavour not to display signs of wealth in public.

h) When camping in remote locations or when not using an approved campground ensure that the area is safe and if possible occupied by other RV's and so do not take unnecessary risks.

i) Refrain from drinking the water obtained from any camping ground unless absolutely sure that it is totally safe to do so, if unsure boil or drink bottled water only.

j) Be aware that in some locations the weather can change suddenly so that very heavy rain and thunderstorms can spring up unexpectedly and when in desert locations the temperature can vary significantly between day and night.

k) Endeavour to carry a mobile telephone but be aware that signals may be weak or not obtainable in some remote areas.

l) Fully appreciate that walking, hiking or even riding a bicycle or taking part in other physical activities at altitude can be very tiring, also it is important to carry adequate supplies of drinking water when in areas where temperatures are high.

m) Be prepared to adjust clocks and watches when entering different US states as they may be operating in a different time zone and of course obtain a good map or set of maps.

n) Wear clothing appropriate to the climate and conditions but be aware that even in hot locations it can turn extremely cold at night.

As a general rule clothing tends to be more economically priced in the US than in the UK, so it may be worthwhile travelling light and then acquire some items while in the United States.

Good fitting comfortable shoes are essential if it is planned to do any real site seeing and in very warm regions larger sized shoes may be desirable as the feet have a tendency to swell in the heat and in sunny conditions it is wise to wear an appropriate hat, sunglasses and suitable sun cream.

RV Camping

As would be expected America is very well served by a vast quantity of RV camping locations ranging from numerous national and state parks to private parks and truck stops, furthermore some hotels and/or casinos allow overnight parking and in some states where no inconvenience is caused to others it seems quite acceptable to just pull off the road in an appropriate place and to dry camp for the night or even a little longer.

Therefore camping in the US is generally very civilised as many dedicated sites are extremely well planned and laid out to permit easy access and exit by even some of the larger RV's and many provide hard standing with full hook-up facilities consisting of electricity, fresh water and sewage connections say from an adjacent island to where the RV is actually docked.

However as the services can vary from site to site it is a good idea to carry a few spare electrical adaptors that will permit connection to 20, 30 and 50amp supplies, it is also useful to carry a mains water pressure reducing valve or regulator so that when it is connected to the mains water supply it will reduce the pressure of the water actually delivered to the RV to a safe pressure of about 40 to 50 pounds per square inch.

Many commercial sites also provide a range of facilities that can include a club-house, laundry, restaurant, swimming pool, a play area for children, boating, fishing, golf, a lake, nearby hiking, cycle ways and much more, some even provide free Wi-Fi Internet facilities.

Some sites may incorporate a combination of RV, tent or even cabin camping and depending on the season, location and popularity it may or may not be necessary to make an advance booking. The National Park Service has something like 26,000 campsite in about 550 campgrounds in just under 80 locations, but it is worth bearing in mind that the average permitted length of an RV, Trailer or Fifth-Wheeler is only 27 feet and that only a limited number of parks are capable of accepting vehicles of up to 40 feet in length, so it is advisable to telephone the chosen park in advance to check availability and whether the site can accept the RV in question.

To ensure a trouble free stay it is always worthwhile taking a few important precautions such as those highlighted and shown below:

- Try and select a pitch that is away from large trees particularly those with dead or low branches.
- Be aware that if parking by a lake or other area of water that insects and mosquitoes may also be in residence.
- Avoid low-lying areas that could flood if there were heavy rain.
- Appreciate that dry brush or undergrowth can catch fire.
- If lighting a fire ensure that it is safe to do so, therefore light the fire in the allocated area and ensure that the fire is properly extinguished after use.
- Ensure that partially eaten or unwanted food and/or waste materials, such as food containers, glass and cans are disposed of in a safe manner and dispose of it on site by placing it in the appropriate waste bins or take it away and dispose of it at a later date in the appropriate and responsible manner.
- Do not be tempted to feed wild animals or even the birds, as it is understood that this can endanger their life.
- Carry a good well equipped First Aid Kit.
- Avoid parking near fragile and hence dangerous cliffs.
- Do not stay in remote locations unless absolutely confident that it is safe to do so.
- Refrain from parking on private land unless prior permission has been given.
- Adhere to site rules and regulations.

Wal-Mart Camping

The Wal-Mart chain was founded by an RV enthusiast named Sam Walton, who believed that if he were to let people in self contained RV's park overnight at his stores then they would probably shop there and so increase the volume of business for the store chain. Therefore it became corporate policy to permit people in RV's to spend a free night in its parking areas and as a general rule there are no formalities or rigid regulations, although it is customary to park away from the store so as not to inconvenience other shoppers and stay only a night or so. The company operates around 1495 discount stores, 1,385 super centres and around 530 Sam's clubs, but nowadays does not permit overnight stays in something like 340 of it's stores and it appears the number that do not allow overnight parking is regrettably increasing possibly because some people have taken unfair advantage of the concession and may have caused problems. As a matter of interest most of the Wal-Mart sites are normally patrolled by a mobile security service that operates on a twenty-four hour per day basis and some of the sites may also be monitored by a surveillance camera system.

Incidentally as not all Wal-Mart stores are easy to find, it may prove worthwhile purchasing a copy of the latest 'Wal-Mart Locator' that is available from **http://rvbookstore/com/shop**.

REGULAR VEHICLE CHECKS PLUS SPARES AND TOOLS

Regular Vehicle Checks

As every caring car owner will be no doubt already appreciate and of course will carry out prior to any journey a few simple routine vehicle checks that should at least include checking engine oil, windscreen washer fluid, radiator coolant, tyre pressures and vehicle lighting etc. But while looking under the bonnet look to see if there are any obvious signs to indicate that there may be something wrong or about to go wrong, look for any traces of leaking fluids or for anything that is loose and that could include say a slack fan belt.

Prior to moving off walk round the vehicle to check and ensure that everything is in-order and pay attention to any loose fittings or accessories and take remedial action should any problems be seen.

Take a moment to check that all the wheels and tyres are OK but look for signs of damage, if necessary check tyre pressures against those recommended by the manufacturer and inflate as necessary and while outside look on the ground and under the vehicle for signs of any leaks or any other indications that could signify trouble.

Before moving off double check to see that the TV aerial, electrical power cable, fresh water and black/grey waste hose is disconnected and safely stowed away and that the drain valves for the waste services are shut and that any open air vents on the roof have been closed.

Ensure hydraulic levelling jacks are safely retracted and do not rely totally on the indicator in the vehicle, for example the system on our Safari Trek tends to be very optimistic indicating that the jacks have been fully retracted when they are still partially extended.

Spares and Tools

As a precaution just in case something needs attention or actually breaks it is wise to ensure that at least a basic tool kit is carried on board so that small running repairs can be undertaken as and when necessary, so aim to carry a few essential spares including vehicle fuses, bulbs, fan belt, engine oil filter, anti-freeze and oil for the RV.

In addition it is always useful to have spare bulbs for interior vehicle lighting, a comprehensive tool kit containing pliers/screw-drivers/open-ended spanners/sockets etc, a roll of electrical insulation tape, a soldering iron kit, tyre pressure gauge, mallet/hammer, a selection of nuts, bolts and washers and possibly a can of aerosol 'tyre inflator'.

Other useful items are a boiler suit/coverall, a strong pair of rubber gloves, (for dealing with dirty jobs, such as the hoses for black/grey waste), a thin pair of rubber gloves, (for dealing with any necessary emergency mechanical repairs), a water pressure reducing valve, (for use when filling with fresh water where mains pressure is high) to connect in line with onboard water tank and water supply.

It is also a good idea to carry a selection of electrical power hook-up connectors with a short length of cable to cope with different on site electrical supplies plus a lightweight folding aluminium ladder.

Fuel, LPG, Water and Emptying the RV's Holding Tanks

Fuel

As a wise precaution always ensure that the RV's fuel tank is reasonably full at all times, as there can be many miles between garages selling fuel, this is particularly important for diesel powered vehicles as according the Diesel Technology Forum just under 45% all fuel stops sell diesel and that is an increase of 12% from the year 2000.

Obtaining fuel in the USA, although not difficult is a little different to the system that is normally used in the UK, so be prepared to pay for the fuel, either by credit card or with cash before it is actually dispensed. Using a credit card is probably the most convenient method and by placing the credit card in the aperture in the petrol/diesel pump allows fuel to be dispensed, on completion press the designated button on the pump to obtain a receipt that will show the amount and the value of the fuel actually taken on board.

Paying for fuel with cash is of course possible, but this can be more time consuming than the credit card method, as it is normally necessary to enter and actually pay for the fuel in advance at the service kiosk and that may be busy. In addition most garages will only turn the pumps on when a specific amount or value of fuel to be purchased is specified and paid for in advance, somehow they are reluctant for the purchaser to 'just fill up' without confirming how much will be taken onboard.

LPG

Fortunately LPG is readily available in the US from garages, campgrounds, fuel suppliers and many RV dealers, furthermore as the LPG tanks on the RV's tend to be of a generous size it is not necessary to have to take the fuel on board very frequently. In all the US states visited it was customary for an attendant to be on hand to take control of the whole filling process, thus relieving the customer of any real active involvement apart from specifying how much gas was required and of course walking to the kiosk to pay once the operation was completed. This means that once the locker holding the tank has been opened the attendant assumes responsible for connecting the supply hose, opening the necessary valves on the RV, monitoring and controlling the quantity of gas delivered and then turning off the RV's valves and disconnecting the supply hose once the operation had been completed. However before filling it is necessary to turn off all appliances, particularly those with any pilot lights, such as the refrigerator and the cooker, as the gas is potentially very dangerous and is of course highly flammable. As a safety precaution even if the attendant is asked to completely fill the LPG tank, he will be restricted to filling the tank to 80% of it's total capacity, to allow for any expansion of the gas due to temperature changes and this is regulated by a small valve that emits vapour once that 'safe fill' capacity has been reached. Throughout the operation the attendant will therefore keep an eye on this valve and the contents gauge fitted to the RV so will turn off the supply once the gas tank registers 'full'.

Fresh Water

With a technically advanced and sophisticated country such as the United Sates of America it is reasonable to believe that there should not be any problems obtaining fresh water that is safe to drink. While in the majority of instances this is a valid belief, this may not always be the case, so care needs to be exercised when obtaining water from a previously untried or unfamiliar source. So although a notice may be displayed proclaiming the water to be potable and therefore fit to drink, it is a wise precaution to boil it first as boiling at one hundred degrees centigrade kills bacteria, viruses, parasites and any other unpleasant gremlins it may just happen to contain. The alternative option of course is to keep to bottled water for drinking, but apparently this is not always one hundred percent guaranteed to be totally free of carcinogens and some supplies have even been known to contain traces of industrial chemicals.

Furthermore to reduce the possibility of any contamination only non-toxic hose that has been specifically produced for potable water supplies should be connected between the RV and the supply and on no account should conventional garden or similar hose be used.

In order to maintain the systems sterility the RV's fresh water tank, supply lines and fittings also need to be kept clean at all times and will need to be sterilised at fairly regular intervals.

This can be achieved by adding to a partially full tank of water some commercially available water purifying fluid or tablets produced specifically for this purpose and adhere stringently to the manufacturers' instructions. Once this has been successfully completed the tank should of course be completely drained and the system flushed thoroughly through with plenty of fresh water.

The importance of this matter cannot be over stressed and is supported by information contained on the website, **www.rvdoctor.com/water/html** that revealed that in 1993 parasites invaded Milwaukee's water system and reportedly killed in excess of one hundred people and made over four hundred thousand people sick!!!!

The same source stated that the Medical College of Wisconsin and the EPA estimated that 7.1 Americans suffer nausea and diarrhea just from foul water!!!!

So always adopt safe, hygienic practices and procedures that will help to safeguard the good health and happiness of the vehicle's occupants, as it is often said 'it is far better to be safe than sorry'.

Emptying the RV's Holding Tanks

Not the most pleasant of jobs, but still not as bad as emptying the good old cassette used on many motrohomes of UK or European origin.

Wear a pair of rubber gloves and remove the RV dump tank outlet cap, then remove the sewer hose from its storage location then carefully connect the hose to the dump valve outlet on the RV, making sure that it is properly aligned, otherwise there is a danger that the small plastic lugs may be damaged or broken.

Open the dump station cover lid then extend the hose inserting it into the stations aperture and if possible use the lid or another reasonably heavy object, such as a stone or brick, to weigh down the hose to prevent it jumping out of position when the dump valve is opened.

If an appropriate object is not available, carefully place one foot firmly on the hose taking care not to exert too much pressure that would distort the hose, but is just sufficient to prevent the hose from dislodging itself from the drain once the dump valve is opened.

Open the black tank valve first then allow the tank to empty completely, then shut that valve and open the grey tank valve and allow that tank to drain until the flow stops, at this stage both tanks can if desired be flushed by partially filling each tank to say ¼ full with clean water and then drain the black tank first followed by the grey tank, in a similar manner to that described above.

Once this has been completed ensure that both dump valves are fully closed and replace the RV dump tank outlet cap then remove the sewer hose and replace the dump station lid cover and if a non-potable supply of water is conveniently available use it to rinse off the sewer cover and the surrounding area. Also run water from the same supply through the sewer hose to thoroughly rinse it inside and out then store it in the RV.

As necessary fill the fresh water tank from a suitable potable supply and at this stage it is recommended that the toilet be flushed two or three times before adding the appropriate treatment chemicals.

Furthermore it is not a good idea to leave the black water tank valve open when the RV is parked at a camp site as the liquids tend to drain off first leaving solids in the tank that are much harder to dislodge, instead leave the tank until it is about 2/3 full and then empty it, as there will be sufficient pressure and flow to ensure that the tank should empty successfully.

It is worth investing in a reasonable good quality sewer hose of 8 feet or more in length and it may also be beneficial to carry an additional hose as well as some spare fittings just in-case it is not possible to get close enough to the dump station for some reason or just in-case something breaks. Carrying an extra water hose can also be a good idea for general rinsing down just in-case there is not one at the dump station, however do not use this hose for filling the RV's potable water tanks or allow it to come into contact with other items that may be contaminated by it and always thoroughly rinse the rubber gloves and try not to touch the outside of them with bare hands.

AN INTRODUCTION TO US DRIVING RULES AND REGULATIONS

The following notes are based on our own personal interpretation and understanding of some of the driving rules and regulations that applied in the state of Oregon, in the year 2004. Furthermore as these Driving Rules and Regulations are understood to be based on national US standards they should form at least a reasonably good if somewhat basic appreciation of the rules and regulations likely to be applicable in other American states.

The notes are therefore provided in good faith and while every care has been taken to ensure that they are as accurate as possible and represent the rules and regulations applying at that time, the authors cannot accept any responsibility for any errors or omissions, it is therefore strongly advised that anyone intending to drive in the United States of America personally undertake their own in-depth research on this important matter.

Introduction

Oregon's traffic signs, signals and pavement markings follow the national US standards.

The Traffic Regulations in cities, towns, counties and federal territories can go beyond state laws, as long as they do not conflict with those state laws.

Fortunately each type of traffic sign has a special colour and shape to aid recognition.

School Zone Signs

A school zone applies to a section of street or road where a reduced **Speed of 20mph** applies as shown on the sign.

The zone commences with a **School** sign and ends with an **End School Zone** sign or other sign indicating a higher speed limit of say 30 mph. Furthermore on entering some zones, in addition to the speed sign the zone may also be marked by a flashing yellow light.

Signs may also indicate the days and hours when the speed limit actually applies.

Signs may also indicate that traffic fines double if the speed limit is exceeded while travelling in the school zone.

Traffic Lights/Signals

As in the UK a **circular Red light** means **Stop**.

But lights change directly from **Red** to **Green** so it is important to note that Red and Yellow/Amber lights do not appear together prior to the lights turning green as they do in the UK.

On entering a two way street it is OK to turn right after stopping at the red light, providing it is clear to do so or unless a sign or police officer indicates a **No Turn** against the red light. However when executing this manoeuvre it is necessary to yield to pedestrians, cyclist and traffic in the intersection.

When entering a one-way street it is OK to turn right or left in the direction of the traffic after first stopping at the **Red light** to ensure it is clear to do so.

A **Red arrow** also means **Stop**.

A **circular flashing Red light** means **Stop**. Look both ways. Yield to traffic and pedestrians etc and then continue only when safe to proceed.

A **circular Yellow/Amber light** warns that the lights are about to turn **Red**.

A **steady Yellow/Amber arrow** means lights are about to change colour so prepare to obey the next sequence of lights that may be a red arrow with a green or red light.

A **circular flashing Yellow/Amber light** means slow and proceed with caution.

A **flashing Yellow/Amber arrow** indicates turns may be made in the direction of the arrow, but only if safe and clear to do so, but that the vehicle must yield to oncoming traffic and pedestrians.

A **circular Green light** means 'Go'. But only if clear to do so having first allowed any other vehicles, bicycles and pedestrians already at the junction to get clear. Movement can be straight ahead, or left or right turns may be made if signalling so to do and it is safe and clear.

A **Green arrow** displayed at the same time with a red or green signal means it is clear to proceed in the direction indicated by the arrow.

Pedestrian Crossings

Pedestrians facing a **Walk** or a **Walking Person** signal, in white, can commence to cross the street and should continue to do so even if the **Don't Walk** or **Raised Hand** signs start to flash.

Pedestrians facing a **Don't Walk** or **Raised Hand** should not commence or attempt to cross the road.

Speed Limits

15 mph applies in **Alleyways**.

20 mph applies in any **Business District** or when in a **School Zone**.

30 mph applies in any **Residential District** and in **Public Parks**.

55 mph applies on all **Highways** and **Roads** not meeting any other definition.

70 mph or if specified a lower speed applies on **Interstate Highways**.

Stopping for School Buses

School buses in Oregon have **flashing Amber** and **flashing Red lights** near the top of the vehicle near to the **front and rear**, they also have a **Stop arm** that extends on the left side of the bus near the driver's window.

Flashing Amber lights indicate the bus is about to **stop**.

Flashing Red lights indicate that vehicles meeting or overtaking the bus from either direction must stop before actually reaching the bus and stay stationary until the flashing **Red light** goes out. At the time the **Red lights are flashing the Stop arm** should also be extended and will be retracted at the same time the Red lights go out.

The **Stop law** applies on all roads with two or more traffic lanes, the only exception is for situations on a divided highway separated by an unpaved median strip or barrier, then only stop if travelling on the same road as the bus.

Bus drivers can report any vehicle contravening these laws.

Church and Worker Buses

Flashing Amber and **Red lights** can be fitted to church buses carrying children as well as buses used to transport workers. In that situation similar rules to those applying to school buses are applicable.

Public Transit Buses

These buses frequently pull over to the kerbside to load and unload passengers and as they rejoin the traffic lane all other vehicles approaching from the rear must give way to the bus when the bus driver signals his intention to pull out or displays a **flashing Yield** sign at the rear of the bus.

Road Construction and Repair Zones

In Oregon traffic fines double for all traffic offences committed in maintenance, construction and utility work zones. This applies at all times and on all roads whether or not there are signs to indicate that fact.

Road Markings

Painted lines on the road instruct where to drive and inform about conditions to be encountered such as stopping or crosswalk (pedestrian crossings) or traffic restrictions etc.

Crosswalk

White lines on the road define the area where pedestrians should cross the road so drive with caution and be prepared to stop.

Stop Line

Solid White Line on the road shows where a vehicle must stop.

Yield Line

Depicted by a **row of Triangles** facing in the direction of motion where the vehicle must yield.

Yellow Centre Line

Dashed or **Solid Yellow Lines** painted on a two-way road define the centre of the road.

Solid Yellow Line

A **solid Yellow line** prohibits overtaking. If passing is restricted in both directions two solid yellow lines will be shown down the centre of the road.

White Dashes

Define the lanes on the road.

Solid White Lines

Define the edge of the road but may also be used to channel traffic into specific lanes or to follow specific directions. Only cross solid white lines with extreme caution.

Double White Lines
Prohibit lane changing.

Solid White Line with a Bicycle Symbol
Defines the lane dedicated to bicycles that must travel in the same direction as the flow of traffic and should not be used by other vehicles.

Yellow or White Lines and Diagonal Stripes
These are frequently used to define fixed objects or islands such as a Crosswalk or Train Crossing.

Two Way shared Left Turn Lane
A separate lane provided in the centre of the road to allow left turns to be made and it can be used by traffic travelling in either direction so extreme care must be taken to ensure the lane is clear before entering it. This lane may also be used when exiting a side street or driveway to temporarily stop and wait for the traffic to clear before merging into the right lane. The lane should not be used for overtaking etc.

Railway Crossings
Railway Crossings are shown by markings on the road that include a large 'X' and the letters 'RR', a 'No-Passing' zone strip and a 'Stop Line'. Vehicles must stop when the flashing lights are activated, or a crossing gate is lowered, or a stop sign shows or a railway official signals vehicles to stop or if a train is approaching and it would be dangerous to try to cross the railway line.

As in the UK it is illegal to attempt to go through, around or under a crossing gate or barrier when it is down or being opened or closed.

School buses and trucks carrying hazardous materials must stop at all railroad crossings and any vehicle following behind is also required to do likewise.

In some areas it may be possible to encounter 'Light Railway Trains' and 'Streetcars' that actually run on tracks set into the road and are frequently powered from overhead wires or cables so extreme caution needs to be exercised when crossing their tracks or when sharing any road with them.

Stopping, Waiting and Parking
Unless in a business or residential area a vehicle must refrain from stopping or parking in the road traffic lanes unless the vehicle breaks down and it is just not possible to pull off the road.

Vehicles must not stop, wait or park, except to avoid an accident, to obey the law, a police officer or traffic sign or signal in the following areas:

* On the road or adjacent to another vehicle

* In a tunnel.

* On the pavement/sidewalk.

* On or within 71/2 feet of a railroad track.

* Within an intersection

- On a throughway where access is controlled.

- On a pedestrian crossing/crosswalk.

- In a bicycle lane between separate roads of a divided road, including crossovers

- Between a safety zone and an adjacent a nearby kerb.

- Alongside or opposite a road works, excavation or other obstruction that would obstruct other traffic.

- On a bridge or overpass.

- At any place where official signs or pavement markings actually prohibit parking. Except for momentarily stopping to collect or allow passengers to get out of the vehicle it is not permitted to park in the following locations.

- In front of a public or private driveway.

- Within 10 feet of a fire hydrant.

- Within 15 feet of a fire station driveway on the same side of the road.

- Within 20 feet of a crosswalk at an intersection.

- Within 30 feet of the nearest corner or intersection if there is no marked crosswalk.

- Within 50 feet of a flashing signal, stop sign, yield sign or similar located at the roadside, if the parked vehicle hides the signal or sign from view.

- Within 75 feet of a fire station driveway on the opposite side of the road.

- At any other location where official signs or pavement markings prohibit stopping or parking.

Miscellaneous Rules and Regulations

It is against the law to play a radio or other sound system at a volume that it can be heard 50 feet or more away from the vehicle.

Televisions are not permitted in any vehicle where it is located that the driver could watch it while driving.

Oregon law requires anyone under the age of 16 years to wear an approved cycle helmet when riding or being transported on a bicycle.

Furthermore the same traffic rules that apply to other vehicles also apply to cyclists.

APPENDIX

Useful Web Site Addresses

The primary search engine used to research and compile the following web site information has been Google, although other engines may of course be used. While the majority of web pages can be easily found via the actual web site address provided, in some instances it may be necessary to follow a slightly more indirect route to the respective site as suggested by Google and in some instances it may be necessary to try each option in turn before access to the desired site is actually achieved.

For example Google may suggest the following routes as follows:

*   Find web pages that are **similar to: www**********
*   Find web pages that **link to: www**********
*   Find web pages that **contain the term: www** **********

Where ********** denotes the chosen web site address.

DRIVING LICENCE AUTHORITIES AND GENERAL INFORMATION

Oregon Driver and Motor Vehicle Services
www.Oregon.DMV.com
Shows DMV office locations and contains detailed data related to driving licence and social security requirements, vehicle title and registration fees, vehicle licence plates and much more.

UK Driver Vehicle Licencing Authority
www.dvla.gov.uk
This is the website of The Executive Agency for the Department of Transport that looks after safety and general law enforcement by maintaining a register of drivers and vehicles. Collects vehicle excise duty (car tax) and is responsible for the import and export of motor vehicles etc.

Traffic Answers
www.traffic-answers.com
The site is intended to answer common queries directed at the legal profession in relation to the law governing the roads in the UK.

Association of British Drivers
www.abd.org.uk
Lobby group set up to fight anti-car measures.

Highway Code
www.highwaycode.co.uk
This site of course shows Highway Code information.

Driving Standards Agency
www.dsa.gov.uk
This is an Information centre and provides news and publications including 'Driving, the Essential Skills' and 'Know Your Traffic Signs'.

Chris Hodge Trucks
www.chrishodgetrucks.co.uk
Contains a commercial directory of 'weighbridge locations' plus data entitled 'law on the web', 'driving licence categories', 'weights and dimensions'. A very informative and extremely useful website that contains much valuable information.

Driver Transport Training
www.drivertransporttraining.co.uk
The company is based in Bury St Edmunds in Suffolk and offers driver-training courses for Light Goods Vehicle, Large Goods Vehicles, Fork Lift Trucks etc. On entering their web site it is possible to select one of their training centres by geographic region.

RV Links
www.rv-links.com
RV Links claims to be the best link system on the Web.

See America
www.seeamerica.org.uk
Very useful site packed full of useful information, including data on outdoor activities, shopping, holiday offers, travel planning, finding a US travel specialist and an important section on Visas.

RV Dump Stations
www.rvdumps.com
Site shows location of approved sanitary dump stations across the US by state. The list shows dump stations accessible from Interstate highways as well as others that may be located throughout the state.

The National Scenic Byways Programme
www.byways.org
The National Scenic Byways programme is part of the US Department of Transportation, Federal Highway Administration. It was established to recognise, preserve and enhance a range of roads throughout the USA. Since the early 1990's the Byways programme has funded nearly 1,500 nationally designated byway projects in around 48 states.

US Locations with Wi-Fi Hotspots
www.rvtravler.com/wifi.html
Site then routes to www.tengointernet.com/forms/form-referral.htm and shows thousands of locations with Wi-Fi Internet access. Sites may be situated in coffee shops, stores, hotels, motels, airports, truck stops and RV parks etc. Just select the region required on the displayed map the system then provides the site location, the address as well as the telephone number of the appropriate Wi-Fi site. Sometimes the actual Wi-Fi connection may actually be free of charge, although there is normally a monthly subscription charge or payment has to be made by the hour.

AMERICAN RV'S FOR SALE IN THE USA

RV Trader
www.rvtrader.com
Covers classified advertisements for new and used RV's and has sections called 'find a dealer', 'RV parts' etc. In the classified section it is possible to sort by make/model/price/length/state or just 'Browse All'. A very good site that shows many, many RV's for sale.

RV Trader on Line
www.rvtraderonline.com
Shows used RV's from private owners and dealers with photographs of most vehicles.

RV on Line
www.rv-online.com
Photographic advertisements for both new and used RV's.

RV Classified
www.rvclassified.com
Covers new and used RV's for sale and more, it is possible to search by Class of RV/make/model/ year/ size/ fuel/state etc.

Free RV Classifieds
www.free-rv-classifieds.com
Site includes RV's for Sale/Parts and an extensive RV Directory.

Recreational Vehicle Trader
www.recreationalvehicletrader.com
Site includes RV's for Sale/Trailers/Fifth Wheelers and Parts.

RV-Mart
www.rv-mart.com
Photographic classified advertisements for pre-owned RV's. Claims to show detailed information about all the vehicles listed.

RV Search
www.rvsearch.com
It is possible to search for an RV by type/year/make/price/length/state. The 'Find a Dealer Section' also contains a very useful 'Buyers Guide'. An extremely useful website that is ideal for anyone seriously looking to purchase an RV.

RV America
www.rvamerica.com
Search for dealers by state or can search by type of new or used RV required. Quite good!

RV USA
www.rvusa.com
RV USA contains classified advertisements covering new and used RV's. Can search by type/manufacturer/ new or used/price/state and claims to show over 15,000 vehicles. A very good and useful site!

RV Sales
www.rvsales.com
Classified advertisements for RV's can search by manufacturer/ state/ model and year.
Can select vehicle categories such as, 'A' class or 'A' class diesel, Travel Trailer.
Has data on What's my RV worth? (it then diverts the user to the NADA guide).
Also has useful information sections entitled 'Buy an RV', 'RV Maintenance', 'Parts and Accessories'.

RV Dealer Network
www.rvdealernetwork.com
Access to this site does currently seem somewhat convoluted as after typing in the web address of www.rvdealernetwork.com it is then necessary to go via the link headed dealers shown at www.dealers.triple7.biz, it is then necessary to type in 'dealers' in the box provided and then press search. This should then reveal a whole host of data on a selection of dealers and much more.

RV Group
www.rvgroup.net
Claim to be America's largest RV sales company with a fairly new UK operations centre that is fully linked to the company headquarters in Florida USA. Understood to represent over two hundred and sixty dealers across the US and the company claim it can locate every make or model of RV either new or used. Information can also be obtained via their web site www.rvgroup.org.uk .The company claim to have sold vehicles in the UK, Germany, Japan and even Saudi Arabia.

RV Advice
www.rvadvice.com
This site contains literally loads of information ranging from travelling with pets to new and used RV's for sale. It also contains information covering state-by-state towing and motorhome laws. There is a questions and answers section that covers all manner of topics. Currently the service is free.

Photo Classifieds
www.RVphotoclassifieds.com
Shows classified RV advertisements.

More RV's
www.morervs.com
A site that advertises pre-owned RV's for sale.

Coast2Coast RV
www.coast2coastrv.com
Shows classified new and used RV's for sale.

100RV's
www.100rvs.com
Features RV's for sale and also claims to show advertisements across a network of 100 sites but there is a fee for this service.

RV Frenzy
www.rv.frenzy.com
Site contains Classified advertisements listing for all types of RV's.

RV Registry
www.rvregistry.com
Shows listing of used RV's for sale.

Classy RV
www.classyrv.com
This is a listing service for RV's, where searches can be made, by category/make/model and this is a very informative site displaying many RV's advertised for sale.

EBAY
www.ebay.com
EBAY is the well-known International Auction Site that promotes the sale of an extensive array of products including RV's, Fifth Wheelers and Trailers. Enter the site and 'browse for all items', then select 'cars, parts and vehicles', scroll down to 'other vehicles', then select 'RV's and Campers'. This should reveal around 700/800 motorised RV's and a similar number of towables.
In-order to bid or buy it is first necessary to register with the site and the acceptable methods of payment include Paypal (credit cards such as Master Card, Visa, Amex etc), as well as cashiers cheque, money order or cash in person.

Prevost
www.prevost-stuff.com
This web site is dedicated for the use and benefit of the Prevost owner and potential owner. It includes vehicles for sale, a discussion forum, a list of Prevost Service Centres together with information on campgrounds that will accept 45 foot long RV's.
It really puts the phrase 'roughing it smoothly' into perspective. Open it if you dare!!!!

Advice on American RV's

RV Doctor
www.rvdoctor.com

This site contains many interesting articles with a question and answer column, video library and much more. The interesting articles cover such topics as RV waste systems, AC power problems, RV maintenance and repair, improving vehicle ride and handling etc. There is even a new technical training programme for owners of RV's that is offered via the Internet. This is a very informative and extremely useful site.

RV Reviews
www.rvreviews.com

RV Reviews contains vehicle reviews by actual RV owners and it is possible to search by name of person filing the review or by manufacturer. An excellent site that is ideal for anyone planning to purchase a new or used RV.

RV Advice
www.rvadvice.com

Contains RV articles, RV travel guide, RV manufacturers, RV advice, RV rentals, Insurance and much more. Have recently introduced a section specifically related to the sale of pre-owned RV's.

RV Chassis Master
www.motorhomechassis.com

RV Chassis Master is located in Florida and specialise in motorhome chassis performance, including suspension, handling and braking systems.

Henderson's Line-up
www.hendersonslineup.com

Henderson's specialise in 'A' Class motorhome suspension, steering brakes and related items. They also design and manufacture after market chassis enhancing products and are located in Grants Pass Oregon, but have a series of shops in various locations.

Camping World
www.campingworld.com

Camping World are dedicated to providing a good range of products associated with RV's and it is possible to 'Shop on Line' or by visiting one of their many stores when in the USA.

The Recreational Vehicle and Campground Directory
www.rv-directory.com

This is a free listing of web sites with campgrounds shown by state in the USA and Canada, it Includes National Parks, RV Parking, Parts and Accessories, RV Rentals, RV Sales, RV Storage and RV Service. Extremely comprehensive and is a virtual 'gold mine' of information.

RV Net
www.rv.net

RV Net contains articles such as beginning RVing, Trip Planning, Magazines, RV Shows and Events. Also has an RV Classified section that goes via www.rvsearch.com

Recreational Vehicle Industry Association
www.rvia.org

The Association represents a $14 billion RV industry and this site contains much useful information.

RV Buyers Guide
www.rvbg.com

This site contains information on RV types, Insurance, RV classified and is run by the publishers of Trailer Life and Motorhome Magazine.

Motorhome Advice
www.motorhomeadvice.com

The site contains Travel Guide, Consumer Reviews, Motorhome Reviews and a Consumer Directory.

Motorhome Review on Line
www.motorhomereviewonline.com

A very useful site, containing general information plus correspondence but also provides access to the Nada Pricing Guide. Can request information on a specific RV's and contains survey results, owners' reviews and manufacturer rankings. Can send in own RV review and currently contains data on RV's from the year 1999 to 2005. This is a really useful and very informative site.

RV Recall
www.rvrecall.hypermart.net

Site provides information about vehicle recalls but unfortunately this is no longer a free service and a fee now has to be paid.

RV Tech Tips
www.rvtechtips.com

An e-mail newsletter featuring articles related to caring for your motorhome that is produced by an RV technician. Anyone interested is asked to submit their respective own E-mail contact address.

RV Service Reviews
www.rvservicereviews.com

Site where owners evaluate and report on companies that provide RV Service Facilities.

Rolling Homes
www.rollinghomes.com

Rolling Homes Press publish a range of publications/books for RV travellers covering locations such as Europe, Mexico and Alaska.

RV Gazette
www.rvgazette.com

RV Gazette is a Canadian RV magazine covering tips and industry news etc.

New RVer
www.newrver.com

This site is dedicated to providing a beginners guide to RVing so the site contains news, information, general articles and information plus reviews on new models. It is also possible to sign up to very useful free e-mail newsletters: a) RV Traveler b) Florida RVer and c) Fulltime RVer.

RV USA
www.rvusa.com

This site claims to be the original on-line guide and it contains data on finding and selling RV's, RV Manufacturers, New and Used RV Dealers, RV Service Facilities, RV Storage, RV Tips and Tricks, RV Shows and a great deal more. Claims to show over 15,000 RV's for sale. Can search by Vehicle Type/Manufacturer and whether it is New or Pre-owned and by price/year or state.

RV Info
www.rv-info.net

RV Info sells a range of RV books, RV lifestyle data, Campground Directories, RV Advice, RV Repair and Maintenance Manuals etc.

RVS-R-Us
www.rvs-r-us

This is good source for appraisals, blue book prices and values of both new and pre-owned RV's.

RV Org
www.rv.org

This is a consumer group that evaluates and rates Recreational Vehicles so contains RV Owner Surveys, Buying Tips, Testimonials, Renting RV's, it also has an informative section devoted to an 'Introduction to 'A' Class RV's'. It is necessary to pay for the information via subscription.

Important note: In the mid to latter part of the year 2004 this site is quoted as reporting that 'All wide body RV's are illegal on American highways if fitted with awning that causes the vehicle to be over 102 inches wide, however it then goes on to say that at this point in time that the enforcement agencies do not appear to be issuing citations'.

NADA Guides
www.nadaguides.com

Nada is the National Automotive Dealer's Association and are reputed to be the largest independent organisation and publisher of used vehicle values in the US and covers recreational vehicles, cars and motorcycles. The guide aims to provide accurate, reliable and unbiased information on vehicle values in America.

Carfax
www.carfax.com

Carfax provide detailed history reports that can be accessed via their web site and checks ownership and vehicle accident records. This organisation claim to have 550 million vehicle records and provide a preliminary 'free of charge' report although there is a fee payable for a more detailed one.

RV Traveler
www.rvtraveler.com

RV Traveler is a free weekly e-mail newsletter literally packed with news and information and advice for RVers, the site claims not to share e-mail addresses with any third party and promises no junk mail. RV Traveler is believed to now have over 100,000 readers. An extremely informative and useful source of information.

RV Bookstore
www.rvbookstore.com

RV Bookstore claim to be the world's biggest and best source for books, e-books, DVD's, videos and magazines about RV's and the RV lifestyle. The company is understood to be owned by Out West Publishing and is operated by the veteran RVer Chuck Woodbury who runs a number of web sites including www.rvtraveler.com and www.newrver.com etc and has been operational since 1989.

Epinions
www.opinions.com

This website provides useful data on a range of vehicles including, cars, boats as well as motorcycles and RV's. Can review the data on RV's by name of manufacturer and the site is packed with information.

Motorhome Facts
www.motorhomefacts.com

Motorhome Facts claims to be a one-stop information source and covers Motorhoming in the UK and abroad it also shows Classified Advertisements and a Dealer Directory. Although it is necessary to register, registration is currently free.

RVers Online
www.rversonline.org

A no cost on line help and advice site covering such topics as RV sites, RV education, Links for RVers, RV information resources, RV bookshelf, RVers mail box (an interactive feature) and much more.

Campervan Club
www.campervanclub.com

Includes data on vehicle rentals and shows some pre-owned RV's for sale. The club provides a free monthly newsletter containing information on American, European and Australian campervans. As of September 2004 the site was still not online.

RV Warranty
www.RVwarranty.com

Claims to provide affordable warranties for both new and pre owned RV's and prospective customers are requested to reply on-line for a quotation.

RV Parts Etc
www.rvparts-etc.com

RV Parts claim to be a full service dealer providing parts and accessories.

Adco Products Inc
www.adcoprod.com

Adco Products manufacture RV covers, RV bras (nose bags) and other soft goods for RV's.

The RVers Corner
www.rverscorner.com

This is a 'How To' web site and covers RV Maintenance as well as tips by a technician for the DIY RVer. Offer a free newsletter and free bulletin board.

RV Basics
www.fulltimer.com

RV Basics contains tips and information as well as listing of books and publications for RV's etc.

New RVer
www.newrver.com

The new RVer web site contains lots of useful information such as RV Buying Advice/Using Your RV/ RV Care and Upkeep. In-fact as the site claims it contains all you need to know about RV's and the RV lifestyle.

RV Service Reviews
www.rvservicereviews.com

Site provides a state-by-state analysis by RV owners who are invited to evaluate and post their own information on the web about the RV service organisations they have personally used.

COMPANIES HIRING RV'S IN THE USA

Cruise America RV Rentals and Sales
www.cruiseamerica.com

Cruise America claim to be the world's leading RV Rental Company that covers America and Canada. The company claim to have a fleet of some 3,000 vehicles mainly from Fleetwood and Thor Industries and the organisation state that they also sell pre-owned RV's and provide a one year 12,000 mile power train warranty and a five year 100,000 mile extended warranty.

El Monte
www.elmonte.com

Established since about 1970, El Monte rent both 'A' and 'C' class RV's from 30 to 36 feet long and have locations throughout the US.

Road Bear RV
www.roadbearrv.com

Road Bear RV is a family owned company that has been in business for about twenty-four years and operate from five US locations namely, Los Angeles, San Francisco, Las Vegas, Denver and New York City. They offer both 'A' and 'C' class RV's and claim to provide seven day twenty-four hour assistance. Their web site contains useful data on National Park services, campgrounds and even some free campgrounds.

Western Motorhome Rentals
www.weternrv.com

Western RV is actually a dealer for Newmar, Travel Supreme, Damon and Country Coach but they also hire motorhomes and travel trailers.

Altmans Winnebago
www.altmans.com

Altmans have been in business for some twenty-five years and are believed to run a modern high specification fully equipped rental fleet and claim that the average vehicle age is just seven months old. The company is apparently the largest Winnebago dealer in California.

Nolans RV and Marine
www.nolans.com

Nolans RV and Marine was originally started in 1969 and are based in Denver Colorado and claim that their rental division is one of the largest in the country with some 200 vehicles. They represent Winnebago, Fourwinds, Dutchmen, Jayco and Fleetwood.

Moturis Ltd
www.moturis.comCompany

The company operates from Boston, Chicago, Denver, Florida, Las Vegas, Los Angeles, New York and California. They claim to offer 19 to 32 feet long RV's, but also hire motorcycles with brands such as Harley Davidson, Honda and BMW.

Bates International Motorhome Rental Systems Inc
www.batesintl.com

The company was started in 1973 and is a member of the RVLA and has a network of locations in US/Canada offering both 'A' and 'C' class RV's for rental. International headquarters is in Las Vegas.

Caravan Abroad
www.caravanabroad.co.uk

Despite the name the company claims to specialise in the hire of motorhomes and motorcycles with a range of US pick-up points that include Las Vegas, Boston, Chicago and Seattle. Caravan Abroad state that they provide individual set itineraries, rentals and pre-paid motoring holidays in the USA, Alaska, Canada, Australia, New Zealand and Europe.

Private Motorhome Rentals
www.privatemotorhomerental.com

Private Motorhome Rentals is a motorhome rental referral service and provides luxury RV's owned by private individuals throughout the USA.

Recreational Rental Vehicle Association
www.rvra.org

Is the Recreational Vehicle Rental Association (RVRA) based in America.

West Country RV Rentals
www.westcountryrvrentals

West Country RV Rentals are believed to rent trailers and are located in Nordogg Alberta.

American Leisure RV Rentals
www.austinrentals.com

American Leisure RV Rentals rent vehicles serving Texas and Indiana.

RV Camping Sites and Camping Information

KOA Kampgrounds of America
www.koakampgrounds.com
KOA boast to having 500 campgrounds in the USA, Canada, Mexico and even Japan. They claim to provide good quality services including clean restrooms, playgrounds and pools plus a variety of lodging options from RV sites, tents and camping cabins. Their web site also contains useful data on RV's such as 'buy one', 'find dealers', 'insurance', 'rentals' etc.

Go Camping America
www.gocampingamerica.com
The official website of the non-profit National Association of RV Parks and Campgrounds sometimes referred to as 'ARVO'. It is reputed to be the premier source of information for private parks and campgrounds across the USA and their website also provides travel tips, pets and parks data, a road trip planner and a message board and much more.

Yogi Bear's Jellystone Park Campground Directory
www.campjellystone.com
Yogi Bear's Jellystone Park Campground Directory covers a significant area of the USA from Washington in the West to New Brunswick in the East as well as some parts of Canada. The organisation provides a range of services including RV's sites and camping cabins. On entering the website it is possible to view the camping site data either by state or park name.

Trailer Life Directory Online
www.tldirectory.com
It is necessary to become a TL Directory Online Member to obtain campground information. However the site covers the US, Canada and Mexico and claims to list over 2,500 Good Sam camping discount sites locations as well as one million RV parks. It is possible to search by city or by state.

Camping Friend
www.campingfriend.com
Initially this site is a little confusing as it is necessary to follow via the Reservation Friend's RV Park and Campground Locator shown as the web site www.reservationfriend.com and then search by the RV and Campground Directory, or the RV Rentals and Campgrounds option or via the quick search facility.

The California Travel Parks Association
www.RVandcampoutwest.com also see www.ctpanews.com
Although at first sight the name tends to imply that this site covers just California, but it provides useful information on over 450 RV parks and campgrounds in California, Oregon, Nevada and Washington as well as some in Canada and Mexico. No club membership is needed for RV'ers to be able to stay at these parks but membership of 'Club Out-West' enables advantage to be taken of discounted park fees. All sites are CTPA members.

California State Parks
www.parks.ca.gov
The California Department of Parks and Recreation manages over 270 park units with almost 1,800 campsites. Can search for a park by region, county/city or activities.

RV Boon Docking Basics
http://rvbookstore.com/shop
This site contains information on a useful book entitled 'RV Boon Dock Basics' that is devoted to dry camping as economically as possible.

Free Campgrounds
www.freecampgrounds.com
Covers free or nearly free sites and it is possible to select a specific campground by state. The site is understood to also provide information on the Wal-Mart sites that do not permit overnight stays. Free Campgrounds is sponsored by www.rvbookstore.com and will take time to grow as it relies on RV owners to contact the site and to add information and comments about new sites as and when they have been located and used.

Bureau of Land Management
www.blm.gov
The Bureau administers over 260 million acres of land covering areas such as Alaska, Arizona, California, Colorado, Eastern States, Idaho, Montana, Nevada, New Mexico, Oregon, Utah and Wyoming. The site related to www.recreation.gov that covers America's public lands that can provide the scenic beauty that RV enthusiasts love and may include RV campgrounds, sanitary dump stations and hook-up facilities. Some areas may even have special RV parking facilities.

RV Park/Campground Directory
www.rvpark.com
Understood to be a family operated business established in 1996 providing a campsite directory covering the US, Canada and Alaska. It is possible to search for a campground listing by state. The organisation also runs another website called www.rvpark.org

Camping Connection USA
www.campingconnection.com/usa
Site allows campsite to be selected by state but also contains useful camping tips.

Campgrounds in America
www.campgroundsofamerica.com
Using the site map it is easy to locate state parks, RV parks and even camping supplies.

Camping America
www.camping-america.com
The site enables searches to be made by state.

Campnet America
www.campnetamerica.com
This site claims to be the original source of camping information on the Web since 1995.

Capitol Reef National Park (National Park Service)
www.nps.gov.care
Contains a vast amount of information and covers the Water Fold Pocket area that is often described as 'a 100 mile wrinkle in the earth's crust'. Capital Reef was subsequently set up to protect this spectacular geological feature and to preserve the associated history. The site also covers other camping sites in the area including Cedar Messa a small 5 primitive, no fee site that is open all the year round, but has no water or electricity and only a pit style toilet. Cathedral City is another primitive site with similar features to Cedar Messa and as it is located at an elevation of some 7,000 feet, so it is recommended that anyone planning a visit should contact the Capitol Reef Visitor Centre to ensure that the roads are passable before attempting to visit this particular site.

Zion National Park (National Park Service)
www.nps.gov/zion
This site covers Zion National Park in Utah that is located at the junction of the Colorado Plateau, Great Basin and the Mojave Desert Provinces. The web site contains a wealth of very useful information on a wide spectrum of activities, educational programmes, news and visit planning data.

Bryce-Canyon National Park (National Park Services)
www.nps.gov/brca
This site covers Bryce Canyon National Park that is located along the eastern edge of the Paunsaugunt Plateau in Southern Utah and includes a whole range of information about activities, educational programmes, news and visit planning etc.

Nevada Division of State Parks
www.parks.nv.gov
The Nevada Division of State Parks was established in about 1963/4 and was set up to manage and to maintain the State Parks within the state. It now manages some 24 parks within the park system that are divided into 4 statewide regions, Western Nevada (Carson, Tahoe region), Eastern Nevada (Panaca Area), Central Nevada (Fallon region) and Southern Nevada (Las Vegas region).

National Park Service
www.nps.gov
The web site is operated by the US Department of the Interior and contains a vast amount of information including 'find a park to visit', 'history and culture', 'nature and science' and 'education'. The site enables the user to see all parks listed alphabetically or alternatively they can be located via a map, by state, region or even zip code. It is also possible to also search by topic of interest, However it is important to note that the maximum lengths for trailers, campers and motorhomes does vary from park to park although the average length permitted is 27feet although some parks may be able to accommodate vehicles of up to 40 feet in length. Some parks have dump stations but there are no electrical or water hook-ups at campsites and most parks adhere to allocating pitches on a first come first served basis. In total there are fewer than 26,000 campsites in nearly 550 campgrounds in just under 80 locations covered by the system.

Oregon State Parks and Recreation
www.oregonstateparks.org
This site provides an on line 'find a park service' with the ability to search by region and features it also contains a vast amount of information including an interactive section all about touring in the state of Oregon.

Washington State Park and Recreation
www.parks.wa.gov
The site provides the facility to search by park name or even park features.

America Best Campgrounds
www.abc.branson.com
Located in Branson Missouri the site was granted the Good Sam 'Welcome Mat' Award for 2005 and was voted 'the most friendly' Good Sam Park in the US and Canada. It is open all the year round with pitches for tents as well as RV's it has a clubhouse, swimming pool and apparently offers free Wi-Fi Internet facilities.

Camping Connection USA
www.campingconnection.com/usa
Site allows campsite to be selected by state but also contains useful camping tips.

Campgrounds in America
www.campgroundsofamerica.com
Using the site map it is easy to locate state parks, RV parks and even camping supplies.

Camping America
www.camping-america.com
The site enables searches to be made by state.

Campnet America
www.campnetamerica.com
This site claims to be the original source of camping information on the Web since 1995.

RV CLUBS AND ASSOCIATIONS

In American

Family Motor Coach Association
www.fmca.com
FMCA stands for the Family Motor Coach Association and members are required to pay an annual subscription. FMCA also produces a regular magazine. They have classified advertisements covering vehicles for sale that can be accessed free via web site with ability to search by make and model of RV. This is a very useful site for locating events and also for trip routing etc.

Good Sam Club
www.goodsamclub.com
Good Sam is a well-known and respected club started some 38 years ago, primarily aimed at promoting RVing and making it safer and more enjoyable. In addition membership of the club provides members with many money saving benefits together with easy access to a whole range of services provided by the club. An annual subscription is required that then allows access to such services as insurance, emergency road service, discounts at parks and campgrounds, membership magazine, trip routing and RV financing etc.

Escapees
www.escapees.com
Escapees claims to be the largest active club with lots of fulltime members.

Family Campers and RVers
www.rcrv.org
This club says that it is the largest family non-profit group in North America with over 17,000 family members.

RV Club
www.rvclub.com
This club also supplies RV Reviews as well as Hints and Tips.

Explorer RV Club
www.explorer-rvclub.com
The Explorer RV Club claims to be the largest national club in Canada.

Important Note: In addition there are numerous dedicated clubs ranging from Airstream to Winnebago.

In the UK

ARVE
c/o 27 Nether End
Great Dalby Leicestershire LE14 2EY
Telephone: 08700 115111 and the Web address is
www.arvm.uk.com

American RV Club
c/o The Spinney Holiday and Leisure Park
Beach Road, Sully, Glamorgan GF64 5UG
Telephone: 02920 531496

UK BASED RV IMPORTERS AND DEALERS

There are a growing number of dealers in the UK that import various ranges of new RV's, but in addition often sell a selection of pre-owned motorhomes produced by a variety of manufacturers. The following highlights just a selection of companies that have been established and operating for several years or more. There are of course various other RV dealers that specialise in marketing and selling nearly new and pre-owned RV's such as Anglo American RV, Dreams RV, American Recreational Vehicles and Premier American Motorhomes whose details can be found from the various motorhome publications, Yellow pages and of course the Internet.

Cheshire American Motorhomes
(Vehicle Sales)
Harringtons Leisure, Chester Road
Delamere Forest, Northwich, Cheshire CW8 2HB
Telephone: 01606 884010

(Headquarters)
C1 Aqueduct Business Park, Marple, Stockport
Cheshire SK6 5LD
Telephone: 0161 4276868
Importers of: Infinity, Windsport and
Thor's Four Winds
www.americanmotorhomes.co.uk

Dudleys of Oxford Ltd
A415 Abingdon Road, Ducklington,Witney
Oxon OX29 7XA
Telephone: 01993 703774
Importers of Winnebago, Dynamax, Thor, Isata
Coachman and Trail Wagon
www.dudleysrv.com

Destination RV International
At the time of writing the company were looking for
new premises. But can be contacted via
Telephone: 07754 196098

Freedom Motorhomes Ltd
Northway Lane, Tewkesbury
Gloucestershire GL20 8HG
Telephone: 0870 7572355
Importers of: Trail-Lite, Forest River and Freedom
www.freedom-motorhomes.co.uk

Gold RV Sales and Service Ltd
Unit 1Caker Stream Road, Mill Lane Industrial Estate
Alton, Hampshire GU34 2QA
Telephone: 01420 544482
Importers of: Triple E, Road Trek, Pleasure Way
and Viking
www.goldrv.co.uk or
www.goldmotorhomeservice.co.uk

Midland International
Wall Hill Road, Allesley, Coventry CV5 9EL
Telephone: 024 76336411
Importers of Georgie Boy and R-Vision
www.midland-international.co.uk

Travelworld
Halesfield 14, Telford, Shropshire TF7 4QR
Telephone: 0845 2305033
Importers of: Holiday Rambler, Monaco/Safari,
Newmar and Fleetwood
www.usrv.co.uk

Transleisure Ltd
Unit 10 Vantage Point
Howley Park Industrial Estate
Howley Park Road East, Morley, Leeds LS27 0BN
Telephone: 0113 2522900
Importers of Chinook
www.transleisure.co.uk

Westcroft Motorhome Centre
Pleasant Acres, Watling Street, Cannock
Staffordshire WS11 1SH
Telephone: 01543 500775
Importers of: Damon, Forest River and Tiffin (Allegro)
www.westcroftmotorhomes.com

Oakwell Motorhomes
65-67 Pontefract Road, Barnsley
South Yorkshire S71 1HA
Telephone: 01226 293300
Importers of Gulf Stream
www.oakwellmotorhomes.co.uk

Itchy Feet
Carvynick Leisure, near Truro, Cornwall TR8 5AF
Importers of: A range of vehicles including Safari,
Monaco, Coachman
www.itchyfeet.biz

THAT'S INTERESTING?

Interesting Words, Spelling and Terminology

In today's world we are all exposed in one way or the other to what could be termed 'Trans Atlantic Speak' whether it is by say exposure to the Television, Cinema, Radio, Books and Magazines or even through the personal experience of visiting the USA. Consequently this leads us to appreciate that there are sometimes significant differences in how the 'English' language varies between the two countries in the choice of words, their spelling as well as the terminology used. So to end on a light hearted note the following are therefore just a few examples that illustrate some of those differences we personally encountered during our all too brief American Dream (the normal English version is shown first followed by the American version).

As they say *'life is just one long learning experience'*.

Motorhome = Recreational Vehicle or RV or Motor Coach or Coach or Bus

Crisps = Chips

Chips = Fries

Wardrobe = Closet

Accident = Wreck

Caravan =Trailer

Bonnet = Hood

Person that owns an RV = RVer

Tyre = Tire

Boot = Trunk

Petrol = Gas

Silencer = Muffler

Generator = Genny

Pavement = Sidewalk

Hamburger = Patty

Colour = Color

Sandwich = Sub

Stock Clearance = Close Out

Push Chair = Stroller

Cattle Grid = Cattle Guard

Cover to protect the front of an RV = Bra

4 Wheel Drive Vehicle = SUV sport utility vehicle

No Standing = No Standees

Short overtaking lane = Turn out lane

Dead end road = No outlet

Sales Assistant = Sales Associate

Dry camping = Boon-docking

A person that lives/travels full time

In an RV = Fulltimer

Location where it is permissible to discharge

RV holding tanks = Dump Station

Pedestrian Crossing = Ped-Xing

Toilet = Restroom

Autumn = Fall

Estate Agent = Realtor

Down and dirty = Cheap and nasty

Marquis = say— 'Markeey'

Prevost = say— 'Prevo'

Mauve = say—'Marve'

Aluminium = Aluminum say—'Aloominum'

Electrical Power Cable = Electrical Power Cord

The authors have taken trouble to ensure the contents of this publication are as accurate as possible but cannot take responsibility for any errors or omissions.